Class, Self, Culture

Class, Self, Culture puts class back on the map in a novel way by taking a new look at how class is made and given value through culture. It shows how different classes become attributed with value, enabling culture to be deployed as a resource and as a form of property, which has both use-value to the person and exchange-value in systems of symbolic and economic exchange.

The book shows how class has not disappeared, but is known and spoken in a myriad of different ways, always working through other categorizations of nation, race, gender and sexuality and across different sites: through popular culture, political rhetoric, economic theory and academic theory. In particular, attention is given to how new forms of personhood are being generated through class, and how what we have come to know and assume to be a 'self' is always a classed formation.

Analysing four processes – of inscription, institutionalization, perspective-taking and exchange relationships – it challenges recent debates on reflexivity, risk, rational-action theory, individualization and mobility, by showing how these are all reliant on fixing some people in place so that others can move.

Beverley Skeggs is Professor of Sociology at The University of Manchester.

Transformations: Thinking Through Feminism

Edited by:

Maureen McNeil, Institute of Women's Studies, Lancaster University
Lynne Pearce, Department of English, Lancaster University
Beverley Skeggs, Department of Sociology, Manchester University

Other books in the series include:

Class, Self, Culture

Beverley Skeggs

Routledge
Taylor & Francis Group

LONDON AND NEW YORK

First published 2004
by Routledge
11 New Fetter Lane, London EC4P 4EE

Simultaneously published in the USA and Canada
by Routledge
29 West 35th Street, New York, NY 10001

Routledge is an imprint of the Taylor & Francis Group

© 2004 Beverley Skeggs

Typeset in Baskerville by
HWA Text and Data Management Ltd, Tunbridge Wells
Printed and bound by Antony Rowe Ltd, Eastbourne
Transferred to digital printing 2005

British Library Cataloguing in Publication Data
A catalogue record for this book is available from the British Library

Library of Congress Cataloging in Publication Data
A catalog record for this book has been requested

ISBN 0–415–30085–1 (hbk)
ISBN 0–415–30086–X (pbk)

Contents

Acknowledgements

Thanks to those who have read all sections of this book. I am truly grateful: Laura Doan, Mike Savage, Sallie Westwood, Andrew Sayer, Rosemary Deem, Tim May, Fiona Devine, Alan Warde, Mari Shullaw, Jon Binnie, Noel Castree, Elspeth Probyn, Lauren Berlant, Sally Munt, including the great 'queer' reading group 'Comings and Goings', with Lisa Adkins, Nicole Vitellone, Sarah Green, Don Kulick, Eleanor Castella, Penny Harvey. To the 'Violence, Sexuality and Space' research team: Les Moran, Paul Tyrer, Karen Corteen, Lewis Turner. Thanks are also due to my fantastic ex-colleagues who remain influential: Celia Lury, Jackie Stacey, Sarah Franklin, Maureen McNeil, Sara Ahmed, Lynne Pearce, and, of course, my new colleagues listed above. To all those participants at places where I've given papers who have enabled me to try out new ideas and rescue badly thought-through ones.

Especial thanks and apologies to my mates: Valerie Atkinson, Nickie Whitham, Graham Day, Jean Grugel, Stuart Baron, John Hobbs, Les Moran, Betsy Stanko, Alan Jamieson, John Phillips, Pat Kirkham, Les Moran, Jeanette Edwards, Henri Kreil and Krystal Packham. I know some have lived the pain of this book with me. Sorry. And of course, thanks and apologies to my amazing parents: Doreen and Ken Skeggs, who continue to sustain me when I should be sustaining them. I really do appreciate the care and loving that all the above have provided.

1 Making class

Inscription, exchange, value and
perspective

According to Manthia Diawara (1998), black working-class masculinity operates
in popular culture as a mobile cultural style available to different characters in
film, be they black or white. Exploring a tradition exemplified in Blaxploitation
films, he shows how a contradictory amalgam of racist stereotypes and resistance
to those stereotypes produces a form of black working-class maleness coded as
cool.[1] This becomes used across a range of sites in popular cultures, most obviously
in film and music. But what is significant is how this inscription, this marking of
cool attached to black bodies, becomes detachable and can operate as a mobile
resource that can be 'transported through white bodies' (Diawara 1998: 52).

Yet the mobility of this attachment and the inscription 'cool' are not resources
that are equally available to all. For when black male characters play 'cool' it
becomes fixed on their body. They *are* cool. They become fixed into playing 'blackness' (Eddie Murphy is probably the most obvious example, where even as an
animation donkey in the film *Shrek*! he still embodies a comedy version of cool).[2]
But black male actors cannot perform 'whiteness' in a similar way, because they
are always inscribed and read as black in our Western colour-coded visual symbolic
economy. They are excluded symbolically from performing 'whiteness'. Yet white
characters that need to achieve 'cool' can move between black and white, attaching
and detaching aspects of black culture and characteristics as and when appropriate.
So what we learn to recognize as categorizations of race and class are not just
classification or social positions but an amalgam of features of a culture that are
read onto bodies as personal dispositions – which themselves have been generated
through systems of inscription in the first place. Diawara uses the example of *Pulp
Fiction* in which John Travolta acts 'black cool' (remember the walk?) whilst Samuel
Jackson *is* cool. A particular version of racial inscription thus becomes a mobile
resource for some whilst being fixed and read onto some bodies as a limitation.
The black male character appears not to be acting; he just *is*. Hence, black
dispositions are culturally essentialized and made authentic. This is an example
of a symbolic economy where the inscription and marking of characteristics onto
certain bodies condenses a whole complex cultural history. Some bodies can be
expanded rather than condensed. At the same time they become a resource for
others. The way some cultural characteristics fix some groups and enable others
to be mobile will be a central exploration of this book. The interest here lies in

how some forms of culture are condensed and inscribed onto social groups and bodies that then mark them and restrict their movement in social space, whilst others are not but are able to become mobile and flexible.

We can chart how similar characteristics are inscribed, marked and stuck on other bodies too – femininity, hypersexuality, criminality, for example – whilst others do not. But before we explore this condensing, sticking and fixing process we need to understand four other processes that provide the framework for the rest of the book. First, how do certain bodies become *inscribed* and then marked with certain characteristics? Second, what *systems of exchange* enable some characteristics to be read as good, bad, worthy and unworthy? Thus, how is *value attributed, accrued, institutionalized and lost* in the processes of exchange? And how is this value both *moral and economic*? Third, how is value produced through different *perspectives* (different ways of knowing, hearing and seeing that represent particular interests)? Fourth, we need to know how these systems of inscription, exchange, valuing, institutionalization and perspective provide the conditions of possibility for being *read by others in the relationships* that are formed between groups; what are the effects? This, therefore, is a book about the conditions of possibility that make class. It is not about how class is lived.

For instance, whilst black working-classness is inscribed on the body as cool, it is also part of a dominant symbolic exchange mechanism that through historical inscription also equates cool with criminality. This cultural equation is useful for film makers yet it does not help those so inscribed to gain employment outside of the field of popular representations where they may be read as interesting but also dangerous and untrustworthy. In exchanging blackness for cool, respectability may be lost. The symbolic value attribution of danger and immorality sets limits on the possibilities for economic exchange. But from a non-dominant symbolic perspective, equating black working-classness with cool may be less tenable, indeed it may even be seen to be highly valued, or valued differently. Different exchange mechanisms generate different values from different perspectives in different fields, hence different possibilities (but all informed by power).

In a previous ethnographic study, *Formations* (Skeggs 1997), I showed how white working-class women were symbolically positioned and how this framed their ability to move through metaphorical and physical social space (the ability to exchange the cultural characteristics by which they had been inscribed and condensed on their body). This marking restricted their ability to trade and convert their cultural resources as these were read and valued as worthless by those who participated in and institutionalized the dominant systems of exchange. The processes of inscription, exchange, value-attribution and perspective put limits on them, not only in becoming economically valued (an exchange-value), but also in generating a sense of self-worth (a use-value). These women, although inscribed and marked by the symbolic systems of denigration and degeneracy, managed to generate their own systems of value, and attributed respectability and high moral standing to themselves. They were both positioned by but also contested the symbolic systems of historical inscription to generate alternative systems of value. This daily struggle for value was central to their ability to operate in the world and their sense of subjectivity and self-worth.

It is the central concern of this book to show how these different processes (inscription, exchange, evaluation, perspective) *make class* in the contemporary. This assumes that class is not a given but is in continual production. This introduction, organized into sections, will establish the central themes that make up the framework for the book as a whole. The first section argues that class is always made by and in the interests of those who have access to power and the circuits of symbolic distribution. The second explores how different forms of exchange (economic to moral) always assume or produce a form of personhood, a form often described as a subject. It also shows how it is not the object of exchange but rather the relationships that enable exchange (hence power) that are important. The third and fourth sections focus on inscription and value attribution, developing these themes through an analysis of Bourdieu's perspective on the symbolic economy. All these themes are then worked through a specific empirical example and extended in the final section into an exploration of self-formation and how this is integral to class making.

Class interests

Class cannot be made alone, without all the other classifications that accompany it. Significantly, the example described by Diawara above is based on a reading of black male bodies rather than female ones, which are inscribed differently through gender. We need to think how bodies are being inscribed simultaneously by different symbolic systems; how inscription attributes difference and how we learn to interpret bodies through the different perspectives to which we have access. These different systems of inscription and interpretation may operate both in simultaneity and in contradiction. This enables us to explore how some people can use the classifications and characteristics of race, class or femininity as a resource whilst others cannot because they are positioned *as* them.

Historically, there are strong and intimate parallels between the generation of classifications of social class and the production of sexuality and gender. So when Foucault (1979) identifies the four discourses that came to produce sexuality (the Malthusian couple, the masturbating child, the hysterical woman, the perverse adult) we can see a similar process occurring with class. The discourses of the dangerous outcast, the urban mass, the revolutionary alien, the contagious women, the non-recuperable, came to produce what was known as class. As Mary Poovey (1995) demonstrates, these were not entirely straightforward designations, and formed part of a long discursive struggle. The category of the contagious woman, figured through the prostitute, presented specific problems. The paradox of needing to name, identify, quantify and know also produced the possibility of breathing life into the figure, making it a lived possibility, and thereby provoking a range of questions about why and for whom the prostitute exists. It was the dilemma over naming the prostitute that floundered James Kay's studies of Irish poverty in Manchester (see Poovey 1995). Also, the sexuality of working-class women became a source of desire and 'scientific' observation for the Victorian male reformers such as Malthus and Mumby. As Lynette Finch (1993) shows, it was the moral reading of women's bodies and practices that initiated the first class categories to be developed in Australia, and as Anne McClintock (1995) and Ann Stoler (1995) maintain, the relationship between race, sexuality and gender generated particular class formations. Another correspondence with discourses of sexuality was the association with negative moral value; sexuality was sin.

The production of sexuality was therefore very much a class product,[3] as was gender. A significant move in the definitional history of class was made by the bourgeoisie who, in order to morally legitimate themselves, drew distance from the figures of the decadent aristocrats above (again sexed and gendered: usually represented by the lascivious woman or the feminized man) and the unruly hoards below. As McClintock (1995) illustrated, hygiene was one of the earliest discourses to combine and condense class, race, gender and sexuality. Articulated as a moral problem, hygiene was one of the first discourses to rely on marketing and commodities as a solution to the threat of those figured as decadent, degenerate and unhygienic. Soap became the solution to hygiene and thus to the problems of threatening race, class, gender and sexuality: the perspective being that if only they could be cleaned for the sake of the empire all problems would be washed away. Thus a combination of figures and discourse were mapped onto moral values so that distance could be drawn. Dirt and waste, sexuality and contagion, danger and disorder, degeneracy and pathology, became the moral evaluations by which the working-class were coded and became known and are still reproduced today (see Chapters 5 and 6).

Bourdieu and Waquant (1992) argue that power works through mis-recognition whereby cultural privilege and power are seen as ascribed rather than achieved – and therefore thought of as natural and legitimate. Bourdieu associated this essentializing of value with the powerful, whose power can be hidden and hence mis-recognized. In an expansion of this argument I'd maintain that the process also occurs in reverse. That is, those at the opposite end of the social scale are also mis-recognized as having ascribed and essential characteristics. They do not have to achieve immorality or criminality; they have been positioned and fixed by these values. This is another form of mis-recognition – not a hiding of the operations of the powerful, but a hiding of the systems of inscription and classification (which work in the interests of the powerful). The powerful not only hide their spurious claims to power through legitimating their own interests, but also through access to systems of symbolic domination, which impose fixity onto those from whom they draw and claim moral distance. Discerning how positioning, movement and exclusion are generated through these systems of inscription, exchange and value is central to understanding how differences (and inequalities) are produced, lived and read.

In this sense this book has a very different perspective on class to some of the ones usually taken. This is not a book about economic inequality, although it shows how processes of inscription and exchange set limits on the potential for some bodies to accrue economic value. Nor is it about 'counting' or measuring classes to see how people fit into classificatory systems. Nor is it about 'refining' these systems to make them incorporate features that enable measurement to proceed more efficiently. It is a step back from these classificatory systems, a move that asks how and why classifications have been established, and why it is that classification is the mechanism by which we know the contemporary. From this perspective, economic discourse and the tradition of measuring class are seen as significant forms of inscription. These systems of knowing re-present the interests of particular groups. Here I ask '*in whose interests?*' do particular ways of understanding class continue to exist or not. This is why the book explores different ways of knowing and inscribing (through academic discourse, to economic and political rhetoric, to popular culture).

For instance, in a study of the making of the middle-class, Loic Waquant (1991) shows how the middle-class does not exist in ready-made reality but is constituted through material and symbolic struggles. The middle-class, he argues, is a historically variable and reversible effect of these struggles. Therefore the middle-class has no frontiers other than those continually produced and transformed through struggle and these cannot be defined abstractly. It is as Bourdieu (1987) argues:

> It is in these intermediate zones of social space that the indeterminacy and the fuzziness of the relationships between practices and positions are the greatest, and that the room left open for symbolic strategies designed to jam this relationship is the largest.
>
> (Bourdieu 1987:12)

Analysis of class should therefore aim to capture the ambiguity produced through struggle and fuzzy boundaries, rather than to fix it in place in order to measure and know it. Class formation is dynamic, produced through conflict and fought out at the level of the symbolic. To ignore this is to work uncritically with the categories produced through this struggle, which always (because it is struggle) exist in the interests of power. Class (as a concept, classification and positioning) must always be the site of continual struggle and re-figuring precisely because it represents the interests of particular groups.

Whilst there have been claims from academics and politicians that class no longer exists, there has also been a massive proliferation of popular cultural output devoted to the expression of class relations. A great deal of this may not be directly articulated as class, via instead what Roger Bromley (2000) identifies as 'euphemistic transference', but this output can be shown to be about class by the forms and perspectives it takes, and the relations it establishes between groups. Part of this book, then, examines the possibilities for how class can be spoken and known, both directly and indirectly, across a range of sites. It analyses how certain legacies from the struggles to produce class linger and become re-figured in different historical circumstances.

This book also explores how class is spoken through other concepts, in particular 'the self' (or the subject) and how certain concepts of personhood make class. The self is seen not as a subject position, but as part of a system of exchange in which classed personhood is produced through different technologies, such as narration for legal claims making. I did not set out to, or even want to, write about the self but found that the more I investigated different forms of class production, the more I became aware that different forms of personhood and individuality were integral to how class interests become inscribed onto different bodies in the name of 'the self'. There is, for instance, an interesting coinciding between the global (International Monetary Fund (IMF) World Bank) definition of the 'subject of value', that is a particular ideal-type of risk-taking enterprising self envisaged for the future generation of global assets, and the 'rational actor' described by 'new' theories of class, which prefigure a self that works to accumulate its own value in its own interests via strategic decisions (see Chapters 3 and 4).

In this sense this book draws on the Foucauldian tradition that demonstrates how the self (and sexuality) was brought into existence through particular discourses. Here I show how particular discourses and technologies make classed selves, not just through productive constitution (namely, bringing the self into existence) but also through *processes of exclusion*, by establishing constitutive limits and by fixing attributes to particular bodies.

Another theme I want to draw attention to throughout the book is *perspective*. This runs from the abstract level of how we can know, to how some forms of knowledge are able to set agendas, to how these are taken up as the methodological techniques by which people come to know themselves and others. Perspective is about taking a knowledge-position on an issue, persons or interaction. Perspective is a technique by which the interests of some people are put into effect. Common-sense definitions of perspective cohere around ways of looking, technical representation and taking a broad view on things. Here I want to argue for a tighter definition which is not just about looking (other systems of knowing such as affects and the aural are evoked when taking a perspective: see Sneja Gunew 2000).

Representation does figure in how knowledge is shaped in order for it to be formed into a perspective. Yet I want to challenge the 'broad view' often incurred by the word perspective. Perspective is not an over-view, but a narrow section of particular interests that are imposed upon others and are represented as a wider-view, when in fact they are the exact opposite. Perspectives are powerful when they eclipse all other perspectives to ensure that they are the only ones that can be taken. To take a position is dependent upon the knowledge to which we have access, the ways we can interpret, and the ways in which we can articulate it and put it to use. Because perspective is always premised upon access to knowledge it is always implicated in power relations (for instance, what type of knowledge? Is it equal access?).

To have a perspective is therefore to take a position. Perspectives are offered through a range of different sites of knowledge production, in a range of guises: as truth, opinion, rhetoric, representation, etc. For the purposes of this book I want to show how perspectives on class are made, circulated and used to produce particular effects. This means not always addressing class directly, but also exploring how it is forged through the perspectives taken on other issues such as economics, culture and mobility.

For instance, Celia Lury (1998) and Marilyn Strathern (1999) show how the concept of the 'possessive individual' (that is a person who is defined through his capacity to own property in his person – see later discussion in the next section) developed from the perspective of a small group, with access to circuits of symbolic distribution, who were able to legitimate their own interests and establish their own authority, by defining themselves against the 'mass'. They represented the mass as the constitutive limit for what an individual could be. As their perspective was taken up by those who also wanted to shore up their own authority it was replicated in various different ways: the political theory of the possessive individual, for instance, can be seen to be the cornerstone of seventeenth century political theory (Macpherson 1962).

The power of repetition across a range of different sites enabled the concept of possessive individual to be taken up, used and reproduced. In doing so it influenced the different formations that were being made of class, such as the unruly, immoral working-class, not capable of being individuals. The concept was then made more powerful and more effective by being institutionalized in law, via property relations and concepts of rights-bearing individuals (this is, of course, a very shorthand and reductive story). What was central to the reproduction of the possessive individual was how particular techniques such as narrative, biography and scientific discourse were used to legitimate their interests through the promotion of particular perspectives. These established the perspective of the possessive individual as the norm, the natural and the good through the attribution of moral value to themselves. In institutionalizing themselves, not just through law, but through different systems of knowledge, they came to consolidate their interests across a variety of fields.

To this day we still have the concept of the 'possessive individual' pervading how to think about self, individuality and personhood. In fact, some of the most challenging recent theory (e.g. Cronin 2000b; Lury 1998; Strathern 1999) explores the contemporary manifestations of this concept via new forms of property, legitimation and economics, via advertising, intellectual property rights and branding. Taking a perspective means taking a position on knowledge. It usually invokes some form of decision (this perspective or that one?) and is thus implicated in judgement. In most classifications, debates and theories we can identify perspectives and it is making these obvious and apparent, as working in the interests of particular groups, in which I am interested. The first two chapters document how economic discourse and theories of risk, reflexivity and individualization work to legitimate a perspective of powerful interest groups.

Now I'm going to develop the framework in more detail.

Exchange

Different systems of exchange can be economic, but are also symbolic, cultural and moral. It was Marx (1967) who, in trying to understand capitalism and class formation, argued for a change of perspective from traditional political economy, based upon understanding exchange, to one that focused on production, in particular on systematic exploitation. In order to understand capitalist accumulation, he maintained, we must turn our attention away from the realm of exchange and focus instead on the realm of production. It is labour, he argued, that is central. Yet, despite this change of perspective to labour, exchange still remained central. For instance, the commodity became dissociated from being a 'thing' (an object in and of itself) to being *an equivalence*, emptied out of its particularity, history and memory. His method was to trace the attribution of value back through all its exchanges to the human labour that actually produces capital. Marx was concerned to show how the commodity was able to eradicate its own production, its labour, in order to generate a value that related only to other things, what he described as fetishism. As Peter Stallybrass (1998) notes:

> To fetishize commodities is, in one of Marx's least understood jokes, to reverse the whole history of fetishism. For it is to fetishize the invisible, the immaterial, the supra-sensible. The fetishism of the commodity inscribes *im*materiality as the defining feature of capitalism.
>
> (Stallybrass 1998:184) (italics in original)

For Marx the problem was not fetishism; rather, it was the fetishism of commodities that dis-engaged people from their labour. Stallybrass, drawing from the work of Pitez (1985;1987), shows how the fetish as a concept had already been radically inscribed when Marx put it to work and was intimately associated with the formation of European personhood. The fetish was used to demonize the supposedly arbitrary attachment of West Africans to material objects. From this the European subject was constituted in opposition to this demonized fetishism. Hence, central to Marx's perspective was the formation of different subjects known through their relationship to objects: those defined as 'primitive' imbued their objects with history, memory, even personality (Mauss 1990/1925). The colonialist, defined in opposition, generated and only saw the value of 'things' in exchange.

Kopytoff (1986) argues that this contrast between individualized persons and commodified things was a central ideological plank of colonialism that served to divorce use from exchange-value, but also, significantly, served to associate certain forms of personhood *with* use and exchange-values. The 'civilized' exercised a relationship to things based on a specific perspective on value; value was always about exchange. As Stallybrass observes:

> It also implied a new definition of what it was to be European; that is, a subject unhampered by fixation upon objects, a subject who, having recognized the true (i.e. market) value of the object-as-commodity, fixated instead upon transcendental values that transformed gold into ships, ships into guns, guns into tobacco, tobacco into sugar, sugar into gold, and all into an accountable profit.
>
> (Stallybrass 1998:186)

This attempt to understand the processes involved in generating profit out of commodity fetishism led Marx to a perspective that produced a distinction between appearance and reality and their respective correspondence to surface and depth.

As Wendy Brown (2001) notes, in this model, the state and ideas become the realm of exchange and the real becomes the realm of production:

> ... [w]e therefore take leave for a time of this noisy sphere, where everything takes place on the surface and in view of all men, and [go] into the hidden abode of production, on whose threshold there stares us in the face 'No admittance except on business'. Here we shall see, not only how capital produces, but how capital is produced. We shall at last force the secret of profit making.
>
> (Marx 1967:176)

And whilst the new colonial Europeans were producing themselves through their disassociation from objects, another subject formation was also taking place according to Marx: alienation, the alienation of the commodity from its owner. Alienation is not merely an effect but a condition of the production of the commodity:

> The existence of things qua commodities, and the value relation between the products of labour which stamp them as commodities, have absolutely no connection with their physical properties and with the material relations arising therefrom.
>
> (Marx 1967:72)

Value becomes established through exchange, but in this exchange the relationship to the commodity itself generates different forms of personhood. There are persons who are alienated from their labour (the labourers), but who have an attachment via use-value to objects, and other persons who can only view objects as the basis for exchange (the European capitalist colonists). These different relations to objects shape the forms of personhood that are established, as well as forming the historical basis for different relationships between groups.

It is significant that it was in the making of this European personhood that the category of the 'possessive individual' was consolidated (see later section), in which it was the ownership of oneself rather than the ownership of objects that created the difference between the individual and others. Carole Pateman (1988) argues that women are structured out of the category of the individual through ownership rights. 'The individual' is defined through *his* capacity to own property in his person. He is seen to have the capacity to stand outside of himself, to separate 'himself' from 'his body' and then to have a proprietal relation to himself as bodily property. According to the perspective of contract theory, the labour power expended in work is detachable from the body of the individual. Therefore, what is seen in an employment contract is the individual's capacity to perform labour, rather than the individual himself. The exchange of the man *himself* would count as slavery and run counter to the principle of freedom expressed by contract theory. As Pateman shows, the constitution of the category individual is also based on the slave contract and the construction of ideas of the European 'self' and the 'savage other' developed through colonial encounters and violent domination of indigenous populations of East Africa. These different relationships to property – in objects, in the person – have resonance today with those who can invest in themselves and those who cannot.

What is also worth remembering at this point is how, for Marx, those who exchanged objects never fully become the possessor of the object, for value is in the relationship of exchange. From this I want to draw out how forms of person-hood are generated, how relationships to use and exchange are also central to relationships between people and objects, and how the perspective of depth and surface pervades the understanding of different persons. The shift of perspective to production, however, still leaves us with the need to understand exchange more fully; for it is in exchange that value is attributed (how does sugar become an equivalence to gold, for instance?). And it is the process of value attribution that is absolutely central to my analysis.

Exchange has long been fundamental to many ways of understanding social and economic relations. As Alphonso Lingis (1994) notes, structuralist sociology was built upon an exchangist model in which values are posited as interchangeable and circulate according to a law of equivalence: for Levi-Strauss, society was the circulation of women; for Marx, it was the circulation of commodities; for Mauss, it was the circulation of gifts; for Homans, it was rewards and punishments; for Parsons, it was about money and power; and, for Bourdieu, it was about different forms of capital.

Strathern (1992b), however, is highly critical of the commodity-logic that underpins these many models of exchange. As an exemplar she critiques Arjun Appadurai's (1986) analysis of the 'commodity potential of things'. Appadurai argues that the social life of any 'thing [can] be defined as ... its exchangeability (past, present or future) for "some other thing"' (1986:13). He refers to this as the 'tournament of value' by which participation in exchange measures the strategic skills and standing of the people involved. In the moment of exchange, charac-terized by Appadurai as the 'flow' of things, value is made visible. Thus the cultural value of exchange determines their value. Part of the problem with this form of analysis, Strathern argues, is that it contains the idea that relationships and value can be reduced to units that can be counted. For Strathern, counting is not what is important in understanding exchange, but rather *the relationships* that enable exchange to take place and the perspective that is taken on the exchange. The attribution of value always depends on the perspective that is taken: for whom is something valuable or not? If we want to understand exchange we need to know from whose perspective and interest is value attributed. Who decides what is valuable, what exists as a resource or asset and what can be exchanged? And what relationships make this exchange and valuation a possibility?

Strathern develops her critique by exploring how an 'equation' is set up between things and persons (such as bride and bride-wealth). These symbolic relations cut across the subject/object divide, so that certain bodies are expected to contain a specific sort of value. She shows, for instance, how Levi-Strauss's model of exchange, based on the trading of bodies of women, assumed that all women had equal reproductive capacities. Not only was value read onto certain bodies, but also the association of certain bodies with certain practices (women and reproduction) simultaneously enabled value to be attributed, making a symbolic connection between body, value and practice. Through the historical repetition and circulation of this symbolic connection, women's bodies are read as being reproductive and thus given value accordingly. Even now, after feminists have substantially challenged this model of exchange, the assumption of fecundity and the value associated with it is still read onto women's bodies. And difference is produced from a moral perspective that makes some women's bodies appear as more suitable for breeding, whilst others are seen to be out of control through excessive breeding (see Chapters 5 and 6 for how working-class women are represented in political rhetoric and popular culture as excessively fecund).

Instead, Strathern proposes a model of exchange based on the capacity for people to extract or elicit from others items that then become the object of their relationship – so persons (or personal dispositions) can be the objects of such relationships. She argues that out of everything that a person has to dispose of – knowledge, artefacts, produce, children, for example – an object is created at the moment when an asset *becomes the attention of another*. Appadurai, she argues, collapses use-value (its worth to the person) into exchange value (its use for exchange), hence reproducing the European colonialist model of exchange value being the defining factor in the construction of personhood.[4] In Strathern's model it is the relationship between people that becomes the crucial factor rather than the object, commodity or item that is being exchanged. In this model it is possible to see people's dispositions, characteristics, culture and artefacts as having use-value only to themselves, both beyond exchange but also becoming an object of exchange the moment another person becomes interested in it/them.

Accepting that relationships are crucial in the formation of exchange and personhood enables us to see how they are produced through struggle and conflict; how power informs the exchange that is made. For instance, an asset a person holds may become the attention of another, but they may not be willing to exchange it. They may be forced to exchange it and it then may be put to a use to which they object but about which they can do nothing. These are relationships of power in which some win and some lose through exchange. Exchange is rarely an equal transaction. Yet the use-value of something, or to which something is put, does not depend on exchange and has a value beyond it.

And it is this I want to keep in the frame when I later develop Bourdieu's model of a symbolic economy. We must keep exchange and use-value separate, for this enables us to see how different groups have different possibilities for evaluation. It is also important not to reduce everything to exchange-value as Appadurai and Bourdieu have done (see Sayer 2001). By shifting attention away from the object/asset being exchanged to the relationships and power that make the exchange possible in the first place, we focus instead on whose perspectives makes something valuable, hence exchangeable. This allows us then to explore the power that exists between groups that enables some to elicit/extract and appropriate dispositions and objects from others.

It is also important to think that value may exist beyond the extraction process. So in Chapter 8, where I explore the extraction of the aspects of working-class culture that are put to use for the enhancement of the middle-class, this does not mean that what has been extracted and attached to the middle-class body is necessarily the same as that which was taken. It is in the relationship that the transformation occurs. The extraction may not generate a gap or a loss for those from whom it has been extracted. Different forms of power and relationships constitute resources differently, so the use-value of working-class culture may remain intact as it is being tried on and exchanged by others. Unlike in Marx, where the value was generated through the commodity form, here value is generated from the power, perspective and relationships that make the exchange possible in the first place.

Inscription

To add another dimension to the model of exchange based on perspective, relationship and power, I now move onto 'inscription'. Lingis (1994) shows how Deleuze and Guattari (1977) challenge models of exchange by focusing instead on inscription. For them, the essential social characteristic is to mark and be marked; this is not about exchange but about the articulation and disarticulation of libidinal energies. To inscribe a body or a body part, according to Deleuze and Guattari, is to interrupt a flow of desire, of libidinal energy. Inscription is about making through marking. Inscription cuts or scars bodies in the process of assembling them into composite forms, segments, strata and habitual modes of behaviour. Class is a form of inscription that shapes bodies in the making of strata and behaviour. William Bogard (1998) maintains that exchange relations already presuppose a complex mechanics of desire that connect some bodies together and disconnect them from others. It is desire that forges the relationships that make exchange possible. Every society, before it is a system of exchange, is, for Deleuze and Guattari, a composition of interrupted desires (Lingis 1994).

Inscription produces the subject via various regimes, classification schema and control of the body.[5] What sociology perceives to be 'society', for instance, Lingis (1994) reveals as a product of inscription – that is, hierarchy, class, race, sexuality and gender are forms of classification. Inscription is not just discourse but a complex set of practices for the deployment and co-ordination of bodies.[6] Bogard notes that:

> There are modes of social inscription that are exclusive, that separate bodies from what they are capable of doing, that demean their desire and distort their sense; and they are modes that are inclusive and connective, that liberate desire, destroy limits, and draw 'positive lines of flight' or escape.[7]
>
> (Bogard 1998:58)

The question is which is which, why and how and in whose interests?

One of the central features by which value-attribution occurs is through inscription. Inscription is established through marking the value of particular bodies, what Foucault (1979) identifies as the 'dense transference point for power'. The emphasis in this book is on the process of inscription, the way value is transferred onto bodies and read off them, and the mechanisms by which it is retained, accumulated, lost or appropriated. It is important not to confuse the process of inscription with the sign itself – which is the product of inscription (Bogard 1998). According to Deleuze and Guattari (1977) there have been many different regimes of signs, of which 'representation' is only the most recent way of understanding inscription.

In building this framework I now want to argue for an analysis that can combine inscription *with* exchange, whereby libidinal energies are not always the driving force, but rather it is the history of inscription that produces the conditions of marking and the possibility for taking perspectives. It is in this process that the value that is attributed to certain markings comes to have an exchange-value. But establishing exchange-value is not enough to control the energies contained by inscription; it is the ability of energy to leak beyond its inscribed containment that makes a class struggle. The refusal to accept inscription and be bound by its value is a significant act in challenging the dominant symbolic order. And it is the symbolic that frames all other forms of exchange (including the economic), as will be explored through Bourdieu later in this introduction. This is why an understanding of inscription, perspective, value and exchange is central to understanding how difference is made. This is more than the economy; it is what makes the economy possible. I now turn to exploring how value is attached and attributed to people and groups through inscription.

Value and institutionalization

We live, breathe and excrete values. No aspect of human life is unrelated to value, valuations and validations. Value orientations and value relations saturate our experiences and life practices from the smallest established microstructures of feeling, thought and behaviour to the largest established macrostructures of organization and institutions. The history of cultures and social formations is unintelligible except in relation to a history of value orientations and their objectivizations, interplay and transformations.

(Connor, 1993:1)

C.A. Gregory (1997) argues that values both describe and prescribe so that people are then both subjects and makers of the values. Values give time and place their recognizable cultural unity. Gregory charts how standards of value arise and become attached to particular categorizations:

Values involve both the is and the ought, the fact and the norm. Values determine the question posed, the mode of description, the evaluation of that description, and the normative judgements that follow. Values are often equated with *ought*, the norm or moral, and separated from *is*, the fact.

(Gregory 1997:7) (emphasis in original)

This suggests that morality lies behind all value. But not just attributed by the dominant systems of symbolic classification (such as class, gender and race), but also by those who study different groups. Underlying the perspective that is taken (the interests that are held) is not just power but also morality. How people are valued (by different symbolic systems of inscription; by those who study them; by systems of exchange) is always a moral categorization, an assertion of worth, that is not just economic (e.g. good or bad; is or ought).

Gregory (1997) also outlines how what he terms 'the value question' can be approached in one of four ways: the power by which, from which, through which and on account of which value exists. The way value is marked on bodies and read, or a perspective taken, is central to the relationships that can be made between people and groups. This is therefore about the politics and perspectives of 'valued relations'. Valuation, when part of the dominant symbolic economy, legitimates, according to Martin Heidegger:

> It is important finally to realize that precisely through the characterization of something as 'a value' what is so valued is robbed of its worth. That is the very valuing, even when it values positively, is a subjectivizing. It does not let things be. Rather, valuing lets things be valid.
>
> (Heidegger 1978: 226)

Thus valuing always works in the interests of those who can name it as such. Their perspective on what counts as legitimate puts valuation into effect. In this evaluation process a distinction can be drawn between use-value and exchange-value. Making legitimate (making things valid) places the thing (be it person or object) that is being valued in the realm of dominant categorizations. As it is inscribed with value it becomes part of the symbolic economy. The moral evaluation of cultural characteristics is central to the workings and transmission of power.

But this is not a straightforward process. Different forms of inscription can work with and against each other. For instance, being marked as black, male and working-class produces a different form of inscription and a different value to that of being white, female and working-class. But this evaluation also depends upon the context (or what Bourdieu calls 'fields'). For instance, my previous research showed how white working-class women were read and interpreted through many different systems of inscription: class, race, gender and sexuality; through discourse of care (motherhood and responsibility); through representations of femininity, race and class. These were all historically attributed through dominant symbolic systems with negative value, so that when amalgamated and stuck to one body they provided a systematic undermining of value and closed down the possibilities for exchange. But sometimes the value attributions contradicted one another and in their local situations the women were able to produce value for themselves from these negative attributions. They re-evaluated the inscriptions. The negative value became less fixed and was more open to contestation. The value attached to their inscription was the most difficult to contest when it was institutionalized, when it was written into social relations by forms of authorization and legitimation. For instance, their mothering practices were regulated across a range of sites (education, social work, health care, media), which made contestation more difficult.

Another important issue is how and why some cultural characteristics can become propertizable and others cannot. What makes some forms of culture valued and others valueless? Propertizing, a term taken from legal studies (e.g. Coombe 1993; Davies 1994; 1998; 1999; Radin 1993), establishes a relationship between property and personality. As a concept it enables an investigation into how some people make investments in their cultural characteristics, which can then be used to realize a value in areas (such as the economic) protected by legal property rights. For instance, being heterosexual enables one to enter parts of the labour market that would be closed off to queers. Inhabiting the position of heterosexual enables people to realize benefits (from welfare and tax systems of the state, insurance systems, property ownership of private capital). It also provides legally-given rights to privacy over one's sexuality – which are not available to male queers, who are constantly criminalized and have no access to the private (Berlant and Freeman 1993). We need to know which cultural characteristics have a legal privilege and entitlement, that enable propriety to be converted into property, legitimated and authorized (see Moran and Skeggs 2001a). It is also worth noting which cultural characteristics become normalized in this process (e.g. heterosexuality) and are infused with moral worth.

New research on the middle-classes illustrates how class is being constituted through the use of *culture as a property* and/or as a *spatialized relation* (Featherstone 1991; Lury 1997a; Savage *et al.* 1992; Strathern 1992a). These studies propose a model of exchange based not only on the sale of labour power, but also on the accrual of cultural resources to oneself, be they commodity objects or cultural practices. Institutionalization also occurs via the ways in which entitlement to space becomes both embodied (as entitlement) and legitimated (through law and policing). The increased spatial apartheid of Western cities is testament to how spatial containment and protection has now become a positional good. And, as Sharon Zukin (1987) points out, the symbolic economy of space is a central dynamic of Western capitalism. This leads David Morley (2000) in an exploration of different mobilities (see Chapter 3), to suggest that difference is being increasingly spatialized. As Chapter 9 suggests, geographical referencing is one of the contemporary short-hand ways of speaking class.

Bourdieu's symbolic economy

To add a further dimension to the frame, I now want to turn to Pierre Bourdieu who develops a perspective that focuses on the centrality of the symbolic economy. By economy he means not just monetary organization, but also the systematic organization of the symbolic, which enables exchange and the attribution of value across a range of fields. In a parallel critique to that made by Strathern above, Bourdieu (2000a) demonstrates how economic theory (and in particular rational action theory) is a very particular (and even peculiar) perspective that confuses the things of logic and the logic of things. Bourdieu is especially critical of the economic as an autonomous domain. Rather, he demonstrates how the history of the economic field is the history of a process of increasing power, autonomy and expansion made in the interests of powerful dominant groups. This, he argues, is because the institutionalization of this field tends to determine the whole of social life, even though it is limited by the existence of other fields. His work is an attempt to locate the economic within the symbolic organization of social space. Moral value is always attributed to the economic domain (as Chapter 2 outlines in more detail), as it is seen to produce good or bad effects and good or bad subjects of value.

Confusingly, though, Bourdieu (1979; 1985; 1986; 1987) uses economic metaphors – of capital – to dispute the centrality of the economy as a separate sphere, whilst also developing a model to illustrate how different resources and assets accumulate in bodies and are carried across social spaces. He develops a model of social topography to demonstrate how relative positions and the *relations* between these positions constitute forms of power, enabling bodies to move in social space. Bourdieu identifies four main types of capital: economic, cultural, social and symbolic:

- *Economic capital* includes income, wealth, financial inheritances and monetary assets – what you own.
- *Cultural capital* can exist in three forms: in an embodied state, i.e. in the form of long-lasting dispositions of the mind and the body; in the objectified state, in the form of cultural goods; and in the institutionalized state, resulting in such things as educational qualifications. Bourdieu defines cultural capital as high culture.

In contrast I'd argue that the value of a particular culture can only be known by the different fields in which it is realizable and can be converted. For instance, femininity can be a form of cultural capital if it is symbolically legitimate (historically a particular version of middle-class moral femininity). But femininity poses particular problems for Bourdieu's analysis because although it is symbolically ubiquitous, it is not symbolically dominant in the same way as masculinity is. Femininity is a form of regulation rather than domination. Yet it is embodied, and operates as a local cultural resource and can be used in local rather than nationally symbolic forms of exchange. So, in marriage a particular form of femininity is enacted that appears as high cultural capital, and is legitimated through the state (legal protection, tax and welfare benefits), yet in marriage the contract is a form of masculine and heteronormative domination that gives women some value but not as much as her husband (e.g. in the exchange of names, the 'obey' command, etc.). This means the value of femininity needs to be analysed in relation to masculine domination and valued accordingly. Yet, femininity as a cultural resource that has to be performed in certain situations can also be given a local use-value and played with (see Skeggs 1997). And unlike traditional forms of capital its value can only decrease with time, for it is youth-specific inscription.[8] The *conversion* into the symbolic is central to understanding power and inequality; that is, what is realizable and propertizable as a resource can be made legitimate, attributed with dominant value and converted into the symbolic. I want to focus on resources (economic, cultural, moral) instead of just capitals, to show how some cultural resources do not operate as forms of capital – hence are not exchangeable but do have value for those who use and make them.

This fits with Ghassan Hage's (1998) idea of accumulated whiteness as a display of national belonging, because it the conversion of one's acquired cultural dispositions of the right kind into symbolic capital that enables one to belong to the nation (see next section). This also brings us back to the difference between use-value and exchange-value. What may have a use-value for one group may not have exchange-value. Along with economic and cultural capital Bourdieu also identifies:

- *Social capital*: resources based on connection, networks and group member-ship: who you know, used in pursuit of favour and advancement.[9]
- *Symbolic capital*: the form the different types of capital take once they are perceived and recognized as legitimate. Legitimation is the key mechanism in the conversion to power. Cultural capital has to be legitimated before it can have symbolic power. Capital has to be regarded as legitimate before it can be capitalized upon, before its value is realizable. It is this conversion process, I'd argue, that challenges the critique made of Bourdieu, that he reduces every-thing to exchange-value (see Sayer 2001).[10]

All capitals are context specific. Thus, according to Bourdieu, all people are distributed in the overall social space according to: the global *volume* of capital they posses, the *composition* of their capital, the relative weight in their overall capital of the various forms of capital, and *evolution in time* of the volume and composition according to their *trajectory* in social space. Moreover, rather than depending on the 'functional equivalence' of all subjects (which informed Thomas Hobbes and Adam Smith), Bourdieu exposes the lack of equivalence between people and the problems with exchange. Different bodies carry unequal values depending on their position in space, on their cultural baggage – the capitals they embody. Inscribed bodies literally embody entitlements. They move in space 'as if they own it', which in the tradition of possessive individualism or in the conversion of propriety into property, they do!

We can add this model of social topography and embodied entitlement as a practice to the frame of inscription which sets limits on the possibilities for the relationships of exchange and evaluation that enable the conversion of different forms of capital. Moreover, Bourdieu (1988) has also drawn attention to the perspectives taken on exchange and the attribution of value, particularly what is presented as symbolically valuable. He explores how knowledge (i.e. particular perspectives) becomes institutionalized. Drawing on the work of Austin and making an argument similar to that of Judith Butler, Bourdieu (1992)[11] argues that theory is performative, that is, theory brings into effect that which it names.

Yet Bourdieu is at pains to point out what he calls a 'theoreticist error', which consists in treating classes on paper as real classes. Social space, he argues, allows us to move beyond the alternatives of realism and nominalism, metaphors enable us to make abstractions about social relations and to think about how they are 'made'. He notes:

> The title of E.P. Thompson's book *The Making of the English Working-class* must be taken quite literally; the working-class such as it appears to us today through the words meant to designate it, 'working-class', 'proletariat', 'workers', 'labour movement', and so on, through the organizations that are supposed to express its will, through the logos, bureaus, locals, flags, etc., is a well founded historical artefact.
>
> (Bourdieu 1989:18)

These classifications are forms of inscription that are performative; they bring the perspective of the classifier into effect in two ways: first, to confirm the perspective of the classifier and, second, to capture the classified within discourse. As Bourdieu (1989:19) notes, 'nothing classifies somebody more than the way he or she classifies'.

Loic Waquant (1991), for instance, charts the production of the categories of *Angestellte* in Germany (a particular sector of salaried employees but developed from the political organization of the industrial working-class) and the *cadre* category in France. In the years prior to 1930 there was no trace of the category *cadre*. It took a long symbolic struggle for people to acquire the principle of *cadre* identity and unity. Drawing on the work of Boltanski (1979) he outlines how the stake of this symbolic struggle was nothing other than:

> The imposition of a ternary representation of society centered upon the 'middle-class' as the 'healthy' and 'stable' component of the 'nation', a representation which was itself patterned after the representation of political space which was being shaped by the vanguard of the new right with its 'Third Way' (*troisième voie*) mediating between the two extremes of 'collecitvism' and 'capitalism'.
>
> (Waquant 1991:63) (italics in original)

Waquant (1991) thus maintains that symbolic and political relations of power enter decisively in the very constitution of class. Lynette Finch (1993) also demonstrates how this process of symbolically locating, naming and classifying was established in Australia, in which the heterogeneity of the urban poor was made homogeneous through the concept of working-class. She demonstrates how it took a considerable amount of time by those so named to recognize themselves by the categories used to describe them (see Chapter 2).

I now want to weave these different perspectives together through Hage's (1998) empirical research into the making of the contemporary national Australian.

National belonging

The nation represents a particularly vivid way of showing how my framework can be put to use. Within the nation, national belonging constitutes the symbolic capital of the field, and to belong is to be legitimate. That is, the aim of accumulating national capital is precisely to convert it into national belonging, to have accumulated national cultural capital recognized as legitimately national by the dominant cultural grouping. National belonging is produced through the 'theory effects' described above in which inscription, the perspectives of the powerful, the relationships that enable exchange, and the dispositions and practices that mark bodies with values, shape the conditions of possibility for national belonging. National belonging tends to be proportional to accumulated national capital.

This framework relies on an understanding of metaphorical space (the space of the nation), the inscription of the nation onto the body (whiteness becomes the mark of national belonging), and the national perspective that marks some bodies as more valuable than others; values that can be exchanged for national belonging. The imaginary and affectivity are also significant for how one imagines one's belonging and the ability to accumulate characteristics, dispositions and goods that display one's belonging. Both of these senses and claims rely on an imaginary space, or on what Hage defines as a 'spatial-affective aspiration'. This is because the imaginary nation does not rely on the inferiorization or essentialization of the other (as previous theories on race have often assumed), but on the construction of the other as an *object of spatial exclusion*. In order to produce spatial exclusion a centre has to be constructed that represents 'real' belonging, and those who really belong have to display and embody the right characteristics and dispositions. In many circumstances essentializing and spatializing work together.

This framework therefore also relies on dispositions and practice (the way one performs being a national subject) and the way relationships are made. It is not just the volume and composition of the right sort of cultural capital (for national belonging) but, rather, that the right sort of capital depends on *the processes by which it is acquired and displayed*. Regardless of how much national capital one accumulates, how one accumulates it makes an important difference to its capacity to be converted. Bourdieu distinguishes between those who only have to *be what they are* as opposed to those who *are what they do* and, therefore, have to constantly prove that they are capable of carrying the signs and capital of national belonging. This process becomes particularly apparent when the concept of the 'self' is investigated.

Personhood, self and property

The self is part of a system of inscription, exchange, perspective and value-attribution. It is a product of and is shaped by the dominant symbolic that contains and leaks the energies of accumulation, loss and practice through affectivity, dispositions and characteristics. The self, as Foucault (1979; 1988) so brilliantly demonstrated, is a category that does not pre-exist the discourses that constitute it. But, I'd argue, it is not just discourses, but the whole system of inscription, exchange, perspective and practices that make it possible. It is always historically and spatially located, especially via national spaces. Yet only some people can accumulate the required cultural capital to become a self (see Carolyn Steedman 2000), only some people can acquire the right dispositions to become the selves that can be reflexive (Adkins 2000b), and only some selves are seen as capable of acquiring the knowledge for self-monitoring and self-responsibility (Vitellone 2002). All the new debates that take perspectives on self-production, -monitoring, -responsibility, -reflexivity, etc., are premised upon the availability of, and access to, discourse and cultural resources, and the techniques and practices necessary for producing, but also knowing, a self.

Roy Porter (1997) demonstrates the centrality of perspective to defining and knowing what a self can be:

> The Greeks believed they were the playthings of fate, Christians saw themselves as miserable sinners, Descartes thought that man was a thinker, Liberals stressed self-determination, Romantics self-expression, while Freud invited you to go and lie on the couch.
>
> (Porter 1997:1)

In an analysis of the histories of the self, Porter charts how the issue of the self has been endlessly posed by those with the time and space for perusal (and hence perspective-making). Yet, as he demonstrates, the answers given are endlessly different; very much part of the cultural, social and political issues of the time. Renaissance Italy has been held responsible as the time and space where the literate and gifted elite males began to liberate themselves from the chains of custom, conformity and the Church and to move into what became known as self-discovery and self-fulfilment. These elite men used and generated new cultural genres, such as the self-portrait and the diary (especially autobiography), to reveal their heightened perceptions of their difference from the powerful Church *and* the mass (Porter 1997).[12] They also used the law (as noted in the tradition of possessive individual inscribed in legal personhood).

In *The German Ideology* Marx (1857/1970) explores how the language of property connects to individuality. He notes how M. Destutt de Tracy undertakes to prove that *propriete, individulite* and *personalite* are identical: 'nature has endowed man (sic) with an inevitable and inalienable property, property in the form of his own individuality' (p.100). He shows how this argument is put to work rhetorically to defend bourgeois existence, that is, 'if you take away my property you destroy me as an individual'. In contrast Marx argues that he only possesses private property if he has something that is marketable, whereas he notes that what is peculiar to him as an individual is not necessarily vendible. The ubiquitous frock-coat appears to make the argument:

> My frock-coat is private property for me only so long as I can barter, pawn or sell it, so long [as it] is [marketable]. If it loses that feature, if it becomes tattered, it can still have a number of features which make it of value *to me,* it may even become a feature of me and turn me into a tatterdemaliaon (transl:

a person dressed in ragged clothes). But no economist would think of classing it as my private property, since it does not enable me to command any, even the smallest, amount of other people's labour.

(Marx 1857/1970:101–2) (emphasis in original)

The frock-coat did certainly become a central feature of Marx's life (forever in and out of the pawn shop (see Stallybrass 1998; Wheen 1999; Kapp 1979): it enabled him to think through the differences between something that has no exchange value but is of significance; inalienable property that cannot be transferred. In the *Thesis on Feuerbach,* Marx (1857/1970) argues that the 'chief defect of all hitherto existing materialism is that of the thing, reality, sensuousness, is conceived only in the form of the *object or of contemplation,* but not as *sensuous human activity, practice,* not subjectively' (p.121). That is, prior theorists do not understand use-value, the worth of somebody or something beyond the exchange relations of the market. I want to show how many of today's theorists are locked into exactly the same conundrum as described by Marx; everything becomes reduced to exchange-value.

Just as particular historical conditions and technologies of inscription enabled the production of a particular self-formation, capitalism now provides particular conditions and possibilities for specific self-formation. As Rouse (1995) notes, the imperatives of specific systems of accumulation influence the shaping of people's dispositions. This debate has a long history, beginning with Adam Smith's *Wealth of Nations* (1776), in which his model of political economy envisages the market place as an arena of sovereign operators, each pursuing personal profit through cut-throat competition (this legacy will be explored in Chapters 2 and 4). This creation of particular conditions for the production of the self has been extensively documented by Nick Rose (1989; 1992), who charts how a whole range of technologies, knowledge systems, including science, psychology and personnel management, have been designed to produce a self that not only fits the capitalist system, but provides it with new resources and services from which profit can be extracted.

Yet many new analyses of the self as a modern Western concept often reproduce the equation of self with the principle of ownership. G.A. Cohen (1995) demonstrates how self-ownership is premised upon the principle that each person belongs to him- (and it was) self and therefore owes no service or product to anyone else. This principle is used to defend capitalist inequality, which is said to reflect each person's freedom to do as he wishes with himself. He also illustrates how the Marxist critique of exploitation implies an endorsement of self-ownership, since it is premised on the fact that the employer steals from the worker what belongs to her, her labour power. The commodity hides this labour. Any concept of the self, he argues, represents a particular perspective that is riddled with libertarian principles of self-ishness, because it maintains that each person belongs to himself and therefore owes no service to anyone else.

Experience is central to concepts of self-ownership. Conceptualizing experience as a property of the individual dates from the seventeenth century in England. It was put to work by the newly forming bourgeoisie (Abercrombie *et al.* 1986), and became central to what we now know as political theory (Macpherson 1962). The ownership of experience became part of what constituted the person and made them unique, hence possessive individualism (see Lury 1997a; Strathern 1992a). And just as only some people could belong to the nation, only some were rendered as having the 'right' experience and could therefore produce themselves as individuals with a self. It was only the bourgeoisie, always white, usually male, who were considered to have *depth* of experience; it was their experiences that were classified as of 'real' value to capitalism (Watt 1957), and it was these different levels of interiority and surface that informed how the working-class became represented; for instance, Herbert Marcuse (1964) considers the mass without interiority as exemplified by his title *One Dimensional Man* (see Bennett 2003).

Steedman (1997; 1998; 1999; 2000) traces how a working-class self came into existence. It was one that had to prove itself to be capable of narrating itself in the ways established by the state-legal system of poor relief. The good self was one that could tell itself in a particular way, one that conformed to the narrative conventions established by the state through law. The self was very much part of a moral discourse. The display of the self was therefore reliant on access to cultural capital to secure economic resources. This also has strong parallels to Hage's contemporary analysis of national belonging.

In this process exclusions had to be made so the good self could be demarcated and known. A site was generated onto which all that was immoral and bad was projected. The excluded were defined as the unwashed mass, the lumpen-proletariat, the outcast – literally.[13] However, the outcome of this projected exclusion was to make the excluded-immoral the site of all that was interesting and potentially desirable. In an attempt to construct the moral self that could be recognized and identified, the immoral marks the site of all that was dangerous, disruptive, contagious, sexual and did not belong; that which threatened its boundary security. This, of course, made it a site of fascination for those who were positioned as the moral.[14] Historically, struggles cleaved this mass into the respectable and the un-respectable, making the un-respectable an interesting categorization; hence the long obsession with black and white working-class danger and sexuality. This process of projection inscribed the working-class as the site of interesting immorality, having no convertible exchange-value for themselves, unless through respectability.

The contemporary reinscription of the working-class as the site of immoral culture and characteristics means that they have an exchange-value, as some of their dispositions are being re-converted into temporary cultural dispositions (such as 'cool') that can be tried on and used as a resource for the formation and propertizing of the 'new' middle-class self (see Chapters 8 and 9).

But there is, I'd argue, a significant moral shift occurring. It is just like the historical respectable/unrespectable divide, that was so significant in the ways the working-class were made and made themselves. Certain historically defined 'vices' have potential marketability (such as the criminality of black and white masculinity – described in a recent newspaper article as 'one of the most pernicious media[15] trends of the last decade'), whilst others have no exchange-value whatsoever (such as the fecund young working-class mother). Even in the local context her reproductive use-value is limited and limits her movement. The splitting of 'vices' into *recoupable* (for exchange) and *abject*, as the constitutive limit for what is valueless (to the nation, for exchange of any kind), is strongly gendered. As the book will proceed to show, it is white working-class women who are yet again becoming the abject of the nation. And different inscriptions generate different boundaries between what is recoupable and what is not; so the one body may carry the 'benefit scrounger' along with the 'naughty criminal'. Characteristics are split and morally valued.

Yet the projection as the site of the immoral also enables the working-class to generate their own use-values *and* to exist beyond moral governance, enabling a critique of the constraints of morality.[16] This, I'd argue, is where the historical critique of pretentiousness emerged (which will become significant later when cultural and class struggle is explored). Anti-pretentiousness was a critique of the constricting morality of the middle-classes, their up-tightness and restraint. The position of non-restraint was seen to be far more fun, making class struggle into a moral struggle. When Mike Featherstone (1991) charts the contemporary interest of the new middle-classes in 'calculated de-control' and restrained hedonism, he is describing a shift in moral behaviour. He shows how the middle-class, who were and are positioned by morality, discipline and restraint, attempt to become less restrained without losing any of the cultural privileges accorded to them by their social positioning. It's like having your cake and wilfully playing with it. There is also a valorization of the 'genuine', which is opposed to both pretension and restraint and which is seen as a real moral value, rather than simply as fun; hence the middle-class interest in the authentic object and the authenticity of the other (see Lury 1997a). For the middle-classes authenticity has moral and exchange-value, but also offers protection against accusations of pretentiousness.

Morality is absolutely central to the different themes that are woven together throughout the book. Morality informs the perspectives taken, the inscriptions made and the value attributed. What this book pursues is: which perspectives become inscribed? What perspectives and relationships enable exchange to take place? How does inscription set limits on how bodies and dispositions can accrue value in different fields and mechanisms of exchange? How do these systems of value attribution position groups socially and spatially? How do these establish the conditions of possibility for not just exchange-value but also use-value? How are dominant inscriptions that institutionalize perspectives and attribute value contested through the generation of alternative use-values?

I will now describe the shape the book will take through mapping the chapter outlines.

Chapter maps

The book begins with an historical interrogation of how different legacies emerged to explain contemporary class. This is not an extensive historical mapping but a discursive mapping, that performs an historical epistemology to establish the terms by which class was spoken and the processes that established those terms. It illustrates how legacies of propriety are established through systems of moral value attribution and how these are always premised on knowing through visuality, because observing is central to governance. It charts how class has always been a moral term and how it has always been a form of cultural property. It then proceeds to discuss how the contemporary classed self is being forged in a very similar manner to that established historically by contemporary academic theorists: their proscriptions of how class should be known focuses on their own experiences. Not unlike the historical possessive individual who self-aggrandized from their own position, we can see how some of our contemporary theorists are doing likewise. These theorists also introduce new ways of formulating class without directly naming it, such as mobility, reflexivity and individualism. A critical analysis is made (in Chapter 3) of these universalizing pretensions; the compulsion to identity is, for instance, shown to be a classed and raced mechanism, a form of cultural property, awash with moral judgments, reliant upon exclusions and central to contemporary forms of governance.

Chapter 4 sketches the contemporary understandings of economic discourse, exploring the terms that are established for speaking class, demonstrating how many contemporary understandings that rely on the economy are underpinned by particular modes of personhood, in particular, the figure of the 'optimizing self': that is, in the contemporary, the rational-acting individual who not only enhances their investments but can also self-govern. This is shown to be in the tradition of the 'self-ownership' (possessive individual) model, in which self and identity become, as they always were, a privileged social position, a cultural resource, that can be optimized by those who are located by it.

In the development of a wider framework for understanding class, the book then moves from the inscriptions of academic, social and economic theory into exploring political rhetoric in Chapter 5. Political rhetoric generates a discursive space where moral evaluation is made explicit. This chapter maps how old rhetoric is re-combined with new to create new evaluations that can be understood by reference to older categorizations. Certain groups become consolidated as *the* problem. This chapter makes explicit how class is ubiquitous without being spoken and how many euphemisms for the term class are being put into effect. It also demonstrates how class is being figured as a spatial problem. And it illustrates how the working-class continues to be cleaved into the respectable and un-respectable with the un-respectable being racialized and made immoral. What is significantly new in this political rhetoric is how the global economy is used to legitimate, as a good and neutral thing, defined *against* those bad things that seek to hamper its development: the moral, racialized (under)class is held responsible for the blockage on unfettered national-global development.

The process of morally-loading different sectors of the working-class with sexuality, gender and race is made even more explicit in Chapter 6, which explores the inscriptions of popular representations. This chapter demonstrates how particular moral categorizations (for example, excess, waste and backwardness) are the ways in which class is exchanged and circulated as a value in the contemporary.

This chapter makes explicit the exchange mechanisms through which symbolic representations of class are mobilized, and begins to chart how different aspects become a form of cultural property, detached from working-class bodies for use as a cultural resource by others. This chapter begins an analysis into how some groups have to be fixed and held in place (guess who?) in order for others to be seen to be mobile, new, interesting and valuable. Whereas distance was once one of the primary ways of marking and knowing class, this chapter proposes that proximity now feeds the desire to know and place bodies via moral attribution.

Chapter 7 focuses on methods and on how certain selves are forced to become, not just through visual systems of symbolic coding but also through ways of narrating a 'self' to make it recognizable to the law, the state, and academics. Techniques of governance require a moral self. The chapter moves from an historical account into an analysis of how self-telling operates in the contemporary, illustrating how telling the self is now being used by social theorists to authorize their own accounts of the world. The contrast between those who claim reflexivity for themselves and those who actually practice reflexivity is explored. The emphasis is on how particular methods (which are usually spoken of as if neutral) are actually techniques for making class and gender difference.

The book now shifts its attention from the working-class to the middle-class. After all, it is about the perspectives that are taken and the relationships that are made im/possible. Chapter 8 explores how 'new' theories of the self rely on perspective-making and resource-use. It analyses how the resource-ful self generates its character through the historical citation of a system of exchange in which everything is reduced to exchange-value and a resource base is widened. This chapter examines how processes of distinction-making have different national inflections, reliant on the institutionalization of the discourse of choice. The perspectives that are constituted by the incitement to choice, or what Strathern (1992b) defines as 'compulsory individuality', depend upon the resources that are available for self-formation and what forms of moral legitimation exist. Access and entitlement to resources (including persons and their culture) are the factors that shape the terms of new middle-class personhood.

The final chapter develops these themes through entitlement and investment. It details how the 'new' cosmopolitan (an entitled, mobile, individualized disposition), reliant on the resources of others for its self-production, is also reliant on a system of exchange that makes some resources, namely the working-class woman, *the constitutive limit*. Propriety, a moral and middle-class attribute, marks her as beyond cultural appropriation as all the prior symbolic systems are inscribed, condensed and read on her body. What is significant is how inscription and spatialization come together through bodies sharing the same space. So, whereas increasing spatial demarcation has occurred to enable the middle-class to be protected from the working-class, in a space of proximity different groups that would not usually encounter each other come together. This makes the readings of each other more acute and serves to put into effect bodily demarcation that is read through all the prior forms of inscription. The moral value attributed to working-class women's bodies in this space marks them as the ground of fixity from which others can become mobile, but also highlights who can be propertized, exchanged, appropriated and attributed with worth.

Ultimately, this is a book about how different forms of class are being made and how in this making value is attributed. This value, which can be read on the body, is produced through symbolic systems which set limits on who can be known and how. This is not a 'turn to culture', or a shift to recognition politics, but a means of showing how bodies and peoples are inscribed with worth (both moral and economic), and how this process of inscription makes entitlements and fixes limits, enabling some groups to *propertize their personhood* and others to be beyond appropriation, as the foundational ground of valuelessness from which others can mark and know their distinctions.

As Wendy Brown (2001) notes, post-colonial, empire and imperialist critiques – by drawing attention to the role of the constitutive outsider as essential to the formation of liberalism – have disturbed the foundational premises of liberalism's most strongly-held beliefs in progress, emancipation and egalitarianism. Here I hope to demonstrate that those who were once considered partial insiders are now being repositioned as the constitutive outsider 'at home': the white working-class. They are constitutive in the attempts by the middle-class to reformulate themselves, but they are also constitutive of new ways of generating value for others.

This book will question some of the wildest universalizing pretensions presented by new theories. It offers a methodology for understanding class relations that does not restrict analysis solely to the economic. Rather, it offers a model that explores different forms of inscription and exchange from academic theory, popular representations and political rhetoric, to methods of narrating, to show how the making of difference and the institutionalization of division occurs, whereby some groups can become resources for others, but also how exclusion is a constitutive necessity in the forging of class locations and relations, and how this necessity works as a constitutive limit holding some groups as the ground of fixity from which others can move. Embodied entitlement is one of the most class-ridden ways of moving through space (metaphorical and physical). It is a way of carrying value on the body, a process in which we are all implicated intimately every day.

2   Thinking Class

The historical production of concepts of class

The strange thing about excavating the history of the concept of class is how it has a remarkably long and dense relationship to other concepts. First, class is always closely entwined with different forms of exchange as an idea in its various manifestations (e.g. markets and capitalism as the contemporary variant). Second, it is always and intimately connected to the concept of the self. Third, it can only be known through other categorizations. Fourth, it always embeds the interests of the theorist in the perspective taken on it, and fifth, it always has a moral value and is connected to systems of moral evaluation just as much as it is to systems of economic exchange.

In this chapter I want to show how class as a concept emerged, reliant not only on particular political interests and social conditions, but also on the ways in which systems of knowledge enable us to know how class came into being. Mary Poovey notes:

> The institutionalization or codification of protocols for knowing and representing facilitates the perception that certain characteristics are common to a number of discrete practices. The reified abstractions that standardized modes of knowing generate then produce effects that are simultaneously symbolic and material – as we see, for example, in the case of the census, where abstractions like 'minorities' (however defined) receive differential symbolic and material treatment according to prevailing assumptions about their relative value to society as a whole.
>
> (Poovey 1995: 5)

It is in categorical production that value is initially attributed, hence a symbolic evaluation. Categories are not neutral terms, but are rather the result of historical struggle. They are not only shaped by the conditions of their emergence, but also by the way in which they get continually cited. This citational process enables flexibility so that some concepts become reshaped to fit contemporary conditions, still carrying their historical legacies, whilst others are abandoned as inapplicable and incapable of being stretched to meet contemporary conditions. This transformation also involves the drawing of boundaries and the codification of rules in order to create new and more specialized conceptual categorizations from what once seemed to be an undifferentiated continuum of practices and ideas. Poovey (1995) shows how these transformations occur, both in the register of representation (what Foucault calls the 'order of discourse'), inscription, and in the register of materiality, producing effects that can be measured or felt. So, the category of class has very real effects for those who have to live its classifications. For the purposes of this chapter I provide a mapping exercise, based not on chronology, but on thematic excavation, to demonstrate how particular ways of thinking class came into being – and also to demonstrate how through citation certain historical legacies are fitted into the present, carrying with them ideas about moral and economic value.

The chapter is organized into four sections. The first explores discourses of economy and markets to illustrate how frames are established for value attribution using class. The second examines the relationship between self and class in formation. The third analyzes how classification is always made from a specific perspective, representing particular interests, and the final section pulls this analysis into the contemporary to reveal how legacies and citation are being articulated through theories of class.

Exchange, economies and markets

Class, as a concept, was formed through the domain of 'exchange'. Exchange encompasses the moral as well as the political and economic. The term 'exchange' can be traced back to the fourteenth century. In the modern context the term 'exchange' is short for the exchange relation that, along with production, is the 'foundation from which the bourgeoisie built itself up' (Marx 1857/1970:40). Analysis of exchange means that we have to address the attribution of value and authority, enabling us to explore inequality as struggle. Slavoj Zizek (1994) claims that it is the abstract nature of exchange, its discounting of morality, social relations and responsibilities, that not only created the conditions for the development of abstract thought, but also determined its nature. Different forms of exchange generate different social and economic relations, as anthropologists have so convincingly shown (Gregory 1997; Strathern 1992b). Exchange also shapes the possibilities for patterns of relationships such as identity or self.

As Don Slater and Fran Tonkiss (2001) note, in an historical analysis of 'markets', different types of exchange – as different means of allocating resources – make sense only in terms of the economic order in which they operate. Exchange oriented to price, as Karl Polanyi (1992) demonstrated, has no meaning outside the large market system. Polanyi's (1992) own account of market exchange is based on a dual understanding of the market – as a socio-spatial artefact and as mechanism or 'gadget'. Michel Mauss' (1990) work on the gift, and later work by Levi-Strauss and Sahlins, on the other hand used an expanded notion of *generalized exchange*. We can only engage in exchange if we share a basic understanding of the terms of social exchange. Two key insights can be drawn from these anthropological perspectives, Slater and Tonkiss argue. First, they point to the practical role of 'non-economic' factors – social ties, cultural norms – in processes of material allocation. Second, they situate specific forms of exchange, including markets, in a realized exchange that provides the basis for social interaction, reciprocity and collective action. Economic processes – including market processes – are thus always embedded in cultural norms and practices. Different forms of exchange are appropriate to quite different social relationships that they each play a part in reproducing or affirming. Modes of exchange are therefore central to reproducing particular patterns of relationships and co-ordinating social identities, functions and actions.

Gary Day (2001) maintains exploitation is central to exchange, but shows how exploitation has been ignored in recent accounts of class analysis. For instance, in the work of David Cannadine (1988) who claims that 'class as hierarchy' was – and is – the most accurate description of the English social structure. Yet, as Day points out, it is possible to give a different history of class in terms of exploitation and this, he argues, is what Marx had in mind when he wrote that '[t]he history of all hitherto existing societies is the history of class struggles' (Marx and Engels 1848/1968:35). The difference between explanations of class based on conflict and struggle and those based on hierarchical description forms a binary division that is still reproduced today (see the following sections). Day contends that exploitation provides a lengthier analysis of inequality. For instance, the historical research of Ste. Croix (1981) charts how exploitation was evident in the forms of exchange of Ancient Greece and has consistently been reproduced in most Western forms of exchange.

Also, when tracing the historical epistemology of class, we can see how it moves between a moral and economic definition. There have been certain periods when it was definable *primarily* by economic, monetary and market value; at others it was defined in relation to moral criteria. During the 1850s and 1860s, for instance, there is less talk of working-class and middle-class, and more of deserving and undeserving poor, of 'respectable artisans and "gentleman"', as emphasis was placed on moral rather than economic criteria' (Crossick 1991:161–2). However, these two aspects are rarely separable and the value attributed to one domain has clear ramifications for the other.

Day (2001) identifies the further paradoxes of exchange: on the one hand, exchange is associated with the rise of the bourgeoisie, and therefore 'class'-based, but on the other hand, it transcends class by assuming the essential equality of all in the market place. It is therefore important to understand the nature of exchange, not just because it is a bourgeois form of economic organization, but also because of the way it insinuates itself into structures of representation and social life. We can see this in the emergence of the 'economic' as a domain.

With the financial revolution of the 1690s, which saw the establishment of credit, the foundation of the Bank of England and the re-coinage of the currency, the word 'economy', Day shows, comes to be associated with money and exchange. These developments represent a further extension of exchange, thereby consolidating bourgeois power.[1] The term and domain 'economic' became consolidated and linked to the political in the course of the eighteenth century. Initially, as Poovey (1995) shows, the term economy referred to the management of a household, with all of the financial, ethical and domestic responsibilities that an early modern household entailed. Yet it came to signal the management of national resources. This linguistic innovation, Poovey suggests, can be seen as an imaginary entity (a representation) that is governed by a specific rationality: in this case, the logic and procedures by which productivity and financial security are ensured.

The economic, then, constituted a domain, an order of discourse, or a form of inscription, when commercial and financial transactions that were once viewed as part of a complex system of management began to seem different from other kinds of practices to which they were once related (Poovey 1995). The represent-ation of 'the economic' stops being recognized as a representation when it begins to seem 'natural' and real. A similar domain construction can be seen in the etymology of the term capitalism. Slater (1997) illustrates how the word 'capitalism' had very little currency in Western thought until after Sombart's (1902) *Modern Capitalism*. Marx rarely used the word, Adam Smith not at all. 'Capital', on the other hand, they show, has a long and busy history from the twelfth century onwards. That capital became enclosed within the economic can be seen to be part of a symbolic struggle to include different perspectives within a domain of knowledge.[2]

Both Callon (1998) and Polanyi (2001) show how the term economy is 'embedded' in political, religious and social relations. Polanyi documents how an inversion was created by the classical economists who, rather than the usual pattern of subordinating the economy to society, reversed the order through the promotion of self-regulating and logical markets. Callon maintains that markets can be seen to be social artefacts, instituted by purposive strategies and technologies of calculation. This analysis has been extensively developed by 'regulation theorists' such as Aglietta (1987) who show how market relations of exchange are instated through cultural practices, social networks, legal and political regulation and organizational arrangements.[3] Theorists such as Granovetter (1981) and Granovetter and Swedberg (1992) argue that exchanges harden into stable social forms as economic institutions become formed by the mobilization of resources through social networks. Fligstein (2001), who uses a political-cultural model from Bourdieu, sees markets as field in the traditional sense. This is the search for stable interactions within the field by which the powerful are able to produce their own kind. The government is then forced to interact with these markets.

In all of these analyses, the market comes to represent the economic institution (Polanyi 2001:47); economic behaviour is isolated as a discrete type of social action, governed by the field and the formal rationality of the market and/or based on impersonal exchanges between buyer and seller. Carrier (1997) calls this 'the Market Idea', meaning that representations of the market have had a central role in organizing the modern West's conceptual and normative universe.

James Thompson (1996) documents how, throughout the eighteenth century, there was a 'drive toward an abstract and consistent and therefore predictable representation of exchange, that is, toward (new) scientific, quantitative, and mathematical modelling' (p.28). These processes involved the calculation and quantification of labour, making the person an object of calculation, subject to domination and to impersonal forces beyond their control. For instance, Slater and Tonkiss (2001) illustrate how Bentham produced the most insanely rigorous rationalist psychology. In Bentham's account people choose their courses of action through 'felicific calculus' in which they compare the relative quantities of pleasure or pain. This is not dissimilar to Ulrich Beck's (2000) contemporary 'mathematical morality' of risk assessment (see Chapter 3).

These processes of calculation became institutionalized in the eighteenth century through the machinery of the New Poor Law, which generated an avalanche of new information and mandated more and more far-reaching fact-gathering, inspection and legislation. This desire for calculation and classification, however, can be seen to have emerged much earlier, in 1665, with William Petty, who set out to calculate the value of the 'people' of England for taxation purposes. Petty is attributed with devising what is now known as the 'political arithmetic' tradition of class analysis in order to enumerate what was otherwise un-measurable (Poovey 1995).

As the domain of the economic emerged, it was accompanied by the representation of an idea of a *neutral market*, the space where exchange could take place. Whereas the old moral economy had validated itself with reference to moral imperatives – what obligations the state or the landowners 'ought to obey' (Thompson 1993a:269), the new neutral market was governed by its own principle: profit. The neutral market placed the emphasis for exchange on individuals. By constructing persons as rational pursuers of self-interest, individuals became detached from traditional 'sources of the self' (Taylor 1989). The market implied a view of the economy as an objective mechanism that operated without regard to moral considerations (made most explicit in Adam Smith's *The Wealth of Nations* (1776)). Thus the moral becomes unhinged from the market itself, but finds a way back in through the self in which it is the attribution of value that enables some bodies to become commodified. Patrick Joyce (1994) illustrates how this became consolidated in the Victorian period, when the transition from an inner- to an outer-directed self was formalized, through not just economic exchange but also state policy. This led to emphasis being placed on systems, laws and regularities, which impact on the way we understand class now as a system.

So, we have an exchange mechanism which enables the development of a separate domain named the 'economic'. This domain comes to be represented as neutral, yet it is predicated upon individualized interest, rational calculation and productive value. This domain also re-shapes self-formation, generating concepts of a proprietorial self that works in its own interests to accumulate, and is directed by inside and outside forces. This self is both enabled and constrained by the exchange mechanisms established; this is how it becomes a self with or without value. This valuation process provides the conditions of possibility for a classed-self. Already the centrality of the visual, quantification and the creation of metaphor to describe social relations are established. The next section explores in more detail how this self is developed as a site of interest and value.

Exchanging the rational gendered split self

Just as the concept of class is produced through exchange relationships, so is the self, and there are close discursive parallels. Day outlines how the operation of exchange constitutes 'the self'. For instance, the split between the bodily form of the commodity and its 'purely ideal mental form', that is, its value (Marx 1857/1970), is implicated in the decline of status and the rise of the 'inner self':

> The difference between the two types of identity is that whereas status is directly expressed in bodily form, for example clothing, jewellery, the 'inner self' has a much more indirect relation to its 'outer appearance'. This 'dual' nature of 'the self, split between mind and body, seems to correspond to the 'dual' character of the commodity, split between 'value' and 'use' and is accordingly an appropriate form of identity for a society based on exchange. The 'split self' also inaugurates the great 'bourgeois' project of self-knowledge whose many forms include the puritan conscience, Freudian psychoanalysis and the stream of consciousness novel.
>
> (Day 2001:60)

He further argues that, just as exchange structures the conception of the self, it also has an impact on the conception of 'reality'. Whereas in the medieval period the things of the world were luminous with meaning, in the Renaissance and onwards there is a divorce between 'appearance' and 'reality'. 'The self', Day maintains, is always class based and, because of that, we can therefore view the contrast between different conceptions of 'the self' as a form of class conflict. For instance, there is a correlation between the Marxist conception of class and Freud's account of the human psyche:

> Freud's conception of the conscious ego constantly under threat from an anarchic id approximates to bourgeois fears of civilization being swept away by working-class radicalism. Similarly, the concern in Marxism over how the proletariat can become fully conscious of itself and so transcend the divisions of class society echoes Freud's early belief that a patient can be cured and become whole only if he or she is made fully aware of the origin of their illness. These very general parallels between Marx and Freud suggest that the concept of class is compatible with that of the individual; indeed, if it is not to push the point too far, we might almost say that a model of class structures the individual psyche.
>
> (Day 2001:142)

This can be seen as a conceptual citation from Adam Smith's *Theory of Moral Sentiments* (1757), which argues not just for a mind and body split, but also for a moral, judgemental split in the self:

> When I endeavour to examine my own conduct, when I endeavour to pass sentence upon it, and either to approve or condemn it, it is evident that, in all

such cases, I divide myself, as it were, into two persons; and that I, the examiner and judge, represent a different character from that other I, the person whose conduct is examined into and judged of. The first is the spectator, whose sentiments with regard to my own conduct I endeavour to enter into, by placing myself in his situation, and by considering how it could appear to me, when seen from that particular point of view. The second is the agent, the person whom I properly call myself, and of whose conduct, under the character of a spectator, I was endeavouring to form some opinion.

(Smith 1759:113)

Smith's self was based on specular, visual relations, a self that could be surveilled by watching one's self. The surveillance was dependent on external ethical systems, which were internalized as a property of the self. One's value as a self depended upon self-control, monitoring and conduct, i.e. propriety. Musselwhite (1987) illustrates how, during the course of the nineteenth century, class conflict becomes gradually internalized as conflict between different parts of the self; internalized morality becomes central to entering exchange circuits. Yet it was not just internalization. Morality was more generally conceptualized within a problematic of visuality. Because the poor were considered to be different from, as well as a part of, the national whole, political surveillance and increased ocular penetration (using social science methods of observation) of poor neighbourhoods were generally considered to be as critical to the inculcation of virtue as the cultivation of taste. (Poovey 1995)

In relation to the development of the self, Day (2001) charts how after the Civil War in England (1642–8) commerce came to pervade everyday life through the emergence of 'character types'. He traces the emergence of 'economic man' in terms of his 'interest' rather than his 'passion' or even position. This process was consolidated by the abstractions made by Adam Smith. Social relations became abstract in the sense that Smith reduces them all to versions of measurable exchange; and individuals became abstract, in the sense that Smith represents 'everyone' as an instance of the same abstract entity, a representative of 'human nature' that wants only to truck, barter and exchange (Poovey 1995:34). So interest rather than position comes to be the defining feature of difference and distinction. This is absolutely key to the development of class, whereby it is the economically interested self who benefits from exchange-value. It is a way of transferring all economic responsibility onto the individual, rather than the system (of exchange) that produces models of the market as a neutral system and the individual as a self, responsible for its own value. The move towards identifying people in terms of their exchangeable, productive capacities also promoted a mechanistic view of the body which, Day argues, could not be more different from the earlier view of the body as an organic unity, whose parts co-operated with one another, which served as a model for the working of hierarchical society.

The metaphor of the divided 'self', therefore, underwrites the division of labour and the new inequalities based on ownership of production. Ultimately, this means that there is not only a division between body and mind, but also that the body itself can be subdivided into smaller and smaller units. The division between the body and the mind, and the subdivisions of the body, were part of a new way of representing the social order; one that relied more on classification than on status distinctions (see Emily Martin 1989, 1994, 1997, for how this conceptualization develops). The subdivision of the body produced interesting associations in the dominant symbolic representations of the time: the working-class became associated with the hands or musculature of the body social; domestic servants, in particular, came to be associated with the care of back passages[4] and the poor came to be represented as excrement. Osbourne's pamphlet on 'Excremental sewage in 1852' represents the working-class as a problem for civilization, as sewerage that contaminates and drains the nation (Yeo 1993).

The divided self was also a self that was split between the rational and the irrational. Emerging from Rousseau, consolidated through Romanticism, the irrational was projected onto women, so that the male character could remain 'intact'. Joanna de Groot (1989) charts how masculinity developed through the dichotomy of reason and nature; in this process men transferred responsibility for emotional and personal needs to women, enabling women to take on the role of guardian. The paradox is, de Groot argues, that this transfer embodied both the male power that made it happen, and the loss of power that dealt with the world of emotion, personal expression and intimacy. This is a significant legacy which combines models of self that – because they operate in the interests of the gendered power of privileged groups – continue to have a long history, cited and re-worked through the contemporary variants of rational action theory, and the association of irrationality and emotion with women.

Valerie Walkerdine (1988) provides a comprehensive history of how rationality came to be such a powerful discourse. Rationality is premised on the fact that initially it is just that – an inscription, an order of discourse, a representational register. She notes how discourse is produced within a specific set of practices that guarantee its applicability. This ensures the 'suppression' of its constructedness and the articulation of its generalizability as the basis of the nature of 'mind'. The power of such discourse is precisely because it forms descriptions and can be read back onto anything. In this sense statements of rationality appear to be without context. De-contextualization is an effect that renders this system of statements as statements of fact precisely because it claims a universal applicability. This, Walkerdine explains, offers a rationality devoid of any content which can describe and therefore explain everything, holding out the dream of the possibility of perfect control in a perfectly rational and ordered universe. Drawing on the work of Rotman (1980), who suggests that discourses of rational action are the product of a particular form of desire:

> The desire's object is a pure, timeless unchanging discourse, where assertions proved stay proved forever (and must somehow always have been true), where all the questions are determinate and all the answers totally certain. In terms of the world the desire is for a discourse that proxies the manipulation of physical reality achieving a perfect and total control of 'things', where no

realizable process falls outside reach. Where no counter-examples or exceptions or errors of prediction are possible.

(Rotman 1980:129)

This is a fantasy in which the world becomes what is wanted: regular, ordered, controllable. 'Reason's Dream', as Rotman calls it, is seductive, for it offers to its subject power over others, oneself, and the prediction and control of events. It is a fantasy of omnipotent power over a calculable universe. The contemporary understanding of 'game theory'[5] is a perfect rendition of this fantasy and, interestingly, it is this that underpins much contemporary rational action theory, which assumes a rational calculating self. However, significantly, game theory argued that for anyone to win, others *must* lose. It was therefore based on *exclusions*. The rational self, the calculating, all-knowing, universal subject, is the result of a powerful group, with access to the circuits of discourse distribution, fantasizing about their own power and effects, producing the forms of exchange and the types of subject that suited them and their fantasies.

For instance, Elizabeth Cowie (1978) also notes how the rational self supposes the very system of exchange that it is intended to explain. For example, the category 'woman' is produced as a sign within mobile and shifting practices. That is, the sign 'woman' in marriage is not exchanged but produced in exchange of actual women. Thus the relations are constituted in the practices themselves, as Levi-Straus showed. So it is the way the subject as a sign is positioned within a practice that produces the possibility of the fantasy of rationality.

Classification and the parts of the social body

One of the central problems for those with power was how to know *exchange*. Just as the economic becomes one domain of inscription, producing different versions of self and class, there is also the issue of how to know the population more generally. Another central trope was the 'social body'. By 1776, Poovey (1995) explains, the phrase 'body politic' was established and had begun to compete with another metaphor, 'the great body of the people', used by Adam Smith in *The Wealth of Nations*. It was used to refer to the mass of labouring poor. Poovey demonstrates how both of these phrases were joined by the image of the social body by the early nineteenth century. The social body was used in two quite different ways: referring either to the poor in isolation from the rest of the population, or to British (or English) society as an organic whole. This enables social analysts to treat one segment of the population as a special problem whilst, at the same time, gesturing toward the social whole. It was only certain parts of the social body that were seen to need both discipline and care. This can be seen as the beginning of the development of bourgeois 'perspective'. Strathern (1992b) argues that it is this perspective on the social body that enabled limited viewpoints to be presented as if they were representative of the whole.

Poovey (1995) also maintains that the conceptualization of 'abstract space' was necessary to class formation:

> [T]he institutionalization of a Euclidian view of space as empty and amenable to mathematical calculation was crucial to the constitution of the social body, because this concept of space authorized treating the poor as an aggregate whose neighbourhoods should be penetrated and subjected to statistical analysis by clergymen and doctors.
>
> (Poovey 1995:15)

Partly as a consequence, Poovey argues, abstract space was symbolically and materially associated with homologies – seriality; repetitious actions; reproducible products; interchangeable places, behaviours and activities – becoming known through the codification of numerical, then statistical modes of abstraction.

Through the system of minute classification, the part was broken down even further: the 'impotent poor', those who could not work, and the 'idle poor', 'vagrants' and 'sturdy beggars' (Kishlansky 1997:28–9). The principle of classification in this case is not only based on the metaphor of an organic body, but it is also a method by which each group is both allocated a potential exchange-value in terms of productivity and classified according to moral principal. That is, the division is drawn between those who want and are capable of work and those who are idle and incapable (think about the contemporary 'Job Seeker' or 'Dis-affected Youth' classification schema). Classification enables moral responsibility, agency and value to be attributed to some parts of the social body, whilst other parts can remain unseen and irresponsible for their power effects (see Chapter 5 for an account of how this is worked through in contemporary political rhetoric).

Moreover, as Day (2001) points out, classification serves the bourgeoisie by describing economic divisions in scientific terms, making division appear as a law of nature beyond change. In the late seventeenth century and throughout the eighteenth, debates centred on the question of representation: for instance, how accurately does a banknote represent monetary worth?

In the early nineteenth century the term 'class' comes to prominence and is consolidated in descriptions of society. Some theorists argue that the term class emerged to coincide with the rise of the 'middle sort' (Williams 1988), which encapsulated divisions and methods that have already been identified. In contrast, Dror Wahrman (1995) contends, middle-class identities emerged after those of the working-class and therefore developed in reaction to them. He maintains that the crucial moment for fixing the idea of the middle-class was around the time of the 1832 Reform Act. The need for political representation allowed the middle-class to be consolidated as a group. A central issue is *how* the middle-class came to conceptualize itself. For some theorists it was through the expression of 'taste' and the generation of distinctive cultures, as Terry Eagleton (1989) notes: 'the ultimate binding force of the bourgeois social order [were] habits, pieties, sentiments and affections' (p.22).

The emergence of the term 'working-class' is subject to a similar debate. Finch (1993) documents how class emerged as a category to define the urban poor. In a detailed study of Australia, she illustrates how class was particularly gendered, conceived through the interpretation of the behaviour of women of urban slums and the classification of them into respectable and non-respectable. In an equally detailed historical analysis, McClintock (1995) suggests that the concept of class has a wider link to more generalizable 'others', who were known through the concept of degeneracy, a term applied as much to classifying racial 'types' as to the urban poor. Domestic servants, for instance, were often depicted by the racialized imagery of degradation – of contagion, promiscuity and savagery. As Engels (1844/1958) notes of the working-class: 'a physically degenerate race, robbed of all humanity, degraded, reduced morally and intellectually to bestiality' (p.33).

The term race was used (in the same way as culture is today) as a kind of summation of historically accumulated moral differences (Stocking 1987). This is most apparent in Engels (1844/1958), who describes the working-class as a 'race apart' (p.361). It is also apparent in other processes of 'racing'. For instance, Poovey (1995) shows how James Phillip Kay's influential pamphlet on *The Moral and Physical Condition of the Working-classes in Manchester* (1832) defines the Irish as inhuman on the basis of their domestic habits. For Kay, the Irish were available both as a scapegoat for national woes and as a resource to be exploited when needed. So observation and empirical description again designates and classifies particular groups. This merging of race and class through discourses of inhuman degeneracy shows how 'natural' and 'biological' legitimation was used to justify difference. As we move into the contemporary we can trace the shift from biological to cultural essentialism (Strathern 1992a).

Gender sexuality, and degeneracy were central to all class definitions. Foucault argues that the middle-class, struggling to find the means to define itself, deployed sexuality. One's relation to one's body and the body of others became the language of expressing one's relation to class.

> The middle-class thus defined itself as different from the aristocracy and the working-classes who spent, sexually and economically, without moderation … It differed by virtue of its sexual restraint, its monogamy and its economic restraint or thrift.
>
> (Foucault 1979:100)

So sexuality, or more precisely, heterosexuality, can be added to the means by which class difference could be known and understood. Sex, gender and race difference were the means by which class came to be known, spoken, experienced and valued. These perspectives, produced in the interests of consolidating the identity and representation of powerful groups via quantifications and empirical observations, came to institutionalize class. As McClintock (1995) puts it, 'the invention of racial fetishism became central to the regime of sexual fetishism became central to the policing of the "dangerous classes"' (1995:182).

For instance, Joel Kahn (2001) maintains that the idea of primitivism was fundamental to the naming, knowing and valuing of the British worker. He documents how, just like the debate and critique of orientalism,[6] a similar distinction was made between 'primitive phobia' and 'primitive mania': primitive phobia provided an account of civilization's triumph over, or mastery of, nature. Primitive mania enabled a critique of the artificiality and decadence of Western civilization, which was seen to have lost touch with the natural and authentic. Primitive phobia was mainly directed at a threat from within rather than outside. Kahn argues that, at times, primitivism was not to do with empire at all, but about the internal divisions inside Britain itself, 'notably the working-classes and everyone else; the unrespectable and the respectable' (2001:61). Victorian notions of respectability were intimately connected with primitivism discourse. Bailey (1998), for instance, details how respectability entailed moral rectitude, economic continence and self-sufficiency; in short, a distillation of evangelical disciplines.

The debates over self-reliance were able to feed into this, showing that those most able to survive had 'natural' talent. For those who made the link between the primitive and nature, vice was seen to be a primitive indulgence of natural desires and physical wants (the behaviour of uncultured savages). The threat to civilization was again seen to lie in the working-class. The unrespectable were seen to be the volcano on which the rest of the civilized nation rested. Kahn charts how most reformers from 'left' and 'right' clung to the primitivist vision of the British worker. What is significant from Kahn's analysis is how terms of degradation (primitive) were used to simultaneously value and devalue: valued by some for being authentic and closer to nature, or valued by others for the proximity to nature that produced the threat to civilization. This is an important legacy, which is worked out in the contemporary, as Chapters 6, 8 and 9 demonstrate.

But what is also significant is that in any definition of respectability, sexuality lurks beneath the inscription. For instance, prostitution, as the constitutive limit to propriety, was subject to particular debate. A target of numerous sporadic reform initiatives in the 1830s, prostitution, like the cities in which it flourished, focused anxieties associated with industrialization and capitalism more generally (Poovey 1995). It operated in the same way identified by Ann-Marie Smith (1994a) to condense anxieties onto a particular visual and identifiable source, enabling the real source of problems to be supplemented and displaced. Investigation into prostitution created several dilemmas for methods of social investigation. Prostitution was seen to epitomize the uncertainty and irrationality of change. Most explicitly, prostitution challenged social analysis because prostitutes were so difficult to count and so difficult to document in minute detail: 'So perplexing were their numbers, in fact, that exaggeration and underestimation presented equal dangers to the would-be statistician' (Poovey 1995:90).

Another issue raised by the classification of prostitution was how enumerating or describing prostitutes could lead to 'exacerbate the evil the moralist wants to control, because realistic representation incites imitation' (Poovey 1995:90). This is not dissimilar to the fears expressed about legislating for the term 'lesbian' (see Lynda Hart 1994). Bringing the lesbian and/or the prostitute into representation meant offering the possibilities for imitative behaviour.

It is, however, not just about bringing sexuality into public discourse, it is always also a matter of governance. For instance, Oxley (1997) demonstrates how in colonial New South Wales, the title 'whore' was earned not by selling sex, but by breaking rules and not behaving like a lady: 'They got drunk, they smoked, they gazed back and they spoke in lewd ways their critics thought reserved for men' (1997:93). This is not dissimilar to Sander Gilman's (1990) research on London's East End, whereby the term 'prostitute' came to stand in for working-class women in general and a range of ethnicities. The key to their grouping together was their perceived immorality and lack of propriety; hence their lack of value, other than in defining the terms of the normative by establishing the constitutive limit of respectability.

Therefore, notwithstanding the historical specificities of class formation, we can deduce that the concept of class emerged through the mechanism of exchange, the inscriptive metaphors of the social and economic body and the methodological principle of classification. This emergence relied on the use of specific methods, such as observation, statistical calculation, ethnography and visual identification, which generated regimes of representation, to enable those classified to be recognized and known. Representations (by classification and visuality) always contained moral de/authorization. Yet by establishing a moral valuing system of exchange in which immortality, nature and authenticity become defining boundaries, a residue of value remains, one that makes those at the constitutive limit potentially much more exciting than those valued through restraint, respectability and propriety. This residual value continues to have significance as it is reworked into the contemporary.

These definitions and valuation of classes also produced particular versions of the self. For the middle-class it was the 'rational', constrained moral individual with reflexivity. For the working-class the self was not a subject-position to be occupied, rather they were *subject to* primitive impulse. The working-class were represented as having deficit 'culture' (be it based on their close proximity to nature), rather than selves. Moreover, their culture was subject to numerous reform initiatives, another powerful legacy carried through into the contemporary. This was reliant on the knowledge and 'expertise' of bourgeois reformers. The discourse of Eugenics enabled proponents such as Galton and Pearson to biologize the superiority and intellects of 'experts', making their culture a matter of national good:

> The nation, however prosperous, however hardy, however big, will fail when it comes to a crisis, when it is suddenly placed in a new environment, unless it has organized brain power controlling its nervous system right away to the smallest outlying points.
>
> (Pearson 1904:14)

Expertise becomes a way of attaching superiority and consolidating power for the proponents of Eugenics across a range of sites (science, education, art); a legacy that continues into the present.

The obsession with expertise, with calculation and classification through observation, and with anxiety over incorporation is played out in debates over citizenship, where we can see how the newly emergent categories of class become divided into new fragments of the social body. Day (2001) documents how, in the early years of the twentieth century, there is a decline in the idea of the individual and the development of the concept of the citizen. However, the individual and the citizen were not entirely antithetical. As Sutton (1985) notes, citizenship was a mechanism by which the dominant class divided oppositional class forces by 'individualizing' them. The idea of citizenship, Day argues, was thus largely formulated in opposition to class, particularly at the respectable section of the working-class who, in return for political rights and social benefits, are expected to labour for the improvement of the race, the economy and the extension of empire.

As a result of this targeting of different sections of the working-class, Sutton (1985) suggests, the concept of citizenship probably increased rather than reduced social divisions. As with previous periods, citizenship relied on the moral distinction between the 'deserving' and the 'undeserving' poor. The language of citizenship, Perkin (1989) argues, located culture as the sole marker of class difference, and it is this that links us into the contemporary. Defining class through culture dislocates it from the economic and firmly locates it within the moral, in which representation and visuality become central mechanisms for knowing and identifying the working-class. Forms of exchange are epitomized by moral worth.[7]

However, in all of these debates over definition, as Finch (1993) documents, the working-class did not recognize themselves as the degraded authentic primitive, or as the lascivious and contagious. Rather, they operated with entirely different value systems (as Thompson (1966) and Vicinus (1974) have shown). Yet not having access to the symbolic systems of representation, they were unable to directly challenge the classifications and positioning of themselves. But there were alternatives, as Martha Vicinus (1974) reveals. They reversed the values, defining themselves through distance and difference from others, in particular the middle-class, heaping scorn on those with pretensions to gentility. It was resentment and hatred of those with the authority to judge and define. 'Putting on airs was the greatest sin anyone could commit' (Vicinus 1974:262–3).[8] Music-hall entertainment enabled the working-class to challenge the moral authority of others and to value their experience differently from the dominant value systems. This is another important legacy weaved into the contemporary. So whilst huge amounts of energy are put into defining, knowing, classifying, recognizing and moralizing the working-class, they go about their business using their own definitions and valuations.

To recap, we can see that class emerges as a domain of knowledge organized by exchange in which the attribution of value is central to knowing what it actually is. This process of value attribution is primarily moral (although economic value is established through labour) and is known through specific methods: inscription, tropes, political arithmetic, empirical observation and epistemologies of the spatial and visual. As class emerges at one point through the discourse of degeneracy and biological essentialism, we can see the parallels that exist to other classifications and how a route is established for the transfer of value. We can also see how concepts of the self are closely imbricated in class and cannot be separated from it, just as our perceptions of social bodies are threaded through class relations. Central to all these points is how inscription, perspective and representation (academic, popular and political) – essentially, how particular interests – frame our knowledge and assessment. I will now move to the contemporary to briefly demonstrate how these legacies begin to get played out in contemporary class analysis.

The study of class always has a particularly national formation. In Britain, analysis of class worked as a means by which British social scientists identified their distinctive expertise *vis-à-vis* other national traditions. Savage (2000) charts how they tried to carve out academic legitimacy by studying the 'social', which was often conflated with 'social class'. He gives four specific points as evidence for his argument: first, the 'political arithmetic technique' (noted above and established by Petty in the seventeenth century), which involved classification, measuring, quantification and distinguishing social classes. Second, as the social sciences grew, this 'political arithmetic' technique itself diversified into new fields, such as social policy, welfare and education. Also, in response to US functionalist sociology, a specific strand of 'conflict' theory was developed, the integral feature of which was class. Within all these fragmentations, adding to the above historical legacies, the definition of the social, as a domain, was still tied to class and the study of class became a measure of intellectual respectability. Third, class was unusual as a concept because it traversed the academic boundaries and entered into the lives of the everyday. Class debates were not just restricted to academic debate (as shown above), but became a site of wider political debate. Finally, class became the foundation by which social change came to be measured. Savage illustrates how this complex amalgam pervades the contemporary with debates about post-fordism, de-traditionalization and disorganized capital, whereby what is being moved from (post, de- and dis-) are class formations. Class then serves as a bench-mark, fixed in place, so that other mobile relations can be identified. It operates as a foundational ground and becomes less a matter of political struggle and more a matter of measurement.

As a concept, class is, therefore, being used to do many things: provide academic legitimacy, frame an academic discipline, speak to 'the people', measure social change, stand in for the social itself. It is hardly surprising then, that some people respond to class in ways that they try to refigure it, dismiss it, trivialize it and de-centre it. For, as Cannadine (1998) has noted, 'the history of class is as much about the history of ideas about society as it is about society itself' (1998:171). How we study (or do not) class is also how we learn to know and speak the social and the self. I will now explore how these different legacies have been put to use.

In 1966 E.P. Thompson published the classic *The Making of the English Working-class*. Thompson's challenge was to show how class was a structured *process*, made by those who lived structural divisions of labour. In contrast to previous debates, Thompson argued that the working-class had been present at its own making, and that the cultural idioms and values of the emerging working-class itself played a crucial role in defining the course of British history and the development of modern democratic freedoms. For Thompson (1978), then, class-consciousness was a crucial defining feature of class itself. His focus was on experience rather than structure, giving preference to those who made history, rather than those who had history imposed upon them. Thompson drew on Marx's point that people make history but not in the conditions of their own choosing. The fact that he gave a considerable amount of 'explanatory power' back to those who were living class provided a new methodological legacy that has been used across a variety of fields. He used specific historical examples to challenge the structuralism of Althusser (see Thompson's *Poverty of Theory*, 1978). Thompson's work also linked to work in the US on slavery such as the *The World the Slaves Made* (Genovese 1975), where agency is attributed to those who 'make' history.

Just as the 'rise and fall' of class as an academic concept has been documented by sociologists, a similar mapping has been performed by historians. Cannadine (1988) notes how some of the stalwarts of the historical left have shifted their attention from class to other objects of analysis, such as nationalism (e.g. Eric Hobsbawm 1992). Even E.P. Thompson noted, in one of his last essays, that class was overworked in the 1960s and 1970s and had become boring. Most of this retreat can be seen in parallel to the retreat from Marxism more generally (see following Chapters 3 and 4).

The more recent historical work on the concept of class draws on a literary and history of ideas tradition, including Day (2001) and Poovey (1995), cited extensively above, and McClintock (1995) and Finch (1993). This tradition analyses not only how the term is *gendered*, *raced* and *sexed*, but also how it prefigures the development of domains, such as psychoanalysis and economics.

There is another methodological issue at stake here too. In contrast to Thompson, these historical analyses have demonstrated how the generation of categories through classification had to be learnt and recognized by those for whom they were designed and how this was a process of negotiated meaning. The gap between classification and positioning enables the exploration of how class actually does and does not work. Academics may define class, but how it is lived may be significantly different. This is why understanding the production of representations of class is so important – it points to the area of negotiation between classification, positioning and experience and it is the site of mediation, challenge and conflict. However, just because some people refuse to recognize the way they are being positioned, does not mean that class has no effect. Rather, the obverse: energy may be put into resisting the classification (Skeggs 1997). This ultimately means that it has significance, but not in a positive, direct or straightforward way.

So, to clarify, ten important processes have already been established:

- How class became known through the *establishment of moral value*, later required for exchange in economic domains;
- How markets became defined as *neutral sites* and responsibility for economic production was *transferred onto people not systems*;
- How the desire for *authority and power* requires 'others' to be designated, classified and *excluded*;
- How this desire for authority was established through *moral discourse*;
- How class is generated through association with *race*, *sexuality* and *gender*;
- How *quantification*, *classification*, *observation* and *visual attribution* are central methods in recognizing the classified;

- How these methods designate others at the *constitutive limit*, thereby making them the site of all that is interesting;
- How one group's cultural capital (their experience) can be *converted* into symbolic power through legitimation;
- How claims for different types of *self* are part of the political struggle of the powerful;
- How the methods and classifications may make no sense to those designated by them and how critiques are produced in opposition.

One of the main ways class has been constantly sustained as a topic of contemporary analysis, withstanding both Thatcher and Blair (and the Third Way sociologists: see following chapter), has been by the British stalwarts John Goldthorpe and Gordon Marshall. We can see, however, that their methods reproduce a long history of 'political arithmetic' in which producing the most accurate classification is the driving force behind the analysis. This analysis concerns itself with how to fit people into categories rather than with questioning the appropriateness of the categories in the first place. It is re-construction rather than de-construction.

Goldthorpe (1996) has spent years refining the UK Registrar General's five categories of class. The seven new categorizations[9] are now being used widely throughout government organizations. These refinements came after sustained critique that argued that traditional classifications did not take into account half of the population (women were only allocated to classes through the position of their fathers or husbands – see Rosemary Crompton (1993) and Michelle Stanworth (1984) – *and* did not take into account economic changes, such as the decline of the manufacturing industry and the rise of the service industry. The new classifications are still classifications based on status ranking, making assumptions about social standing, that create a measurement classification and then try and fit people into it; not dissimilar to the legacies of classification. Erik Olin Wright (1985) argues that descriptions of class are 'static' concepts: all they can do is classify and label people and ultimately evaluate.

However, even the 'political arithmetic' tradition establishes an important challenge to the liberal agenda of social mobility. Goldthorpe and Marshall demonstrate that life chances based on social class have not changed radically, and that inequality is still a major social problem in the UK. They also show that Britain is not becoming a classless society.

Moreover, one of the most recent turns in class analysis has been to rational action theory, in which the historical citation of the fantasy of the calculating rational self is seen to be the prime mover of class inequality. Yet, as we have seen, this fantasy of the rational calculating individual was a particular bourgeois perspective that benefited the interests of the powerful. It is a theory that not only legitimates particular interests and posits them as universal, but also stresses the individualism of action, thereby placing responsibility for structural inequalities upon those that are subject to them.

Conclusion

This chapter has shown how certain historical legacies, forged at particular times, are repeatedly cited, enabling a resonance for what we know when we speak about class in the contemporary. These citations will be examined throughout the rest of the book. There are clearly a large number of debates from the 1960s and 1970s that have not been included because I wanted to draw out the main strands that are pertinent for my analysis.[10] It is the purpose of this book to reveal how class is always a matter of inscription, representing partial perspectives, power and particular interests. It is the aim of the rest of the book to explore how class is spoken euphemistically, in ways that do not directly name it or ignore it but, nonetheless, represent a classed perspective. This chapter has demonstrated that drawing together particular ways of looking at, measuring and creating an object, i.e. class, enables it to become known. Once in place these perspectives – depending on the power of those doing the looking, knowing and speaking – can be legitimated and even become part of law (e.g. The Poor Law) or the major system of exchange (e.g. the economic) or known morally (e.g. as part of the social body). So the concepts are performative; they have very real material, economic and political impacts.

Whilst class is taking shape through academic battles, it is also being re-formed through market discourse and circulated in popular culture and political rhetoric. In a remarkable consistency with the historical legacies generated to legitimate market neutrality, Thomas Frank (2001) describes how, whereas in the past markets were figured as neutral, then inevitable, now they are being promoted as the basis for democracy, an expression of the will of the people. He points out how the representation of the market suggests that it is a friend of the powerless, occupying a new position in the expression of class struggle. The significance of the economic domain as a register of representation will be woven into the next three chapters to show how unlikely characters are speaking class when sociologists are not.

When we come across the terms economic, social body, exchange, market, self, interest, rational action, abstract space, etc., we need to think about how they articulate a specific relationship to class. Such terms may appear to have nothing to do with class, but they constitute it nonetheless, primarily through their reiteration of value on a daily basis. Class will always be a site of struggle, as it encompasses interests, power and privilege. An acquaintance of mine recently said: 'I don't know why you talk about class, it's so distasteful.' When one of the major mechanisms of global and national inequality, one that determines how we know and evaluate ourselves and others, becomes reduced to a matter of etiquette and taste, we know there is something clearly very wrong and very bourgeois happening.

3 Mobility, individualism and identity

Producing the contemporary bourgeois self

Mike Savage (2000) asks why sociologists have found it less useful to use the concept of class at the very same time that economic polarization has reached unparalleled depths. The sociological retreat from class mirrors retreats in political discourse and popular culture, where enormous efforts have been put into denying the existence of class. But why?

This chapter begins to answer this question by providing an analysis of how and why class is being refigured in academic discourse, in order to show how and whose agendas are being set and who is being obliterated from history. The argument is ultimately about agenda setting and power; that is, authorizing who is authorized to know, to speak and to be. In other words, it is about how systems of knowledge, inscription and representation enable some things to be known and perspectives taken, whilst other things and perspectives are made invisible, irrelevant and lacking in importance. In this sense, the forms of knowledge that are made available to us offer the potential for reading and knowing ourselves and others. This chapter shows how the legacies of the classed self, perspective, exclusion and value are interwoven and reproduced in the present.

I begin from the premise that categorizations and theory are 'performative', both in Bourdieu's (1985) sense of theory producing the effects it names, and in Butler's (1997a) use of Austin to indicate how the utterance is both productive and constitutive of action. They produce what Lorraine Code (1995) identifies as rhetorical spaces, the kind of utterances that can be voiced with an expectation of uptake, and what Patricia Williams (1991) argues is crucial to the operation of law, namely categories that have meaning for those who operate and institutionalize power. What we know about different classifications is a matter of where and how we are positioned in the classification schema. For, as Bourdieu (1988) notes, knowledge is always a matter of positioning. It is the space from which we speak, the political, disciplinary and social inheritances that we travel through, which leave traces and marks upon us, enabling us to see some things and be blind to others. This is, of course, tautological, because it is our social positioning and categorization (of which class is one) that enables our only ever partial perception (Haraway 1990; Strathern 1992a). Yet theory alone cannot generate the effects that it names – the methods that make the theory are also significant (see Chapter 7). Moreover, as Antonio Gramsci (1971) argued, in relation to hegemony, the theory also has to have a particular resonance to be effective; that is, it has to speak to people and make sense. But to whom does contemporary theory speak? We seem to have entered a time when speaking of class is not acceptable (even distasteful). But why? This is not the first time class has appeared and disappeared, as Barbara Ehrenreich (1990) demonstrates in an analysis of the theorizing of class in the US, where the poor, the culture of poverty, the urban mass, at first stood in for class. These were then replaced by the term 'the working-class' and great efforts were made to identify and document the minute details of the lives of those who might fit into the new category:

> For the next few years media people, intellectuals, and others of their class would work overtime to make up for their embarrassing neglect of this new social 'other'. They would examine, fearfully and almost reverently, that curious segment of America: the majority. And within it, they would find that supposedly extinct – or at least thoroughly assimilated – category, the working-class. They did not discover the working-class that was in the late 1960s and early 1970s caught up in the greatest wave of labor militancy since World War II. They discovered a working-class more suited to their mood: dumb, reactionary, and bigoted.
>
> (Ehrenreich 1990:100–1)

Class, directly articulated, and as an object of analysis, has largely disappeared again, although, as Frank (2001) shows, the language of class is very apparent in the new 'marketspeak' in which the class positions have changed. He maintains that, in the US in the 1990s, there was a spectacular revival of the language of social class, accompanied by a new moral climate against elitism (defined by Clinton as wrongful authority, false expertise, and class arrogance). This, he argues, produced a 'righteous indignation towards the claims of the unrich' (p.43). The implication is that the rich and poor had somehow exchanged class positions (at least for the purposes of moral righteousness), a cliché repeated in management literature as well as more radical places such as *Wired* magazine. Frank contends that the fantasy of the market as an anti-elitist machine made the most sense when couched in the language of social class. Businesspeople and a range of Republican politicians depicted the workings of the market as a kind of permanent social revolution in which daring entrepreneurs were endlessly toppling 'fatcats' and snatching away the millions off the lazy rich kids: the 'New Economy', he maintains, was a narrative of class warfare as much as anything else. The most extreme example is probably Rupert Murdoch's effort to cast himself as a man of the people against the institutions of the British aristocracy. As David Harvey (1993) notes, only the upper classes feel able to articulate their interests in class terms. The use of the language of social class by capitalist market pioneers and the lack of use of class in the language of social theorists is an interesting juxta-position. The different uses and absences of class formulations will now be explored.

This chapter is organized into four sections: the first examines the continuing retreat from directly speaking about class in academic spaces, showing how class is being spoken without naming it, via theories of mobility. The second section explores how middle-class experience is being spoken without naming it, via the 'new' condition of reflexivity and individualism. The third investigates how class is being avoided but re-made through gender, and the fourth charts another way in which class is not spoken but reproduced through identity politics.

I have earlier and elsewhere documented the academic retreat from the study of class outside the arena of social policy, where terms such as underclass dominated the agenda, referring back to 'culture of poverty' debates. These have more recently been eclipsed by the discourse of social exclusion, which does not name class, but still refers to pathological culture (Skeggs 1997) (see Chapters 5 and 6 for a more extensive debate). However, more recently there has been a resurgence of interest in class in feminist theory, queer theory, geography, media studies, history, and in some parts of sociology (see in particular: Bondi 1998; Bonnett 1998; Brenner 2001; Cannadine 1988; Carter 1990; Charlesworth 2000; Cook 2000; Crompton *et al.* 2000; Day 2001; Devine 1997; Devine 1998; Dowling 1999; Ehenreich 2001; Erickson 1996; Featherstone *et al.* 1991; Field 1995; Finch 1993; Fraser 1999; Fronsman 1992; Griffin 1992; Hartigan Jr. 1992; Harvey 1993; Healy 1996; Hunt 1998; Lamont 1992; Lamont 2000; Lawler 1999; Lawler 2000a; Lawler 2000b; Longhurst and Savage 1996; Lovell 2000; Lucey and Reay 2000; Mahony and Zmroczek 1997; Massey 1994; McClintock 1995; McNall *et al.* 1991; Milner 1999; Mooney 2000; Moran 2000; Morris 1994; Partington 1990; Patrick 2001; Reay 1997; Reay 1998; Reay 2000a; Reay 2000b; Roberts 1999b; Rowbotham and Beynon 2001; Savage 2000; Savage *et al.* 1999; Savage *et al.* 2001; Savage *et al.* 1992; Sayer 2001; Seiter 1990; Sklair 2001; Tasker 1998; Tyler 1991; Valocchi 1999; Wahrman 1995; Walkerdine 1989; Walkerdine 1990; Walkerdine and Lucey 1989; Waquant 1991; Wray and Newitz 1997; Zweig 2000). This research will be interspersed in this chapter and throughout the rest of the book.

Mobility

In 1993 Crompton (1993) identified how the influence of the sociological equivalent of the 'new individualism' in the late 1980s impacted on the study of class. Coinciding with and enhanced by Reaganism and Thatcherism, the new individualism produced a retreat from class analysis. The study of class was also abandoned during this period, I argued, because the fantasies of authenticity and revolutionary potential that the middle-classes projected onto, usually male, members of the working-class, failed to materialize. So, the academics *who could* looked for something else as the site of social change, usually themselves, via theories that could explain *their* mobility and *their* social networks. When they had power they tried to establish and institutionalize it by creating academic agendas and employment practices. This agenda setting is powerful, as it establishes the exchange rate and market value for knowledge and employability (in the UK the Research Assessment Exercise (RAE)[1] can be seen as crucial to this agenda setting and thereby fraught with struggles over what counts as academic knowledge). The recent move toward theorizing around mobility is an example of attempts to shift the sociological agenda. This is most clearly displayed in John Urry's[2] (2000) proposals for the 'new rules of sociological method' based on mobility. He argues that we need: 'To develop through appropriate metaphors a sociology which focuses upon movement, mobility and contingent ordering, rather than upon stasis, structure and social order' (2000:18).

Urry (2000) maintains that we now live in a post-societal culture in which mobility is the determining feature that frames social relations, not structures or positions. This, he argues, re-figures the whole of sociology, as the loss of unity of society (a statement he makes) has been transcended by mobile forces. He notes: 'In such a maelstrom of social and intellectual mobility I ask whether any fixed points can remain?' (p.17).

Urry also believes that mobility can be understood best through a horizontal rather than a vertical sense, thereby flattening out the differences that have to be crossed. Lois McNay (1999) draws attention to the problems of analyses that flatten out difference, enabling certain subjectivities to become amenable to change and self-fashioning, whilst others remain intact. This flattening out of difference contrasts sharply with Bourdieu's analysis (see introductory chapter for explication). His spatial metaphors of capital (economic, social, cultural and symbolic) are about how bodies *can* move through social space, with volumes of different capital in different networks/fields developing the dispositions (habitus) as they move. The central difference between Urry and Bourdieu is that Bourdieu's metaphors enable us to understand who *can* move and who *cannot*, and what the mobile/fixed bodies require as resources to gain access to different spaces. Also, Bourdieu contests mobility as a universalizing condition.

The arguments for mobility also suggest that 'new' theory has become orientive and regulative: it describes what exists for a privileged few and then suggests this is a perspective that applies to many others. The way in which mobility is put to use is explored in a recent study of 'home' by Morley (2000). Morley demonstrates how mobility and fixity are figured differently depending on national spaces and historical periods. He identifies how the bourgeois desire for fixity, knowing and naming their place, was closely tied to their self-formation. The desire for fixity was initially a bourgeois achievement, restricted to a few, producing a representation of a particular kind of self. The home offered a form of interiorization. He traces how in Britain up until the nineteenth century this kind of privatized lifestyle was open to the bourgeoisie alone, and has only become more widely available to some other sections of the population in the period of affluence after 1945.

Davidoff and Hall (1987) also illustrate how the struggle to establish a clear division between the external world of work and community and the internal, private space of the family was crucial for the nineteenth-century middle-class attempting to establish its respectability. Thus the evolution of domestic comfort, Rybczynski (1986) argues, can only be understood in that specific context, because it begins in the appropriation of the house as a setting for an emerging interior life. The home becomes the location for the split-self, identified in Chapter 2. It mirrors the interior in the interior and the exterior in the exterior. But only some groups were deemed capable of claiming, having and knowing a split-self. Domesticity, privacy, comfort and the concept of the home and the family are, Morley demonstrates, principal achievements of the Bourgeois Age. So the desire to establish fixity, in that historical period, was a desire to display a respectable self, known through its being 'in place'. There are contemporary legacies of this as Mike Davis (1990) shows in a study of the US.

Davis points out how the contemporary theorists of mobility are usually writing (literally) from their own safe, secure spaces. His analysis of 'Fortress LA' shows how 'good citizens' (that is, respectable ones) are off the streets, enclaved, usually gated, in seemingly interiorized, private consumption spheres. The power to fix and protect one's self by excluding others is a defensive measure by the privileged, allowing access to the resources of the home to a select few. The continual emphasis on respectability, on becoming a 'good citizen' through self-protection, is also a move replicated in contemporary 'risk' literature,[3] which suggests that the moral order has been spatialized in the production of particular classed selves figured in mobility debates. Moreover, as Doreen Massey (1991) explains, beyond the class differences in degrees of mobility, there are also important differences in its styles. The mobility of choice of the affluent British middle-classes, conducted in relative ease, is quite different from the mobility of the international refugee or the unemployed migrant. In a similar way to Mike Davis's analysis, Massey examines a group of middle-class hi-tech male scientists based at Cambridge University, UK, who live thoroughly internationalized and highly mobile working lives (communicating by e-mail, fax and phone, travelling to international conferences, etc.) and concludes that this type of mobility is premised on a strong commitment to a very settled form of residential localism. One can be highly mobile from a fixed location.

Not only does middle-class mobility require located security, but for the affluent, Davis argues, physical gatedness is also matched by an increasingly comprehensive system of electronic surveillance which constitutes a virtual scanscape – a space of protective visibility that increasingly puts others under surveillance. Morley (2000) notes that this replicates a long history, from the Greeks and the Romans onwards, of imaginary geographies, in which the powerful and privileged members of a society locate themselves at the centre of the universe, secure their position and then represent others at a distance. This projected perspective can clearly be seen in the colonial imaginary.

Critiques of mobility have been plentiful and come from a range of different directions. For instance, Massey (1991) further argues that the politics of mobility is premised on 'power-geometry': that is, who moves and who does not. She contends that the idea that 'we' all somehow experience the same form of post-modern nomadology can be seen as little more than a cruel nonsense. Her key argument is that some groups are more mobile than others and have more control over both their own and the mobility of others. Mobility and control over mobility both reflect and reinforce power. Mobility is a resource to which not everyone has an equal relationship. For instance, as Morley (2000) shows:

> For those living in sink estates with little local employment, nothing but poor-quality run-down local shops, no car and with poor (or in some cases non-existent) public transport links to enable residents to get elsewhere, and in situations where those from elsewhere (from doctors to pizza delivery services) are reluctant to enter their territory, it is their very disconnection which is both most symbolic and, in practical terms, constitutive of their material poverty.
>
> (Morley 2000:142)

Or, as Graham and Marvin (1998) note, issues of mobility are also about *connectivity*. In poor inner-city areas in the UK the proportion of households with telephone connections can still be as low as only 25 per cent. The ultimate issue is not who moves or is fixed, but who has *control* – not only over their mobility and connectivity, but also over their capacity to withdraw and disconnect. The point is that the poor have to put up with that from which others can move. The 'white flight' from US inner cities is a classic case in point. This leads Davis (1990) to view security as a *positional good* and that, in the USA, a person's social status is increasingly marked by the degree of their insulation in residential, travel, working and safe environments. Voluntary mobility is therefore a social good, a resource, not equally available to all. Moreover, Morley (2000) argues, immobility increasingly acquires the connotation of defeat, of failure and of being left behind, of being fixed in place.

Keith and Pile (1993) stretch this argument further by charting the emergence of a discourse of a reactionary vocabulary of the identity politics of place by drawing attention to how it is used to '*name origins*', so that some people are considered to be located and others mobile. Identity politics is used to attribute locatedness to others in order to generate a means of fixing in place. This mechanism of trying to fix others is well known in racist discourse, e.g. 'Where do you come from?' is a question frequently asked of black British subjects. Our recent research project on Violence, Sexuality and Space,[4] also shows that class was spoken in terms of geographical location, so that anybody from one of the local housing estates was regularly named by its location (e.g. 'people from Wythenshawe' as potentially disruptive of the safe cosmopolitan space of the commercial gay village – see Chapters 6 and 9). Locatedness, a geography of placement, becomes a way of speaking class indirectly but spatially, through geography and physicality. Just as the middle-classes have changed their interests and perspectives from fixity to mobility (although remaining located to become mobile), the working-class have shifted historical locations from once being the dangerously mobile, threatening to contaminate the respectable through their movement and proximity, to now becoming firmly fixed in order to be identifiable and governable.

The desire to identify others by place is made explicit in the experience of the migrants Rouse (1991) studied, where fixed identity was forced onto people, requiring them to display their 'origins'. The migrants moved from a world in which identity was not a central concern to one in which they were pressed with increasing force to adopt a particular concept of personhood (as bearers of individual identities). This forced identity was often at odds with their own understandings of their situation and their needs. Rouse shows how for these migrants, the taxonomic pressures of various state authorities to enumerate and certify their individual identities was often something to be avoided, neutralized or strategized, in order to maximize their own flexibility of manoeuvre and action. In a similar move by Swedish authorities, Martinsson and Reimers (2002) identify what they call 'disharmonious pluralism' whereby diversity is enforced by the state based on taxonomies of identification, which bear little relation to how people identify themselves. Just as the working-class did not recognize themselves by bourgeois classifications (as documented in Chapter 2), the migrants Rouse studied also produced different strategies for dealing with the institutionalized demand to identify.

This leads Morley (2000) to argue that for some people, fixed places may also be symbolic habitats, a performative way of life and of doing things, in which one makes the most of the cultural resources to hand. What is essential is how resources are accessed and how we are positioned in relation to them. This is evidenced well in Aihwa Ong's (1999) study of trans-national citizenship. She refers to this resourcing process as 'flexible citizenship', in which the cultural logic of capitalist accumulation, travel and displacement induces subjects to respond fluidly and opportunistically to changing political-economic conditions. To do so trans-national citizens rely upon the resources they have accumulated and strategically use them when appropriate. It is therefore a matter of access to resources and resourcefulness than mobility that is the issue. Moreover, she notes how the diasporan subject is now vested with the agency formerly sought in the working-class, in order to generate credibility for the theorists: 'Academic interest in how diasporas shape racialized, gendered, sexualized, and oppositional subjectivities is often tied to scholars' attempts to shape their own cosmopolitan intellectual commitment' (1999:13).

For instance, John Hutnyk (1998) demonstrates how the more the anthropologist James Clifford discusses travel, the more stationary he becomes. Rather than engage in what Cora Kaplan (1996) calls 'theoretical tourism' – where some attempt was made to connect to the margin as a new poetics of the exotic – now theorists of the other stay safely at home. As the fascination with the 'other' has shifted, different objects are produced. But what remains the same is the desire on behalf of the knowers to name, place, identify, quantify and thereby offer the possibilities for the control and governance of others, whilst considering themselves mobile.

It is also worth noting how mobility is itself gendered on a variety of scales. Gupta and Ferguson (1997) describe the often gendered opposition posed between global and local, in which the local is understood to be that which is natural, authentic and original, while the global is seen as the realm of the external, artificially imposed or inauthentic. The local is associated with femininity and seen as the natural basis of home and community, into which an implicitly masculine global realm intrudes. Moreover, the various projects of travel have been 'reserved' for men: women have been constituted in immobile, place-bound domesticity and symbolic geography (Enevold 2000). Teresa de Lauretis (1984) demonstrates how male subjectivity is discursively linked to narratives of travel, adventure and discovery, whereas female subjectivity is mapped as a fixed place on the itinerary of the male journey. In response to these formulaic narratives, Jokinen and Veijola (1997) suggest a new metaphor for the mobile postmodern, invariably male subject, by replacing male gendered 'stroller', 'tourist', 'vagabond' and 'player' with the figure of the au pair.[5]

So when people argue that mobility is the new universalizing condition replacing class, we need to think what concepts of self and personhood this involves? Is it voluntary? Is it gendered, sexed or raced? How is fixity figured? Who is being fixed in place so others can express their distance from them? Who is being forced to inhabit an identity in order to be known? These questions become even more pertinent when we explore how mobility becomes theorized through the new forms of reflexivity proposed (again as a universal condition) by Ulrich Beck and Anthony Giddens.

The individualism of Beck and Giddens

By showing how individuals reflexively construct their biographies and identities, Beck and Giddens suggest an erosion of class identities in 'late modernity'. They see class not as a modern identity, but as a traditional, ascriptive one, which has no place in a dynamic, reflexive and globalized world. Beck is more explicit than Giddens in departing from class via theories of 'reflexive modernity'. Savage (2000), however, argues that Beck and Giddens radically misconceive the relationship between individual and class identities. What Giddens and Beck read as the decline of class cultures and the rise of individualization, Savage argues, would be better understood as the shift from working-class to middle-class modes of individualization, but classed, nonetheless.

Savage charts how, in the last three decades, there has been a subtle reworking of the relationship between class, masculinity and the individual, enabling the emergence of a new form of self-developmental individualization, premised on particular kinds of middle-class employment relations, defining a new mode of individual identity. This is apparent in both Beck and Giddens' arguments.

For Beck, 'the individual himself or herself becomes the reproduction unit for the social in the lifeworld' (Beck 1992:130). And, '... class loses its sub-cultural basis and is no longer experienced' (1992:98). Individuals, Beck maintains, although unable to escape structural forces in general, can decide on which ones to act and which to ignore.[6] This, he argues, does not create a 'free' individual; rather, it creates individuals who live out, biographically, the complexity and diversity of the social relations that surround them. This self, this biographical production, Beck calls 'reflexive modernity'. Central to this theory is an incredibly voluntarist individual who can choose which structural forces to take into account and which to act upon. However, as Savage (2000) points out, individuals still need to situate themselves socially in order for them to assess what kind of risks they are likely to encounter. They also need access to social resources, including forms of interpretation such as discourse, by which they can make sense of the 'risks' that surround them and act upon them. In this sense they are always/already implicated in a process of positioning, cultural differentiation and resource access, that by necessity involves the making of social distinction. Thus individualization cannot be anything but a cultural process involving differentiation from others and differential access to resources.

In a similar mode to Beck, Giddens sees institutional reflexivity as fundamental to the development of a new universal 'life politics' where (like Beck) individuals search to create a coherent biography in a fractured world. Here the self becomes a project on which to be worked. It is a dual model of the self which (similar to Adam Smith, as outlined in Chapter 2) requires a self that reflects upon itself, simultaneously externalizing the self from social relations, so that the former can reflect and plan its future actions, and then reinsert itself back into society through internalization: it is a self that therefore knows its self. But it is also a self that is detached from structure. There is no sense in Giddens that the possibility of having a self may itself be a classed, raced or gendered issue (as the previous chapter showed). The self appears in Giddens as a *neutral* concept available to all, rather than an inscription, a position of personhood produced to retain the interests of a privileged few, requiring for its constitution the exclusion of others. The method of constructing a biography is seen to be a *neutral method*, something that one just does, rather than something (as Chapter 7 shows) dependent upon access to discourse and resources. Like Beck, Giddens relies completely on everybody having equal access to the resources by which the self can be known, assessed and narrated. Again, this is problematic since, as Savage (2000) notes, it must involve social differentiation and therefore always invoke positioning, not just in terms of structure, but also in the perspective from which we can know the types of personhood we can inhabit (Strathern 1992a).

Savage (2000) demonstrates how the arguments of Beck and Giddens are rhetorical ploys, designed to convince by claiming plausibility and having more 'commonsense' than other accounts; accounts that resonate with middle-class experience. Their sociology can thus be viewed as part of a symbolic struggle for the authorization of their experience and perspectives. In Gidden's case these rhetorical ploys have powerful outcomes as they frame the shape of a new neo-liberal politics that influenced the governments of Clinton and Blair through the more general formulation of 'the Third Way' (Giddens 1998; 2000; Callinicos 2001; see Chapter 6).

Savage's point is given further weight by Andrew Milner (1999), who describes the huge gulf that has developed between empirical sociologists, who demonstrate that the class character of culture is as undeniable as ever, and the more theoreticist sociology that is less likely to accord significance to class. Paradoxically, Milner quotes from one of the 'founding fathers' of postmodernism, Fredrick Jameson (1981), to argue that there is a history outside of theory, a 'history that hurts, a history that might hurt theory, which is itself the result of class forces' (p.102).

Thus we need to ask, why is it that some theorists conceive of themselves as mobile, reflexive individuals? Also, why is there a division between those who theorize the social and cannot see class within their perspective and those who study it empirically and note its ubiquity and increased inequality? Why do these divisions exist at this historical moment?

One way to explore these questions is through Bourdieu's (1988) analysis of class formation and intellectual knowledge. These academic agenda setters can be seen to embody what he identifies as a *middle-class habitus*. So, for him, a retreat from class is just the expression of the class interests of a group of relatively powerfully placed professional intelligentsia. John Frow (1995a) confirms this by showing that what he calls the 'knowledge class's own interests' are actually based upon representing their own position, their perspective, their own cultural politics openly and without embarrassment.

As Savage (2000) observes, this suggests that the kinds of globalizing forces that Giddens sees as a systemic, background feature of late modernity, might be better seen as exemplifying the embodied habitus of particular types of socially located individuals. Rather than globalization being a neutral fact facing individuals, a few culturally privileged individuals construct a globalized world to allow them to shrug off responsibility for their local, social activities (Bourdieu and Wacquant 1999). This exposes Beck's and Giddens' arguments as a particular kind of intellectual manoeuvre, a celebration of a cosmopolitan intellectual ethic, that can only be realized by a small minority of people (Savage 2000:108).

These 'new' speculations of Urry, Beck and Giddens, therefore, should be seen for what they are: that is, projects for intellectual grandizement (Bauman 1998). Class is displaced and effaced in these new modes of mobility and individualization, by the very people whose ideas are institutionalized and help to reproduce class inequality more intensely – especially in Giddens' case as friend of Clinton and Blair. This enables a particular middle-class habitus to be institutionalized in government policy, evidenced in the 'New Labour' agenda on social exclusion as a way of speaking class, knowing, naming and positioning others (see Chapter 5). This also enables the abdication from acknowledging class relations, from occupying and recognizing the positions of power and privilege they inhabit and the resources they can access.

Class retreat/gender reproduction

Lisa Adkins (2000b) develops these critiques even further by exploring how gender intervenes in the classed project of Beck and Giddens to expose how they authorize their claims for reflexivity. She shows that there is some disagreement regarding the exact meaning of reflexivity (see, for example, Beck *et al.* 1994), yet Scott Lash (1994) defines two forms of reflexivity: first, 'structural reflexivity', whereby agency reflects both on the rules and resources of social structure and on the conditions of existence of agency itself: 'the more societies are modernized, the more agents (subjects) acquire the ability to reflect on the social conditions of their existence and to change them in that way' (Beck 1992:174). Second, Lash writes of 'self-reflexivity' in which agency reflects on itself and there is increasing self-monitoring: 'We are, not what we are, but what we make of ourselves' (Giddens 1991:75). Such intensified tendencies towards reflexivity are often understood to be constituted by a destabilization of the significance of structural forms of determination, a destabilization described as progressively 'freeing' or 'unleashing' agency from structure (Adkins 2000b). This leads Paul Heelas (1996) to show how external, traditional forms of authority are giving way to the authority of the individual: 'Individual subjects are themselves called upon to exercise authority in the face of … disorder and contingency' (p.2).

Adkins (2000b) demonstrates how the potential for self-reflexivity in the individualization project and the freeing of agency from structure actually involves less a transformation of identities than the re-traditionalization of gender relations. She maintains that modern subjects are not free to 'be' whatever they like, but remain constrained by the social relations which produce women workers as a social group and men as individuals; in the absence of formal economic structures, social relations continue to determine the organization of production according to gendered processes.

Adkins further suggests that since women are – continually and through a series of ongoing processes – positioned as members of a social group with a *fixed identity* rather than as individuals who perform an identity, the agency and autonomy of women workers is always limited by the social category of gender. She illustrates how, despite prevalent conditions of reflexivity under late modernity, a simple detachment or dis-embedding of individuals from social categories does not take place, *but rather* a continual, processual re-embedding in circuits and networks in which re-traditionalized rules, norms and expectations occur.

Anne Cronin (2000b) also examines the apparent shifts in the subject formation of modernity. By focusing on contemporary consumerist discourses of self-actualization, self-transformation, will power and choice, Cronin demonstrates how the modern self, who can will itself to be (through consumption), is not freely accessible to all, and that women, as well as other marginalized groups, remain excluded from this reinvention of the bourgeois liberal, reflexive, mobile subject. She documents how the gendering address of consumerist imagery via femininity is used to restrict the access of women to the individuality it offers. In this sense individuality operates as an unequal resource. Moreover, individuality is not just a resource that can be attached to the person, but requisite knowledge is required in order to know *how* to operationalize it. For instance, in Adkins' (2000a) analysis of new worker flexibility, gender reversals *appear* to be equally available to all workers to perform for rewards. Yet, in the workplace socialities she studied, access to gender as a workplace resource is unevenly distributed. Occupation and position determine whether it can be deployed or not. So, if men deploy aspects of femininity to make them more caring managers they are rewarded, if women employ femininity in the same way, they are just seen to be doing what they are expected to do.

Adkins (2000a) also shows how sexuality can either be deployed as a resource – a diversity dividend, used by companies to demonstrate that they are modern and open – or negatively, to sack people when sexuality is exposed. Lesbian employees, she notes, may be forced (in a similar way to the migrants studied by Rouse) to perform an identity category (lesbian) to which they feel they do not belong, or do not want to be known and positioned by. These intricacies of becoming an 'individual' in different settings are not explored by individualization theorists.

The fixing and forcing of identity positions are not recognized by those who do not theorize beyond their own experience.

As Don Slater (1997) recognizes, the generic model of 'the individual' which forms the basis for conceptualizations of the consumer is founded on discourses of Enlightenment rationality, which (as Chapter 2 showed) exclude women. Feminist theorists have rigorously argued that gender and other categorizations, such as race and class, have been 'structured out' of the historically embedded epistemological pedigree of 'the individual'. Just like the self, and often in parallel to it (as a concept), the individual is an exclusive and politically privileged category (see Cornell 1993; Diprose 1994; Fraser 1989; Pateman 1989; Yeatman 1994). Yet it is the very exclusion of these categorical 'differences' that creates the boundaries for the interiority of the individual. 'He' is self-present in that 'he' has discursive access to the ideal of a unitary, temporally and spatially bounded selfhood: a coherent, 'rational' biographical account of privileged identity defined against others (Cronin 2000b; see also Diprose 1994). Just as it occurred historically, 'Rational Man' as the ideal of self-possessed self-control is set against frivolous, consuming 'Woman' lacking in self-control. As Cronin (2000b) extensively demonstrates, the exclusions that constitute the category 'the individual' impact upon the very terms of 'individuality' as an available form of unique selfhood.

Moreover, Charles Taylor (1994) documents the imperative to make the introspective search for the essence of individuality, in which the self is seen as having inner depths, and is situated within more general rhetoric of identity politics. This is an explicit politicizing of individual self-definition in which discourses position individuals as having a right to self-expression (Miller 1993). In these discourses the self is directed to embark on processes of self-monitoring through the production of 'authentic self-knowledge' of the self's interiority, whilst being encouraged to engage reflexively with the self as 'project' (Giddens 1991). Taylor (1994) argues that contact with this inner-self takes on a moral accent or form of 'duty' to oneself. Added to this morally inscribed interrogation of interiority is the idea that each person has a unique, original inner essence that is considered as individualized 'potential' (Taylor 1994; Cronin 2000b). But, as Chapters 2 and 7 show, the individualized essence is only available to the privileged few and is premised upon the exclusion of others.

Cronin (2000b) asserts that we are now in a historical period of 'compulsory individuality'. She uses the work of Strathern (1992a) to document how discourses of choice are central to the Western production of ideas of 'individuality', providing what she calls 'proscriptive individualism'. Thus, forms of control are manifested in inner-directed technologies of the self, which in consumerism are expressed as technologies of choice. An individual is defined by the 'innate' capacity of 'free choice' and this choice expresses the inner authentic individuality of that person. The abstracted notion of 'choice' becomes an inherent ideal as well as the route to the expression of individuality. Yet, as Strathern notes, within this politics of choice, we have no choice but to choose, if we are to express ourselves as individuals and if self-expression is the cornerstone of the politics of identity.

Thus Giddens and Beck faithfully reproduce the consumer market rhetoric that not only promotes individuality as necessary, but also makes it a moral prerogative. As Nick Rose (1992) notes, self-management through choice is framed as an ethical duty to the self and to society. Yet the self is not a pre-constituted, neutral category, but must be performatively produced through the very discourses of 'choice', an exclusion reliant upon the requisite resources. Performativity as a method, I'd argue, is not universal; it is specific, always related to positioning and access to rhetorical space, utterances, resources, possibilities and interpellation. This contemporary version of the middle-class imperative to produce oneself as a choosing, self-managing individual can be seen clearly in the rhetoric of identity politics, as the next section will illustrate.

Displacing class through identity

Many different routes have been cited as the reasons for the emergence and dominance of identity politics in the West. Zweig (2000) argues that in the US it was based on the combination of the Cold War and the Vietnam War, generating a specific form of anti-communism and discrediting class as a fundamentalism of Marxism and socialism. In the UK identity politics appears to have developed much later, partly, I'd argue, as a result of the individualism of Thatcherism, but also the ability of powerful trade unions to keep the figure of the heroic working-class male on the British political agenda. When Thatcherism became entrenched and desperate searches began for sites of change (see *Marxism Today* 1983–90), many theorists turned to themselves via psychoanalysis and attempted to establish an academic agenda. McClintock (1995) argues that Marxism is the theory of the proletariat whilst psychoanalysis is the theory of the bourgeoisie (after all, you need classical Greek training, don't you?). This again draws attention to the cultural capital of the theorist and their interest in themselves (if Lacan argues that it takes at least 11 years of dedicated reading to understand him – who is going to say they wasted their time?).

The interest in, and move to, self and subjectivity (often via Freud and Lacan) had parallels to the political campaigning around identity. This campaigning was not usually based on a coherent systematic theory, such as psychoanalysis, but methodologically similarities do exist. Feminism, for instance, embraced a form of identity politics: 'I am a woman' = therefore 'I am politically oppressed.' The methodology of feminism in the 1960s of consciousness raising was based on telling stories of one's horrific experiences and one's oppression. This put the focus on the individual. Identity politics in this early formation embraced a form of possessive individualism (see introductory chapter) whereby the individual became known through their ownership of pain and oppression. During this methodological and political climate shifts were made between taking a standpoint and having one; taking a position and owning an identity.

Identity politics, as Nancy Fraser (1995) shows, has had devastating consequences for the articulation of class politics; it is also, she argues, unhelpful for feminism.

She documents a shift from the 1980s politics of redistribution to a politics of recognition in the 1990s, in which the grammar of political claims-making is forged through identity claims, rather than through exposure of structural inequalities. For Fraser these identity claims are based on a desire to be recognized as something (fill in appropriate category). This political claims-making is usually based on singular categorizations (that is, identity claims are usually made from one identity position), invariably tied into a neo-liberal discourse of rights and assimilation, what Brown (1995) identifies as the politics of bourgeois individualism.

Brown (1995) shows how 'the wounded attachment', developed from Nietzsche's notion of ressentiment, energizes a particular impulse to feminist politics that focuses in on itself and celebrates its misery. (For an example of how this is put to work in a variety of political struggles, from Australian reconciliation policy to the rhetoric of Simone de Beauvoir, see Ahmed *et al.* 2000.) According to Brown, feminism must retain and reproduce the pain of marginalization in order to maintain itself as a political project.

Brown contends that the injuries, insults and agonies embodied in the politicized subject become a necessary fetish for the gaining of visibility and credibility in late modernity (Taylor 1994; Fraser 1995). The subject, in effect, is what she feels, and she desires recognition of her pain as her primary identity. For Brown, as a result of this complete identification with pain, the politicized subject is either unable or unwilling to break its hold or envision a less self-absorbing and retributive politics.

The wounded attachment is premised on the belief that the experience of pain, hurt and oppression provides greater epistemological authority to speak. Lauren Berlant (2000) reveals how concepts of privacy and national attachment have been forged out of a limited understanding of (specifically heterosexual) women's pain, enabling the development of a particular national formation, in which the currency of distress, hurt and pain are the means by which groups make claims for recognition. This produces a political terrain that is increasingly figured through not just individuality, but also morality premised on injury.

The rhetoric of identity politics is, therefore, dependent upon the individual morally authorizing themselves through their own experience. Urry, Beck and Giddens do this without claiming pain or acknowledging the location from which they speak; rather, they pursue a traditional masculine fantasy of the 'rational' risk calculating individual. In contrast, feminism made identity (as woman) the precise grounds for speaking. So whilst one group makes their experience the condition of universal knowledge, the other marks their specificity through experience. But what both have in common is their reliance on their own experience as the basis for understanding oppression and as the basis for producing their self as a possessive individual.

The emphasis on wounding and pain as a measure of injustice can be exposed as unreliable measures of justice claims. This is because only some groups can articulate their identities through wound and pain, and only some would want to. Only some groups can produce their subjectivity in this way and focus on themselves and their experience as the basis for knowledge. This methodology of moral authorizing has a long historical route through the development of the bourgeois individual. Apart from eclipsing structural inequality and suffering, it also leads to a relativist collapse in the pain alphabet so that major forms of distress and death, such as the holocaust, are read alongside narratives of personal trauma.

Identity has thus become refigured as something to be *owned and articulated as a property of the person*. It has become figured as a property right, and struggles around gender, sexuality and, in particular, race, compete for moral authorization. Lisa Jones (1994) shows how this was literalized in respect to race when certain cultural markers of race in the US actually became copyrighted.

Moreover, exploring how political struggles have been 'branded' in order to generate identifications and commitment, Karyn Sandlos (2000) charts how visual images of pain are played out in the 'grammar of indisputable knowledge'. She traces how the visual image of Gerri Santoro (a woman whose body was found after an illegal and fatal abortion) was deployed in political claims-making. Outlining the visual battles over the representation of dead women and dead foetuses, she details how forms of citizenship and personhood are generated, using a moral economy in which personal outrage is necessary for mobilization. Drawing out the implications of this, Lisa Bower (1997) points to how struggles based on branding and visualizing pain for entitlement within the law can produce pathology and readability; as the law encompasses new forms into an already known vocabulary, the rhetorical space is stretched. So the foetus in the Gerri Santoro case becomes a body, then a person, then a citizen with rights, through the process of making visible and legal. She argues that this leads to the sedimentation and ossification of certain categories in feminist mobilization around rights, closing down ways of knowing rather than opening them up. If images of pain become central to political rhetoric, visual struggle and legal entitlement, we need to ask where and how can class figure in this? And, more importantly, should it?

Central to the whole basis of identity and recognition politics is the assumption that people can:

* articulate their pain via individual experience;
* access the forums in which their pain will be recognized and heard (and not read as something else);
* be recognized as worthy of having that pain;
* make identifications with a category in the first place.

People who cannot authorize themselves through their individual experience of pain, because they do not see everyday suffering as exceptional, are unable to participate. When everyday suffering is pathologized as an individualized problem the pain of endurance is not recognized. When dis-identification is made from the categorizations under which the working-class are expected to stand, they are left only exclusion, disenfranchised from the current form of justice claims. Identity politics has thus served to reinforce bourgeois individualism that renders some groups outside of the need for justice and places others at the centre of moral authorization. Whilst some groups are able to play with categories of identity, others may find it impossible because they do not have the requisite resources and knowledge (Skeggs 1997).

If we begin to think of 'identity' as an effect of the deployment of feminist (or other political) strategies, tactics and rhetoric, rather than its origin or cause, we can then consider how class has been mobilized or not, in particular times and places, through the deployment of different theoretical explanations that work both to explain and rhetorically seduce. The attention to rhetorical strategies exposes the gestures that are made within the politics of alliance, which articulates a pretence to include whilst excluding. Differences are frequently invoked in rhetorical forms (often as a mantra), whilst racism and class inequality not only remain intact but are also reproduced through lack of attention. Attempts by the state to deflect attention away from class inequalities, through rhetorical signs of 'lone mother', 'smoker', 'unhealthy school', create moral divisions between worthy and unworthy recipients, the respectable and good citizen and the socially irresponsible and excluded. Self-responsibility and self-management, precisely the features identified by Giddens, become the mechanisms by which class inequality is reproduced and refigured, individualized as a marker of personal volition and inclusion, excluding groups from belonging and participation through assumptions about their own take up of a particular form of agency, one to which they do not have access.

Conclusion

This chapter has shown that whilst class is being displaced by theories and claims of mobility, individualization, reflexivity and identity, it is simultaneously being institutionalized and reproduced. This is, in effect, a re-legitimation and justification of the habitus of the middle-class that does not want to name itself, be recognized or accept responsibility for its own power. What these theories demonstrate is how the historical legacies, identified in Chapters 1 and 2, have contemporary relevance as they come to be reproduced and refigured, particularly the ways in which the salience of the way the self (articulated via individualism and identity) comes to be absolutely central to what is known and spoken in the name of class, and the way in which particular ways of representing oneself rely on the placing and fixing of others. Theorists of mobility rely on a safe and secure place from which to speak and know. This has depended not only on the theorizing and legitimating of their own experience of mobility and self, and claiming it as universal, but also on a projection into the space of others as immobile, potentially dangerous, inhabiting fixed identities.

Just as class was always known through gender, race and sexuality, here in the contemporary, race and sexuality are constituted through the same processes; as Ong showed, it is now the raced diasporean subject who is the object of the projected fantasies of mobility theorists. Yet for this subject to 'work properly' (to be properly known) it needs access to the requisite resources that can produce it as a mobile object. A difference appeared to emerge between the mobile subject (the individualist of Urry, Beck and Giddens) and the mobile object (identified by Rouse and Ong). The former forged itself, whilst the latter was subject to the definitions of the theorist or the state. It could only make itself through the terms of the powerful. In this sense mobility can be seen to be a positional good, a resource that is only available for some, whilst forced on others.

These points were substantiated through Strathern's (1992a), Adkins' (2000b) and Cronin's (2000b) analysis of how 'compulsory individuality' was also only available to some, and how the debates about individualizations, flexibility and reflexivity relied on a particular conception of the self; one that was not female, raced, homo-sexed or classed. In this sense the 'new' theories relied on an old model of the self that was not available to all. In a similar reproduction of history, this self was expected to display its own ethical sensibility through its own management and governance. To convert the self into a recognizable identity was also shown to be the way in which political claims were forged, illuminating the middle-class basis of some dissident politics. The claim to moral authority was the way in which subjectivity was converted into political identity. This relied on making pain a property of the individual in which identity became a form of propriety through which political claims could be made. So, whilst the securely positioned selves of Urry, Beck and Giddens could universalize their own positions, feminists were particularizing theirs to make the same claims for legitimacy. Both, it became clear, operated to displace class from the political/academic agenda, whilst also declaring it loudly to those who knew the underpinnings through which their class identities were being forged and claimed.

What is also significant is how different sites produced different use of the language of class to articulate interests. Market-speak, as Frank identified, used class as a position to incite consent, by positioning the 'freedom' of the market against entrenched elite interests. Discourses of consumption broke this down by inciting individuality, but broadened the address of individuality to wider consumers[7] (rather than the few privileged individuals for which the term was designed); yet these discourses were still premised on gender exclusions. Academic theorists, using suspiciously similar discourse to those of consumerism, promoted individualism and individuality[8] as not only compulsory, but inevitable and universal. It was only when empirical analysis interrogated these assumptions that the academic discourse was exposed as simply that, a discourse; used where necessary to gain advantages, but usually deployed traditionally to keep people fixed in place.

This is why we need to know how and where and for whom discourse is being produced, exchanged and used as well as the conditions that put it into effect. These concerns will be the focus of the next chapter. Taking economic discourse as its focus, it explores how class relations are again being put into effect through particular conceptions of the self, a self that is not equally available to all, but one that exposes how class relations are being refigured.

4 The subject of value and the use-less subject

The centrality of the economic to how we speak and understand ourselves should not be underestimated, yet the economic has not always been this central, as the previous chapter showed. In the contemporary, the economy, often articulated via the term market, returns as the neutral way of speaking capitalism. Or even, as Frank (2001) suggests, the market works to articulate new positions in class struggle. The economy has always played a specific role in all understandings of class, but more recently this has also been accompanied by neo-liberal understandings of governance, in which particular forms of self are deemed to be necessary to the functional working of the global economy, enhancing the value of the nation. The work of this chapter, then, is to show how class is being refigured and reworked, even effaced, through contemporary understandings of, and ways of speaking, the economic. In these articulations, the 'self' is again central and assumed.

This chapter is organized into five sections. The first outlines the discursive characteristics of the economic-framed self, demonstrating how it became a 'subject of/with value'. The second explores how class is articulated when unhinged from the traditional labour theory of value, and the third examines how this affects recent neo-Marxist understandings of class. The fourth shows how, for some theorists, class has been abandoned in favour of a more general model that makes the economic cultural by focusing on the self. This leads to the final section, which maps how new theories of subjectivity establish the moral prerogatives for the self to become enterprising, hence establishing its value.

To move beyond the 'political arithmetic' tradition identified in the previous chapter, the initial focus here is on how recent debates in Marxism have taken shape. For Marxists class is an *objective* relationship. It does not matter what people think about their location (their subjective class position); it is where they are placed according to economic relationships. The economic (specifically capitalism) is absolutely central to determining how class is formed. The economy is therefore not represented as neutral, as it works to generate and legitimate capital for powerful groups. But it is, nevertheless, seen as an objective structure, outside of, different to, and often determining culture. New neo-Marxist analyses all provide a challenge to the traditional labour theory of value, that shows how one class can extract surplus value from the labour of the other class, because one class owns the capital that enables it to employ labour, whilst the other only owns its own labour power.

In this formula, value is determined through the extraction of the value of labour from the value of commodities that are produced and sold on the market. What is interesting is how this theory of the objective economic is premised upon, but also constitutes, a particular model of the self: one that can sell its labour, potentially – *the optimizing interested self*, first identified by Adam Smith. This self is both a moral self, because it takes responsibility for its actions, but is also rational, because it can calculate its value on a labour market. Also, culture plays a role in mystifying the transaction between the sale of labour and its transformation into a commodity. The role of fetishism in Marxism is to hide the presence of labour in the commodity. (See Chapter 1 for an analysis of the development of the concept of fetishism.)

Economic invasion?

Economics has invaded, pervaded and impinged upon or swamped sociology, argues Fine (1999), Fine and Lapavistas (2000) and Thompson (1999). This swamping, they maintain, can be seen particularly in the work of US theorists, such as Becker (1996) and Granovetter (1981), who utilize and extend the notion of the *optimizing individual* to every aspect of social life. Fine and Lapavistas (2000) draw attention to how this signifies a shift of perspective from the social to the individual, and from capitalism to markets, where emphasis is put on money (see Zelizer 1988; 1994; 1996), rather than the social relations of production, exploitation and the commodity, reducing every exchange to a form of monetary exchange. This puts emphasis on individual behaviour in which the 'market' is figured in the same way as it was historically, as a neutral and 'flat' space, where everybody competes from an equal position. This discursive neutralizing of capitalism is a highly morally-charged issue, as it shifts our perception from capitalism as a force that generates class inequalities to a flat, neutral and equal space where everybody is free to exchange. Moreover, as Hodgson (1988), Mackintosh (1990) and Sayer (2000) have noted, there is enormous confusion over what markets actually are. Mackintosh, for instance, found at least three different meanings used in a major World Bank report. Sayer warns against seeing the world through a 'market optic', either imaginary, latent or implicit, in which everything becomes subsumed to the logic of market forces.

We therefore need to remind ourselves of the historical legacies that generated the economic terms. As the previous chapter demonstrated, the economic was not a neutral term, but developed to consolidate bourgeois power. Moreover, whilst the terms market and exchange existed long before capitalism, the fundamental properties of capitalism, Marxists believed, were responsible for class divisions. This elision of interest is particularly apparent in the use of the term globalization, which stands in for the terms market and economy. In a detailed study of the discourse of *The Economist* magazine, Martha Starr (2002) shows how globalization is represented as the natural and normal form of economy, in which utopian neo-liberal aims can be achieved and anxieties assuaged by supporting global policies. Targeting an elite readership – nearly all readers have a degree, over one-half has a postgraduate degree, and over one-half earns an annual income of $100,000 or more[1] – *The Economist* represents globalization not only as the sole way to organize an economy, but also as a way in which only economists know how. So economists are presented as the people with real knowledge, as opposed to a host of different 'others' who only have opinions. *The Economist* positions the knowing self of global-supporting economists in opposition to the mass of less knowing (but self-interested) others.

Yet within this claim for legitimation, a contemporary version of the 'self' is produced, based on rational self-interest, drawn from Adam Smith:

> Globalisation continues and intensifies the extension of market-based capitalism to new spheres of production, distribution, consumption, and invest-ment and to new parts of the globe. This is inevitably good: although pursuit of profit and self-interest sound rapacious, we know from Adam Smith and the 'good old invisible hand' that, when brought to bear in competitive markets, they unlock all sorts of opportunities for mutually beneficial gain.
>
> (Starr 2002:4)

This self-interested self of globalization becomes even more apparent in a study of German unification. Paul Smith (1996) documents how a global rhetoric of market was used to generate an appropriate willing subject of labour from com-munism into the market. In a textual analysis of the influential economic rhetoric that was deployed, he shows how, even though elaborate or theorized descriptions of the subject are scarce in the works of economists, they always assume a 'common-sense' version of a subject defined almost exclusively as a function of some kind of *original appetitive desire*. Smith quotes Sinn and Sinn (1994) as an example of the standard and normative within the field of economics. Their work, he shows, was central to the policies put into practice by Brigit Breuel who, as Head of the Treuhand, led the privatization of GDR (East German) state industry. This, then, is not just an example of textual rhetoric, but rhetoric made to work in the incorporation of communist workers into a capitalist system; the institutionalizing of rhetoric; rhetoric with effects.

Whilst Smith maintains that mainstream economists almost never bother to go beyond the assumption of the appetive, self-interested, subject, he notes how some neo-Marxists, namely Amariglio and Callari (1989), have recently begun to think of the constitution of subjectivity as central to the understanding of economic processes. For instance, they propose that capitalism works for the preparation of an individual who might be:

- endowed with an ultimately self-interested rationality;
- convinced of the principle of equality;
- dedicated to the concept of private property.

This leads Smith to argue that their work has begun to define the contemporary 'subject of capitalism' and its characteristics more specifically and historically in terms of capitalism's various processes of extracting surplus value. He names this as the *subject of value*: the requisite for specifiable regimes and modes of value production. The current mode of capitalist unification in the West can be generalized as one where 'it has become increasingly necessary to legislate the "subject of value" and thus consolidate such a subject as a norm' (Smith 1996:350). This, Smith maintains, is made clear in the much-vaunted rationality of the free market.

Paul Smith also charts the position of Lawrence Brainerd (1991), a consultant for the IMF (International Monetary Fund), who claims that success in unification depends on the conversion of East Germans to the necessity of putting themselves *at risk*. This, it appears to him, is the essential difference between market economy and planned economy: in the latter, subjects are not agents. Capitalism, Brainherd argues, by contrast, works through the construction of subjects who must come to see themselves as 'responsible', and responsible because they 'naturally' protect their own stake in private property (note here the development of the elite possessive individual of political discourse, now being made available as a moral prerogative to the mass). So again, through the discourse of the powerful, we have the constitution of an interested, morally responsible self; but this time the self is figured as one that is prepared to take risks in order to accumulate.

However, as has already been noted, these formulations of self are deeply imbued with traditional gender relations and, from his analysis of contemporary rhetoric, Smith notes that: 'If one definition of the subject of value is that it be endowed with an ultimately self-interested rationality, women are now returned to the traditional non-self-interested roles of reproduction' (1996:358).

The next two sections explore how this subject of value is theorized by neo-Marxists who both abandon, but also use, class in their understandings of exchange.

Abandoning labour theory of value

Mike Savage (2000) charts a movement away from class, which he associates with analytical Marxists, notably Cohen (1988), who has exposed the logical problems entailed in using the labour theory of value by demonstrating how value changes over time, so that the extraction of surplus can never be a known quantity. Therefore, the central underpinning to Marxist class analysis becomes unstable.

Another Marxist response, identified by Savage (2000), is to recognize the 'transformation problem' that emphasizes the distinction between price and value, and accepts that the price (though not the value) may change according to contingencies. This is part of Postone's (1993) claim, drawn from Foucault (1966), that Marx did not break with the neo-classical assumptions of his day, but in fact consolidated them (see also Polanyi 2001). Just as Foucault argues that Marx's work embodies an implicit bourgeois concept of the human subject, so Postone maintains, the 'labour theory of value' is simply a model adopted from Ricardo and other bourgeois writers. This is echoed in Miller's (1993) identification of neo-classical liberal economics as a structuring discourse determining the terms of truth and positionings for the subject.

As Savage shows, Postone's critique questions traditional Marxism's reliance on 'surplus value' as the device by which the working-class is exploited by the capitalist class, in favour of a system approach which sees all labour as being based on instrumental abstract labour. Hence, within this perspective, Savage notes, there is no room at all for any developed or elaborated class theory which is dependent upon the labour theory of value.

However, Savage observes that it is doubtful that these writers would deny the existence of surplus value extraction. Rather, it becomes a kind of background condition, so ubiquitous that it plays no fundamental or determining role in explaining the specificities of particular capitalist systems. Some Marxists have taken this deconstruction even further. Arrighi (1994) argues that the dynamics of capitalism are organized much more around financial cycles than around any obviously class-related tensions. He maintains that since the fourteenth century there have been cyclical patterns, in which phases of production tend to give way to 'monetized' and financially driven modes of capital accumulation. So the history of all previous societies being premised on class struggle is replaced with cyclical economic patterns.

All these diverse Marxist currents, Savage maintains, have therefore turned their attention away from class to focus on the economy more generally. They do not deny that contemporary capitalism is a society divided by class, but they do not see the processes driving contemporary social change as class processes. The only exception to this general trend in new academic Marxism is, paradoxically, that associated with analytical or rational choice Marxism, found in the work of Elster (1985), Roemer (1986), Wright (1985; 1997), Cohen (1988; 1995) and Carling (1990). These theorists have attempted to place Marxist theory on secure 'micro-foundations' by formally considering how exploitative relationships can be defined in ways that are not dependent on the labour theory of value but still make class central. This leads Savage to conclude that it would appear that while Marxism continues to be a live intellectual force, it no longer has the mutual constitution of class and capitalism at its core. Indeed, he argues, it seems that Marxists have travelled down one of two roads, either choosing capitalism *or* class as their focus. They have either developed their arguments around the systemic properties of capitalism, or they have sought to find new foundations for the definition of class, but they have not linked the two together in any theoretically coherent way.

However, what we see seeping through this 'new' Marxism is again the old definition of the rational self. Central to their definition of exploitation is a theory of 'self-ownership', whereby all individuals are deemed to properly control themselves, and hence the capital–labour relationship must involve workers losing such control. This can be seen as a contemporary way of attributing different forms of personhood to different groups. This self-ownership occurs when the 'subject of value' realizes its value, acts in its interests and controls itself.

This becomes even more apparent in the way self and agency are figured in another set of neo-Marxist arguments based on the shift from seeing labour as something that is embodied and owned, a property of the self, to one that is based on the knowing self who *rents out* her or his labour. The impetus behind the debate is less a retreat from class than a shift of focus from labour to assets, with an inbuilt assumption about self-formation.

It should be noted, however, that the overuse of economic metaphors leads to ambiguities and confusions within these theories. The German economists (identified earlier) who talk about risk, transpose economic risk onto a theory of the subject. Moreover, it is difficult to separate the attribution of moral value from that of economic interest as it coheres to the agency of the worker.

The Sorenson debate

New approaches, which try to link across from economic organization to market processes to class formation, have been suggested by Eric Olin Wright (1985) who uses 'game theory', and Sorenson (2000a), who uses 'rent theory'. These approaches do not abandon class, and both have Marxist legacies, made apparent in their attempts to understand *process*, and in their concern to retain the concept of exploitation. Whereas Marx saw humans exploited through their labour, Wright and Sorenson suggest that humans *rent out* their labour. Rather than being just exploitable, this gives workers a form of agency (and, of course, requires a different conception of self), in which they are responsible for renting themselves out in the labour market. Sorenson defines 'exploitation class as structural locations that provide rights to rent-producing assets' (p.1,525).[2] Sorenson maintains that different contracts are being drawn up between labour and capitalists on the basis of what is necessary for current market competitiveness.

In a symposium on class analysis conducted in the *American Journal of Sociology* Sorenson (2000b) critiques the concept of exploitation based on antagonism and conflict. He challenges the idea that the source of inequality resides in the relations between the classes. Like the analytical Marxists above, he also abandons the labour theory of value, arguing that even the broader concept of exploitation proposed by the economist Roemer (1986) does not explain how antagonism is produced through exploitation to generate classes. Sorenson argues that a more useful distinction is between class as conflict groups, where conflict originates in exploitation, and class as a determinant of individual actions and mentalities, where these consequences originate in the life conditions associated with different classes. From Barzel (1997) he notes:

> Both class concepts have properties that reflect the extent and type of resources or assets possessed by incumbents of class positions. My proposal sees class based in property rights, as did Marx's, but the concept of property used here is broader than the legal property rights definition usually employed. It is a concept of property rights defined as the ability to receive the return on an asset, directly or indirectly through exchange (Barzel 1997).
>
> (Sorenson 2000b:1,525)

This defines class as:

1   a life condition – based on a person's total wealth;
2   exploitation – based on a person's control over assets that produce economic rents.

This can be seen as a model based on assets owned (1) and assets controlled (2). Exchange becomes an essential mechanism for any accrual to occur. Sorenson also defines exploitation class (2) as structural locations that provide rights to rent-producing assets – what he calls a 'geography of social structure'.

Whilst other theorists such as Ossowski (1963) and Wright (1985; 1979) have formulated class categories through cross-classifying ownership with authority, Sorenson refutes this, because he cannot see any economic rationale for the effect of authority per se. Conversely, Roemer (1982) and Wright (1985) contend that authority can be seen as a form of asset, namely 'the control of organizational assets'. Sorenson argues that authority is not a necessary prerequisite for exploitation to occur. This is because he limits his exploitation class to inequality generated by ownership or possession of *rent producing assets*. Rent producing assets or resources create inequalities where the advantage to the owner is obtained at the expense of non-owners. Exploitation is thus simply a matter of *economic advantage* obtained at the expense of someone else. Rents are advantages to the owner of assets that are not necessary to bring about the use of these assets.

Economic property rights, therefore, for Sorenson, reflect an individual's ability to consume a good or asset directly, or through exchange; that is, to control the use of a good or an asset. Such economic rights may be enforceable by law, but not necessarily. This means that all individuals usually have some property right to assets under some circumstances, even if it only consists in the ability to execute a task that can be exchanged for a wage. The total wealth controlled by people, according to Sorenson, defines their class situation with respect *to class as life conditions*. The individual's total wealth, as defined by control of their assets, determines their life conditions and, thus, class location. The rent-generating part defines class as exploitation and so the individual's ability to exploit their own assets constitutes class.

The challenge, Sorenson argues, for a theory of exploitation is to define a process by which some holder of an economic property right obtains an advantage *at the expense of persons without these rights*. When people act on their interests they create social organization and processes to protect or destroy rent benefits. Alongside other interest theorists (that is, most economists and the Rational Action Theorists who appear to be pervading sociology and political theory) this again presupposes a model of the knowing, accumulative, self-interested self. It is based on what Smith above identifies as the 'subject of value', an individual with an innate desire to increase his own accumulative potential. But at least Sorenson can perceive the disadvantages of those who do not have assets to exploit and obtain advantage.

The ability to perceive future returns on wealth reflects the different life conditions, as those with fewer assets can see less chance of future gain. The distinction between temporary rents and enduring rents is central to the analysis of class formation as process (it depends on stability and change). This process is also about who can mobilize resources to work in their interests, hence *resource mobilization*. Sorenson describes how cultural capital can be a source of rent, as it operates as credentials; class action in contemporary society is therefore about rent seeking and the protection of property rights to rent-producing assets.

There have been many challenges to Sorenson's 'rent shift'. For instance, Wright (2000) believes that rent is not enough for understanding class formation, because it cannot provide a full account of the explanatory mechanisms of exploitation. The first problem he identifies is how Sorenson's model is built upon an idea of perfect competition, which he contends is just never possible, because it would need perfect information and a complete absence of any power relations. The logic of Sorenson's argument, he notes, would be a classless society. Wright's point is sustained further when he scrutinizes the idea of everybody being able to own assets, thus eliminating the relationship between the exploiter and the exploited. For Wright, it is precisely the dependency of each group on the other that constitutes a social relation that creates class antagonism by pitting interest against interest, hence against each other. Capital still needs labour: labour does not want to be exploited. Those who hire rented labour determine the price they are willing to pay. Only in conditions of scarce labour are the renters likely to gain an advantage.

Wright further asks how we can identify which properties of social relations generate antagonistic interests based on rent. It is not possible, he believes, to have a theory of class divorced from capitalist property relations. Employees who are the recipients of various forms of rents within their earnings should be regarded as occupying privileged appropriation locations within exploitation relations (Wright 1997). Wright points out that this challenges his own earlier formulation, which regarded both skill and loyalty rents (rents appropriated especially by managers because of their control over organizational apparatuses) as the distinctive forms of exploitation.

Goldthorpe (2000) also notes that Sorenson's leaning towards interest groups fighting out for the potential to enhance or destroy rents does not show how rent-seeking itself may inhibit class formation and reduce strategic action though class organization; and Rueschemeyer and Mahoney (2000) observe the lack of moral grounding in Sorenson's theory of class exploitation which is not based on the injustice of exploitation. As a result there is little reason for believing that rents will consistently generate class-consciousness and collective organization. Sorenson's framework only makes sense if rents have no significant social consequences beyond the zero-sum gains and losses they distribute to owners and non-owners. Even if some rents do generate antagonistic objective interests, it is unlikely that the exploitation will carry the moral authority to produce broad-based class formation and mobilization. Rueschemeyer and Mahoney (2000) insist that we need to abandon the idea that rents are a universal basis for exploitation, and instead develop a more specific hypothesis about the conditions under which actors come to perceive rents as exploitative. People, they suggest, are more likely to mobilize around life conditions than exploitation.

To add another dimension, Savage (forthcoming) traces how assets have come to play such a prominent role in class theory. He focuses on the economic assets that can be deployed to produce a capital return, introducing the dimension of 'expertise', and arguing that it is the organization of expertise that has come to play a key *structuring role*, as significant to class dynamics of late modernity as property relations were in Marx's time. Developing Savage's earlier work, Savage *et al.* (1992)

delineate three causal processes that generate class inequality – property, organization and cultural capital – to show how assets are linked to particular occupational
groups. They describe the difference between managers, who enjoy the rewards
of organizational assets, and professionals, who benefit from cultural capital.
Savage's argument is that different assets can contingently give rise to diverse
kinds of occupational structuring. There is no attempt in his analysis to embed
class in the occupational order, but rather, to show how the division of labour is
structured through the processes of organization, property and culture. The most
serious task facing asset-based approaches to class analysis, he maintains, is how
to distinguish assets, as generative entities, from contingent forms of social advantage and disadvantage. Or, to put it more simply, how do we recognize an asset?

This leads us back, however, to the question of exploitation because asset-based
approaches do not automatically invoke a labour theory of value, and have often
been associated with 'game theory', e.g. Wright (1997), in which the traditional
three social divisions – class, status and party – become re-translated as property,
skill/culture and organization. This comparison, Savage argues, is not particularly
helpful. He suggests instead a focus on the *accumulative potential* of assets because,
as Bourdieu (1985; 1987) notes, assets can be increased over time and they involve
social relationships over time. Bourdieu demonstrates how cultural capital can be
detached from one setting and is, by definition, mobile, although within limits. So
if we developed this analysis, we could have an understanding of what assets can
be accumulated over time, which ones are worthless, and which generate optimal
potential. We would need to have a theory of how access to assets is acquired and
how exclusions are produced. But does this explain exploitation?

Fine and Lapivistas (2000), however, urge caution; they reveal how the use of
assets reflects the increasing hegemony of economics within the social sciences.
This is because asset approaches conceptualize class differences without resorting
to a labour theory of value. Fine draws attention to a more radical potential of
asset theory which disrupts the 'market logic' by showing how the causal powers
of particular kinds of assets are not only necessary for market processes, but often
prevent free markets from operating, which leads to structural inequality. Thus
shifting our perspective from accumulation to disruption may offer a more extensive
understanding of how assets work. To this I would further ask, why and how is it
that some groups would find acquiring and disruption impossible?

Moreover, how do we understand what Adkins (1995; 2000a) shows to be a
requirement of certain divisions of labour; namely, the use of gender and sexuality
in the structuring of the work-place, or the use of lesbian sexuality as a 'diversity
dividend'? Part of the problem here is how a sharp division is drawn between
culture and economy, in which property, capital and accumulation are only seen
to be products of the economic. Exchange-value seems to have become reducible
to economic-value, whereas in fact all exchange is always informed by the symbolic
value attributed to that being exchanged and the relationships that enable it to
take place. This has led some theorists to locate gender, sexuality and race to the
'merely' cultural (see Fraser 1997 and response by Butler 1997b, and also Adkins
2002c).

We, therefore, need to understand the symbolic valuation of culture, labour and property, which enables it to have an exchange-value for either selling, rental or asset accrual. Also, how do different fields offer different accrual or renting possibilities? Where does their value come from? It is now almost a truism that capitalism does not care about the sex, gender or race of its workers. As long as value can be extracted, it does not matter. However, workers enter the labour market with different values, hence making them more or less amenable to the potential for exploitation. So, in this sense, sex, race and gender do matter. A woman might only be employed in the first place because she is young, beautiful and sexy. Thus, it is her gender value that matters and gives her access to the potential to be exploited in the first place.

A shift of perspective is therefore needed that enables us to understand what is embodied in order to be exploitable, but also what makes accrual possible, or not. We need to be able to hold together exploitation (the extraction of surplus) *with* an understanding of how people accrue value by obtaining assets, which enhance their value and may protect them more from exploitation. We also need to understand how some people can only be exploited. They are forced to enter the labour market with little value that offers minuscule possibilities for accrual over time. In fact, their value may depreciate.[3]

The debate over rent is still about property, the introduction of assets, resources and expertise into the equation, ultimately reducing class formation to the owning of particular forms of cultural property. The shift that occurs in this analysis is from ownership of economic goods to the ownership of oneself thorough one's labour power, to the ownership of cultural properties. A central difference then appears. On the one hand, there are those who are depicted as rational and accruing individuals, who can secure the necessary properties in order to either exploit themselves or avoid exploitation, and who, as a result, become a subject of value. On the other hand, there are those who are depicted as not having the potential to be a subject of value, without access to the resources required to produce them-selves as such. This latter group are born into positions where resources may be given different values. It thus becomes a matter of how different forms of culture and labour are given value and how these can be exchanged or not.

Exploitation then continues to be a useful concept as surplus value is still extracted. Some people may have greater control over their value – through their ability to accrue valued assets – and can, therefore, protect themselves more and generate greater value for themselves from the renting of their assets and expertise. Underpinning this analysis is a morality, not based on social good but on individual advantage.[4] Others will not have access, or the ability, to acquire the requisite assets to rent themselves; but, as this book will proceed to show, they do have cultural properties upon which others can capitalize, even when they themselves cannot. And this is an important intervention; to capitalize upon one's own cultural properties is central to the ability to accrue assets over time (and in volume). Exploitation also occurs when one group is able to use the resources of another, not to directly extract surplus value, but to increase individual value in order to increase the volume of marketable exchange-value. This relies upon a model of one class being comprised of 'subjects of value' and another class having 'culture'. To develop this argument further, I will now explore theories that make subjectivity central to forms of economic exchange.

Culturalization of the economy

Whereas the renting, asset and rights theories of the economic have assumed and relied upon an unreconstructed theory of the self and subjectivity, Rose (1989) develops Smith's 'subject of value'. He makes explicit the formation of a range of 'technologies of subjectivity', in which political power has come to depend upon expert techniques, for shaping and enhancing the psychological capacities of citizens. This, he claims, is a new form of political rationality grounded in the entrepreneurial self. His focus is on work, and he begins with the traditional Marxist view:

> No amount of the re-jigging of the details of work, the organization of the enterprise, the conditions of the labour process, or levels of reward could transform the basic alienation that lies at the heart of work. Workers work because they have to. They work at the behest of others in a process they do not control, to produce goods or services they do not enjoy. It is the wage, not the pleasure of work that drives them to the production line, the office, desk or shop floor each morning ... As far as the worker is concerned, it would seem, work is made up, principally, of the elements of obedience, self-denial, and deferred gratification – it entails an essential subordination of subjectivity.
> (Rose 1989:55–6)

Yet, he argues, during the course of the present century, types of work and conditions of working have radically changed. Now the path to business success lies in engaging the employee with the goals of the company at the level of his or her subjectivity. The subjectivity of the worker has thus emerged as a complex territory to be explored, understood and regulated.

Rose traces how, since at least the early nineteenth century, the significance of work for public order has been as important as its directly economic function – its moralizing effect upon the worker, and its capacity to enmesh the individual in the network of expectations and routines that make up the social body (1989:63). He illustrates how a range of technologies, including management, human relations, Taylorism and personnel, made the subjectivity of the worker central to understanding how the economy could develop. Following the Second World War, he shows how, in the UK, a new form of government of labour had been established in which work was considered to be the means by which the individual achieved a relationship with society at large. Following this, Rose charts how psychology became increasingly used to understand worker relations through 'meaning'. Discontent was traced not to the actions of managers, but to the meanings that these actions had for workers. He calls this the 'new social psychology of industry' and shows how it was translated into the self-evaluations and self-judgement of each individual.

The governance of the self is thus a central mechanism of state control, and the instinctual and affective life of humans comes, as Bernstein (1971) noted, under more embracing forms of self-control, of becoming responsible for one's own governance. Self-regulation then is a matter of establishing a moral code under which the self can be assessed as being or becoming responsible.

Forms of ethical conduct are a form of labour and governance imposed upon the self by the self. The self becomes obliged to 'become' in a particular way. But all ways are not open to all, and some positions are already classified as in need of help, of being irresponsible, of having deficit culture, or of being pathological. There is a conflict here between theories that show how subjectivity *has to be* produced in order to work and consume (e.g. Adkins 2000b; Rose 1989; 1992; Cronin 2000b), and those that assume an optimizing individual without establishing the conditions of possibility by which any individual can become optimizing. There is also a problem in suggesting that all workers can, and need to, produce subjectivity for work. Many are not seen as capable and remain the constitutive limit. This is clearer if we turn to debates about the 'enterprising self'.

The enterprising self

Rose's 'new worker subjectivities' and renting one's labour, or becoming a 'subject of value', have close links, which depend on turning oneself into a marketable product, into a commodity and, ultimately, becoming more easily controlled through ethical self-governance. 'New workers' have to create themselves as a marketable product, to be sold and re-sold on a rapidly changing market. But this is not just about skills; the worker also has to persuade the buyer that they, as workers, have the right dispositions, affects and attitudes. For instance, they are reliable, will do the work, can be trusted, are ahead of the field, etc. The sort of labour that is being sold is related to the wider qualities of *being a particular sort of person* and having a *particular composition of cultural resources*. Certain personality characteristics are required, and it is more likely that these will impact upon a person's subjectivity, of who they think they are. So, for instance, a mechanic may think of herself as a mechanical-practical type of person. Those who perform caring work often come to think of themselves as caring people, merging 'caring for' with 'caring about' in order to attribute moral worth to themselves (see Skeggs 1997).

Developing Rose's analysis, Paul du Gay (1996) identifies a new 'enterprising self', whereby people are required to become entrepreneurs of the self. This is similar to the work of Devine (1997) and Granovetter (1995), who show that social skills based on cultural and social capital are becoming increasingly necessary as requirements of the labour market, as more people gain similar level qualifications and employers need to differentiate between them. Their social and cultural dispositions make the difference. Du Gay's work adds cultural analysis to 'renting' theory, but sadly it has little to say about class formation. Again, it assumes a level playing field, in which access to assets are available to all and, therefore, it is a matter of technique, of learning which assets are most lucrative. In this sense, it can be seen as reproducing the very conditions it sets out to explore: the enterprising self is enterprising because it has the requisite skills to make it enterprising. In this circular argument we again need to ask what are the processes by which some groups become more enterprising? Are they enterprising all the time or only at work? How does their enterprising self impact upon other areas of their lives?

Brooks (2001), for instance, in a study of the 'new bohemians' (whom he terms 'bobos' because they combine the counter-cultural 1960s and the achieving 1980s into one social ethos), documents how this group of 'enterprising selves' enterprises their whole lives, so that even sex becomes something to be 'achieved', travelling becomes an 'education', and they adopt the moral code of utilitarian pleasure, evaluating all time through its accomplishments. For them, the intangible world of information merges with the material world of money, and everything becomes a matter of accrual, of exchange-value.

Yet 'new worker subjectivities' are not particularly new, if we take into account the work of feminist theorists. Previous work on women workers, such as Hoschild (1983) and Adkins (1995), reveals how women have always had to embody enterprising gender characteristics, i.e. they are employed on the basis of their dispositions as well as their skills; particular occupations require employees to have 'feminine' characteristics. This is not part of the job description, but is a prerequisite for employment. This is, therefore, not an optimizing, enterprising or reflexive individual, but one who is forced to display skills she is already assumed to have, through her positioning by gender (or sexuality). She has no choice. She does not optimize. She was optimized. And then exploited. Exploitation is then a matter of forcing a person to use the cultural attributes by which they are positioned: forced performativity, culturally essentializing.

Adkins and Lury (1999) demonstrate how studies that emphasize how the self-identity of workers constitutes a key resource in new regimes of accumulation, do not take into account how some workers may be denied authorship of their identities. Adkins and Lury warn against universalizing an analysis of 'self-possessing workers with performable identities' (p.598). In a study of employment in tourist organizations, Adkins (1995) outlines how workplace identities are not universally available as resources and, in particular, that identities are not constituted as the cultural property of the self (or individual) which all workers are equally free to exchange. Certain gendered and sexed identity practices are rendered intrinsic to women workers through relations of appropriation. This, Adkins and Lury (1999) maintain, is a self that cannot be performed as 'enterprising', as an occupational resource, and is therefore unlikely to be rewarded.

Adkins and Lury illustrate just how difficult it is for many women workers to achieve identities beyond that of 'woman worker', because their labour of identity is naturalized as part of their selves and cannot be used and exchanged as a mobile resource. In another study, Adkins (2001) demonstrates how feminist theories of flexibility and performativity at work, reproduce and re-traditionalize gender divisions by showing the limits to who can actually mobilize gender at work. And, in a further study, Adkins (2000a) observes how sexuality is similarly fixed. The already evaluated categories and classifications put limits on what is seen to be a useful resource in the making of the enterprising self.

The cultural capital of the working-class is often read in a similar way by employers, through gender and race. A working-class man is recognized as embodying physicality and endurance, rather than cleverness and self-governance. Black working-class men, in particular, are read in highly racist ways by employees, suggesting that their cultural capital cannot be optimized at work, or used as an asset to rent as cultural property, because it is nearly always perceived and valued negatively. Hence, black working-class men cannot enterprise themselves 'up' as they are not given access to spaces for exchange (work), and are mis-recognized symbolically as negative. This process of mis-recognition and negative evaluation has been extensively documented in studies of education, where the cultural capital of the working-class (black and white) is always read as deficient and in opposition to the ability to accrue educational credentials. So, the working-class begin from a very different starting point where their culture is not valued, thereby limiting its potential for use in the development of the subject of value who can enterprise themselves legitimately.[5]

The self is always located by prior historical classificatory schemes of value. These classifications are not 'merely cultural' but are part of a wider symbolic economy, of which the economy is itself a part. They enable and constrain what can be exchangeable, propertizable, exploitable, appropriable, and what can be used as a resource and asset. They establish the conditions of possibility for exchange. Being classed, raced, gendered or sexed by culture places limits and/or enables advantages.

Some theorists of the 'enterprising' or aestheticized self, however, investigate *how class not only intervenes, but actually constitutes* this process. Savage *et al.* (1992) argue that a performing self, especially in regard to the stylization of the body, including an emphasis on appearance, display and the management of impressions, is key for membership and constitutive of the new middle-classes. In their substantive empirical research from 1992 (Savage *et al.* 1992), they document how the professional middle-classes have been able to consolidate their position through cultural practices, such as taking more care of their bodies, increasing their education, staying healthy, thereby making themselves more productive, a greater subject of value (see also Featherstone 1991). The middle-classes, therefore, start from a position of advantage and optimize from this. Savage *et al.* argue that, in order for the middle-classes to secure their position, they have to maximize the assets on which they can draw. Hence, Brook's description above of the new bohemians is a perfect description of middle-class culture being optimized. The moral code of utilitarian pleasure enables all cultural activities to be put to use to optimize the self (see also Florida 2002). This is an asset-acquiring self, obsessed with increasing the volume of its cultural capital. This suggests to me that these theories of the enterprising self are premised upon models, ideals and the experience of the middle-class and as a model of exploitation, labour relations or exchange, mainly redundant for the working-class, who do not have access to the same starting point, the same approach to accrual, access to the knowledge of how to accrue effectively and access to the sites for optimizing the cultural capital that they may have acquired (see Chapters 8 and 9).

The recent emphasis on self-agency as necessary for exchange was, Morris (1991) argues, developed through the emphasis put on enterprise by Thatcherism, and some social theorists appear to be caught up in this rhetoric. Morris maintains Thatcherism produced a cast of characters informed by two distinct kinds of morality: on the one hand, what Tipton (1982) calls the 'moral culture' of 'utilitarian individualism', and on the other, an 'authoritative style of ethical evaluation' (pp.3, 7). Both begin with the individual person as an agent seeking to satisfy his own wants or interests. So, within each of these new contemporary developments lies a dormant historical model of a self informed by moral authority which enables exchange to take place. Rose (1989) develops this by showing how the practices of the self are being organized. He identifies:

> First, the moral codes, the languages they use, the ethical territory they map out, the attributes of the person that they identify as of ethical significance, the ways of calibrating and evaluating them they propose, the pitfalls to be avoided and the goals to pursue. Second, there would be the ethical scenarios, the apparatuses and contexts in which the moral codes are administered and the means by which they are enjoined – in the school and the courts, in the practices of social work and medicine ... Third, there would be the techniques of the self, the models proposed for setting up and developing relationships with the self, for self-reflection, self-knowledge, self-examination, for the deciphering of the self by oneself, for the transformation one seeks to accomplish with oneself as object.
>
> (Rose 1989:241)

This shift to explicit self-production is important as it exposes the contradictions in generating a particular sort of labour value through the production of a particular sort of person. It also exposes how the economy is just one part of the symbolic order, put into effect through social and cultural relations. The ability to capitalize (or not) upon culture and use it as a mobile resource is fundamental to the arguments promoted in this book. It is also important, as the most recent trends detected in the economy are towards de-materialization in which there is a predominance of symbolic exchange with hyper-commodification and the industrialization of culture (Slater and Tonkiss 2001). Dodd (1995), however, points out that this is not a new trend but that the economy has always been premised on the symbolic; he uses the example of money to argue this point. Money is, after all, a representation of value. And, Callon (1998) argues, culture makes the representations that constitute the market and economy as objects of knowledge, which are simultaneously objects of action. What is significant is how these representations enable and constrain the conversion of the resources of labour and subjectivity, fixing some as already performative and others with the potential for optimization.

Conclusion

Analysis of recent economic debate and class analysis alerts us to the significance of cultural assets and how culture can be used as a form of capital, as a resource, to accrue property to one's self. Methodologically, we can also see that, as with previous class analysis, the ability to mobilize and accrue property produces a 'new' model of the self, premised on middle-class experience that constitutes its boundaries through the exclusion of others, and reproduces a static (objective or neutral) model of the economy. This also draws attention to the significance of the social, to the way in which cultural practices become institutionalized – not only through work, but also by governance through self-moralizing and authorizing. As Miller (1993) notes, the will of the producing and consuming subject is a desired object of control, where the sense of identification is with a responsible, internalized obedience. These are central processes of middle-class formation, highly inappropriate to the conditions of the working-class.

What these theories seem to be lacking is a theory of positioning, a way of understanding how birth into categorizations, known and recognized through inscription, representations, discourse and narrative, but also institutionalized and surveilled, sets limits on the potential for exchange (whether it be through the labour theory of value, renting, asset accrual, or conversion of cultural capital). Sorenson, for instance, relativizes the potential for rent. It is as if anybody can do it, if they have the requisite assets. We need to ask, though, where do they get them from and what enables forms of exchange to take place? This would show how the market is not a neutral playing field, but an already divided historical entity, premised upon classification with historically generated value, into which we enter with differential access to different types of resources.

I'd argue that what is missing from all these new class analyses (with the exception of Bourdieu and Savage) is an understanding of the symbolic economy, of the significance of representations and categorizations in attributing value that sticks to certain bodies, fixing some in place and enabling others to be mobile. We need then to understand how these value processes become institutionalized beyond the economic. How does propriety become property, for instance? How does the law (legal texts and institutionalization) hear, know, legislate and enable certain bodies and certain goods to be seen as property? As Foucault shows, the systems of categorization are an effect of state power, of struggle for authority. What forms of mis-recognition are put into effect by employees, the law and theorists?

The present configuration of the economic relies upon a particular conception of self – one that not only owns itself, but optimizes itself, in order to prove itself amenable to capitalism. This involves turning one's culture into a property of the self. The self, as Rose (1989) notes, does not pre-exist the forms of its social recognition. The technologies which come to produce the self are not floating around a diffuse field of culture, but are embodied in many institutional practices through which forms of individuality are made visible through specification and governance. Yet only some can utilize their culture as a property of the self: others are forced to perform it as a 'natural' part of being. We have different access to becoming a subject with value. That is, our prior historical categorical positioning will always inform how we enter these technologies. Some groups (such as white working-class women) do not have access to class as an 'identity', to be deployed as a resource; they are also forced to perform gender, fixed in place as naturalized, regularly pathologized. These groups are most definitely not on the same playing field (of cultural capital) as the one on which the enterprising self plays. This means that they cannot utilize their culture in self-making in the same way, one that can be converted into other forms of capital. It cannot be used in the same way as a workplace resource. Positioning by the categorization of the working-class means exploitation can occur by the extraction of surplus value from labour, and also from the use of their culture, but the working-classes cannot capitalize on their culture because it has already been devalued as that which is not optimizable.

The next chapter maps how working-class culture is evaluated through its formulation in political rhetoric. It establishes further how the symbolic attributes value to different forms of culture, making this value legitimate, economic and/or moral, enabling some forms of culture to be converted into a property of the self, and some not.

5 The political rhetorics of class

Rhetoric is the science of persuasion, involving both an aesthetic and a pragmatic agenda. Rhetoric persuades people to believe or to suspend disbelief, to accept the claims for verisimilitude as well as political claims; literally, to be heard, understood and accepted (Silverstone 1999). Different contemporary approaches to rhetoric stress its various functions: as persuasion (Burke 1962), as argument (Billig 1987) and as the structuring of knowledge (McKeon 1987). Roger Silverstone (1999) outlines how rhetoric is comprised of different elements: invention, arrangement, expression, memory and delivery; forms of argumentation: figures and tropes and its mechanisms of engagement. Rhetoric, he demonstrates, has been divined in: the perambulatory rhetorics of everyday life (de Certeau 1988; 1998); the homological narratives that link the literary and personal and that structure time (Ricoeur 1980; 1983); and the metaphors of everyday life. Rhetoric involves appeals that are both cognitive and critical, intellectual and emotional – for attention, for assent and, in the sharing of communication and understanding, for both common sense and community (Billig 1987). Rhetoric is one of the mechanisms through which class struggle occurs and can be identified. This book has already explored historical classifications and academic perspectives; the next two chapters turn to other sites of symbolic production – political rhetoric and popular representations – to explore how value becomes attributed and attached to particular cultures, selves and classes.

The rhetorical address produces a distinct discursive space, which combines a range of techniques, methods, frames and forms of communication. The exploration of these is the purpose of this chapter, which is organized into five sections. The first explores contemporary recombinations and recitations of class discourse identified in earlier chapters. This provides a frame for the second section which outlines how the nation state abdicates responsibility for its own policies through the discourse of global development; through what Bourdieu and Waquant (2001) call the 'rhetoric of impossibility', in which the inevitability of global 'progress' is presented as impossible to resist. This brings into focus, in the third section, the way in which the term 'social exclusion' is also used to enable responsibility for inequality to be transferred from the state to the individual via the diagnosis of pathological culture. The use of the rhetoric of 'moral underclass', which has a long historical tradition, is central to the rhetorical ploys used. The fourth section concentrates on how the contemporary discourse of multiculturalism is used in these rhetorical manoeuvres to racialize the white working-classes, enabling them to be identified as *the* blockage to future global competition and national economic prosperity. This identification of a pathological cultural hindrance to modernity is the means by which structural problems are transformed into an individualized form of cultural inadequacy, in which a position of self is offered to the working-class; but this is not the optimizing self or the subject of value identified in previous chapters, but rather a self who is immobile, useless and redundant, who cannot, because of their location in pathological culture, make anything of themselves. This self becomes not just an individual's problem, but a threat to all respectability, a danger to others and a burden on the nation. The final section examines the seepage of these rhetorical ploys as they become solidified in other sites of symbolic production.

The chapter builds a picture of how class is produced as a cultural property figured through difference and moral attribution, rhetorically ubiquitous and profligate in its expression, just rarely named directly. This is very similar to how sexuality existed in public, through euphemisms rather than being named directly. For instance, Foucault (1979) identifies how different discourses came to produce and frame what was known as sexuality. The discourses produced not only what came to be known as sexuality, but also served to concentrate extremely potent transfers of power, enabling considerable influence on the social order. Such discourses articulated what was desirable, undesirable, legitimate and illegitimate – hence, moral and immoral. Foucault describes how what came to be known as sexuality was a dense transfer point for relations of power. He identifies:

> … the wide dispersion of devices that were invented for speaking about it, for having it be spoken about, for inducing it to speak of itself, for listening, recording, transcribing and redistributing what is said about it; around sex a whole network of varying, specific, and coercive transpositions in to discourse.
>
> (Foucualt 1979:34)

In this chapter I develop aspects of this method for an understanding of class. For Foucault, an analysis of a discursive formation deals with statements in the density of the accumulation in which they are caught, and which they never cease to modify. Discourse is always produced in response to other discourses, and it has meaning only in its relation to complex networks of other meanings. Language is always language in use rather than an abstract system of relations. Utterances, as Mikhail Bakhtin (1981) has shown, are always history-laden; they are always part of an ongoing historical process. And as Michael Holquist (1990) has suggested, an utterance is never in itself originary. Rather, it is always an answer, conditioned by and in turn qualifying the prior utterance. What is significant is how, through processes of transference, condensation, crystallization and citation, value (usually moral) becomes attributed to positioning.

Developing Foucault's analysis of sexuality through a postcolonial reading of his ideas about race, Stoler (1995) maintains that Foucault does not depict different racial discourses as totally distinct; rather, he identifies not the end of one discourse and the emergence of another, but the refolded surfaces that join the two. By using the term 'fold', Stoler identifies the recursive, recuperative power of discourse itself, in a way that highlights how new elements in a prior discourse may surface and take on altered significance as they are repositioned in relation to new discourses with which they mesh. This enables us to see how the historical legacies described in Chapter 2, and the populist academic discourses identified in Chapter 3, are put to work in the contemporary. Political rhetoric, a mechanism of persuasion to win legitimacy, works within these discursive spaces. It draws on, folds in and recombines discourses from other sites.

Norman Fairclough (1991) demonstrates how discourse is not a redefined closed entity, but rather a set of tendencies – transformations within fields, which are of a diffuse nature and cannot be located in any one text. He therefore argues that the focus needs to be on processes across time and the social space of text production, plus the wider strategies that text production enters into. Linguistic and discursive conventions, hence class struggle through rhetoric, in which discourse operates as a dense transfer point for relations of power, has to be continually put into effect to legitimate power.

Recombinations in political discourse

Fairclough (2000) charts a contemporary 'mediatization' of politics and government in which the terms of governance are continually constituted and reconstituted. In the UK the political discourse of New Labour, he argues, is a process rather than a finished product, in which the government attempts to shift from one construction of the social relations of welfare to another. These shifts can be identified through political texts. Texts are processes in which political work is done, as well as the rhetorical work of mobilizing people behind political discourses. Political discourse weaves together different discourses through relations of equivalence, antithesis and entailment. This Fairclough calls the 'texture' of the text, which gives it a distinctive form of materiality. The work of politics or government is partly done in the material of texts – in the case of New Labour, the political discourse of the 'Third Way' has brought new right and social democratic discourses, as well as communitarian discourses, into a new combination; so, changes in the way of governing have taken the form of changes in the set of genres which are brought together in government.

Although the discourse of New Labour is a new discourse, some of those elements are derived from prior political discourse. For instance, Phillips (1988) documents how the Thatcherite thematization of 'value for money' and 'waste' within public services folded and recombined in the language of the Labour Party from the early 1990s.

Fairclough (2000) calls the moral and contractual discourse of New Labour an *individualist discourse*, which stands in contrast with traditional collectivism. The moral discourse also slides into authoritarian discourse and, as Tony Blair represents the continuity between family and community, he constructs the family through a discourse that is more usually applied to public institutions, such as schools. And he represents family life in a formal and distanced way by emptying it of its intimacy, speaking of the family through public categories, such as 'mutual respect' and 'acceptable conduct' (Fairclough 2000:43). Fairclough notes:

> My impression is that the most morally loaded term, 'duties', is increasingly being used, although probably 'responsibilities' (which has legal as well as moral connotations) is still the most common. Moral discourse is combined with contractual discourse which interprets the distribution of rights and responsibilities metaphorically as a 'contract' or 'deal' between the individual and society (the community) or the individual and government.
>
> (Fairclough 2000:39)

Fairclough demonstrates how the value that is consistently omitted is 'equality'. Also, the meaning of 'social justice' has shifted through the omission of 'equality of outcomes', which entails redistribution and substitution by 'fairness' and 'inclusion'.

In a close and detailed reading of the texts of Old and New Labour Fairclough notes:

> 'Values' occurs 19 times in the 'earlier Labour' corpus. Six of these relate to 'value' in an economic sense (4 occur in the collocation 'socialist values', 2 others in collocation with 'socialism' or 'Socialists', and 3 more in collocation with 'Labour' – (totalling 9). The remaining 3 are: 'civilised values', 'political values' (of 'monetarism'), the 'values and ideals which will guide the nation', and the 'relative values' of standard English and other varieties of English. A striking feature of these examples is that in 8 out of 19 occurrences of 'values' the context is one of political antagonism – conflict between Labour and its political opponents.
>
> There are 64 instances of 'values' in the New Labour corpus, none of them in an economic sense (so all in the moral sense). In contrast with the 'earlier Labour' corpus, 'values' never collocates with 'socialist' and only once with 'Labour', and there are no contexts of political antagonism. The predominant context is rather 'change' – 'values' occurs 29 times in contexts of change, modernisation, or more specifically applying traditional values to the modern world.
>
> (Fairclough 2000:45)

Alex Callinicos (2001) has developed this, showing how value is translated into individual duty and a moral imperative. Those who cannot perform their state-defined 'duty' are thus morally suspect. Value thus becomes duty that is individualized, even though it is imposed and defined by the state, so that those who cannot perform 'duty' properly are seen to be culturally and individually at fault.[1] When rhetoric becomes an individual moral prerogative and responsibility, its most pernicious effects can be seen.

The following section charts the various ways governments transfer responsibility from themselves and their policies onto others through recourse to global political rhetoric.

Global inevitability

In contemporary political rhetoric what stands out is the lack of contestation over capitalism. Just as we saw in the last chapter how the market historically came to be seen as neutral, we can now see the global economy being figured in the same way. Those who aspire to exist in a more global economy routinely represent it as already in existence – that is, they presuppose it. This Bourdieu and Waquant (2001) identify as the discourse of the 'planetary vulgate'. They argue that the terms 'capitalism', 'class', 'exploitation', 'domination' and 'inequality' are conspicuous by their absence, having been dismissed under the pretext that they are obsolete and non-pertinent. This rhetorical ploy is the result of a new type of imperialism whose effects are all the more powerful because they are pernicious: 'globalization' is not a new phase of capitalism, but a form of 'rhetoric' invoked by governments in order to justify a voluntary surrender to the financial markets and their conversion to the fiduciary conception of the firm. Far from being the inevitable result of the growth of foreign trade de-industrialization, growing inequality and the retrenchment of social policies, the rhetoric is, rather, the result of domestic political decisions that reflect the tipping of the balance of class forces in favour of the owners of capital. This makes even more sense when we see how global rhetoric is invented, arranged and explained through the market-speak identified by Frank (2001), who shows how it is put to work as a supposed expression of the 'will of the people' (see final section for a development of this position).

The take up of aspects of globalization can be identified easily in New Labour rhetoric. The themes and tropes of national renewal, individual responsibility, maximizing competition, and the limitations of government are all there. Such themes constitute elements of an international neo-liberal politics: governments promoting the globalization of the economy in order to legitimate and win consent for a drastic revision and reduction of the welfare state, by adopting a punitive stance towards those who are the victims of economic change and the retreat from public welfare. Accompanying this argument about inevitability, Lois Wacquant (1999) identifies the international spread of the new 'penal state'. He documents the institutions, agents and supporting discourses (advisory notes, committee reports, visits by officials, parliamentary exchanges, specialist seminars, academic and popular books, press conferences, newspaper articles, television reports, etc.) through which the rhetoric of new penal common sense (incubated particularly in the US), is produced, directed at criminalizing deprivation, and thereby normalizing insecurity in employment. This process, he argues, is becoming international.

Bourdieu and Waquant (2001) note how this emergent rhetoric that displaces class is not just restricted to national states. It is not only governments that are incorporated within this new international order and discourse, but also various other types of business and community organizations and, importantly, powerful international agencies, such as the World Bank, the International Monetary Fund and the Organization for Economic Co-operation and Development. Part of international harmonization of policy is the emergence of an international political discourse in which class does not figure but, as we saw in Chapter 4, the 'subject of value' does, with its moral prerogative of risk-taking in optimizing and enterprising its value, and exercising its own self-governance.

As Fairclough (2000) illustrates, the responsibility attributed to people via slogans of citizenship, community and self-management is significantly absent from the responsibility attributed to government or the global economy. This, as he points out, means that all change, all governance, all responses, become inevitable and non-agentic. The 'logic of appearances' generated by this political rhetoric once again takes out the subject and the process, concentrating instead on outcome, symptom and calculated evidence. The new 'global economy' is represented as an accomplished fact and change is represented as an inevitable feature of global forces for which there is 'no alternative'; neo-liberalism is something with which we just have to live (Fairclough 2000). Interestingly, as Rouse (1995) shows, there is less of a concern in the US with naturalizing and neutralizing global capitalism, but more of a concern with nation-building. This, I'd argue, points to the complacency of imperialistic power (see also Hardt and Negri 2000).

The evasion of class, and the attempt to nation-build, are identified by Rouse (1995) who documents two major approaches used in US political rhetoric. He traces how new efforts have been launched to reinvigorate and recast the divisive power of taxonomies through the generalizing discourse of identity. Identity, he maintains, 'is the most ubiquitous, the most vivid idiomatic symptom of the anxieties and opportunities that the recent challenges to the old topographies of difference' have produced (p.381). He details two different ways in which difference is presently being reinscribed. The first discourse is 'conservative monoculturalism', and the second is 'corporate-liberal multiculturalism'. Conservative monoculturalism has been used to garner support predominantly for white men, whose privileges have been supposedly under attack. The rhetoric presents the need to break down divisions in order to create an unmediated relationship between generic individuals and a national society, that is, the bearer of a single culture and identity. It is the character of individuals and their willingness to fit into the nation that count. The practices considered antithetical to this core national white culture are coded through taxonomies of racial and political difference. They have built 'a discriminating, panic-driven picture of a virtuous core increasingly imperilled by a horde of dangerous others' (Rouse 1995:382).

In contrast, corporate-liberal multiculturalism has taken a different route in order to build a centre-right alliance that can incorporate the cosmopolitan members of the professional managerial class. The corporate-liberal multicultural approach has been double-voiced in its approach to difference. This rhetoric does not use narrative to tell a story of a nation united around a single set of substantially defined values, but focuses instead on formally defined political processes and procedures that promise equal rights. Inequalities are thus based on the failure of these procedures as mediating sources of affiliation. Equal representation is at issue, and this depends upon people developing knowledge and pride in their identities. Yet, as Rouse points out, the central focus has been on questions of efficiency, making cultural diversity a resource to be used. The differences between these two dominant discourses are not substantial:

> As old taxonomies of difference and division have become increasingly problematised by changing patterns of residence and work, these discourses reassert the primacy of taxonomic differences along lines of gender, race and national origin and amplify the distinguishing force of these taxonomies by suggesting that they are matched by differences in ways of life. They both attribute the material deprivations of those at the bottom of the contemporary class structure primarily to the ways in which differences in identity and way of life have been handled in political terms.
>
> (Rouse 1995:385)

This has striking parallels with the ways in which cultural difference is being refigured across Europe, where cultural practices – seen as a property of the person, as a form of cultural essentialism (for those who do not have the mobility to move beyond cultural designation) – are held as responsible for inequality. This US strategy has more recently been translated into the UK: on 9 December 2001, the Home Secretary, David Blunkett, announced in a White Paper that one becomes British through having a British identity. By this he meant not having 'another' primary identity, such as Indian or Pakistani. In all these different (US, UK) discourses outlined above, one either owns an identity and can protect it, or one can use cultural diversity as a resource, assuming access for middle-class cultural capital, which can be converted into value. Neither of these is an option for those who are not offered identity as a positive value, or who do not have the recognized type of cultural diversity, considered to have a cultural value that can make a claim on the state.

The terms underclass and middle-class are still being used in the US and, for Rouse (1995), are symptomatic of the anxieties that surround the processes that they mark and the moral divisions that are drawn. This is nothing new, as the historical analysis and the next section will show, but it figures class through morality in a way that has not been seen since its initial inception. The major difference is the extension of the concept of self, so the rhetoric of 'compulsory individuality' is now seen to address all – whilst only being applicable to a few who have access to the requisite resources – and their lack of take-up is read as a consequence of their own individual failing. This is the cultural politics of class that is being consolidated in a variety of rhetoric and representations, made incredibly explicit in the discourse of social exclusion and, in particular, in the rhetoric of the underclass.

Social exclusion and the moral underclass

Social exclusion was in part defined by the quantification of the unemployed. It was then institutionalized through the Social Exclusion Unit, established to deal with the five million individuals who live in households where there are people of working age, but no-one in paid work, and the three million who live on the 1,300 housing estates identified as the worst in Britain. In its first phase the Unit produced three reports that identified specific aspects of social exclusion: truancy and 'school exclusion', street living, and the worst housing estates. The concept of 'social exclusion', as Fairclough (2000) notes, is a relatively new one in Britain, although regularly used in the European Union (EU), and its adoption in Britain can be seen to be part of an EU harmonization (Curran 1999). The use of social inclusion incorporates Britain into an established continental European discourse, and an especially French focus on marginalization as detachment from the moral order of society, as opposed to the Anglo-Saxon liberal view of marginalization as redistribution, of not commanding sufficient resources to survive in the market.

Fairclough (2000) documents how the Social Exclusion Unit uses listings to generate the appearance of evidence that a 'problem' exists, because it can be seen, identified and recognized. Note the similarity to the methods discussed in Chapter 2, whereby a 'social body' is established through quantification, observation and the demarcation of its parts. Rather than trying to find explanations, including cause/effect relations between different problems and agencies, people are just listed and counted. Emphasis is placed on the *state of being excluded*, whereby social exclusion becomes an *outcome* rather than a process. It is a condition people are in, not something that is done to them. Their culture is at fault. Correspondingly, although the lack of paid work is seen as the primary reason for social exclusion, there is no specification of economic processes or agents that are responsible for producing unemployment.

In the first leaflet produced by the Social Exclusion Unit the verb 'to exclude' is used only once, whereas the nominalization 'exclusion' occurs 15 times. This in itself, Fairclough suggests, shows that the 'outcome' sense of social exclusion rather than the 'process' sense is predominant, because one effect of nominalization is to de-emphasize process and foreground outcome. This effect is linked to the fact that nominalizations tend to involve the omission of the subjects and objects of verbs, which specify who the agent is and who is affected. So subjects are taken out of exclusion; they are not the equivalent of what Smith (1996) identifies in Chapter 4 as the *subject of value*, but are the calculable result of this new discourse.

According to Ruth Levitas (1998), there are three different discourses associated with social exclusion and inclusion, and different constructions and combinations of discourses they privilege. The three discourses are: first, redistributionist, which focuses on poverty and attempts to reduce it by redistributing wealth; second, social integrationist, which sees exclusion as primarily due to unemployment and inclusion as getting people into paid work; and third, moral underclass, which attributes exclusion to deficiencies in the culture of the excluded and inclusion as entailing cultural change. Levitas traces a shift away from redistribution rhetoric to increasing emphasis on culture. This is particularly apparent in the term 'underclass'. Lydia Morris (1994) charts how the 'underclass', as cited in current political concerns about the emergence of a 'culture of dependency', is figured in a remarkably similar way to Victorian discourse on 'dangerous classes', that is as the immoral and unrespectable.

Levitas (1998) also elaborates on the contradictory nature of social exclusion by showing how remnants of the underclass discourse are used to actually attribute blame for wider (even global) social processes to individuals. She identifies a 'moral underclass' in which the poor are blamed for their own situation, and references are yet again made to a 'culture of dependency'. This neo-conservatism concern with the family, nation and morality is developed alongside neo-liberal economic policy: for example, privatization, by which the state relies on the market and the threat of unemployment as a source of governance and social discipline.

This shift also impacts on the proposed solution to exclusion, leading to an emphasis on social integration and a changing of culture, rather than a redistribution of wealth. The focus on social exclusion suggests that the inherent importance of language in government is enhanced in the case of New Labour, describing the focus as a promotional way of governing – that is, the management of 'perception' through media spin. Fairclough (2000) describes this as 'cultural governance' (p.157), or the rhetorical management of culture, which necessitates the gaining of acceptance for a particular representation of the social world, through particular discourses. These become particularly effective when they spread beyond the confines of political rhetoric and enter the wider public imaginary.

Chris Haylett (2001) documents how the discourse of 'underclass' became part of the personal, public and political imaginations of British culture in the 1990s, via entertainment in crime-genre television programmes, as closed-circuit television (CCTV) evidence in 'factual' documentaries and news items, and as the backdrop for announcements of new social policy initiatives. The representations unleash a chain of signifiers in which an underclass is not only represented, but also shaped by disparate discourses of familial disorder and dysfunction, dangerous masculinities and dependent, fecund and excessive femininities, of antisocial behaviour, and of moral and ecological decay. As a way of crystallizing a number of social, economic and cultural issues into one, these different moral discourses become produced through the shorthand of the term 'underclass', continually cited across a range of sites so that it becomes normative. A newspaper article describes:

> Those who no longer share the norms and aspirations of the rest of society, who have never known the traditional two parent family, who are prone to abuse drugs and alcohol at the earliest opportunity, who do poorly at school and who are quick to resort to disorderly behaviour and crime.
>
> (*The Sunday Times*, 23 May 1995:3)

This is a reworking of the 1970s 'culture of poverty' discourse, in which the culture of the working-class, rather than the structures that create inequality, are seen to be problematic (see Ehrenreich 1990 for a summary). The cultural properties that stick to some bodies and not others can be seen in this example to be: addictive (only usually attached to those who have no control over themselves and are not attributed with agency); out of control – both of themselves and others, again having no subjectivity of value; ignorance, with a desire and quick to resort to criminality. The only thing missing is the gender differentiation and the spatialization (and, for a change, no housing estates are mentioned). This media condensation is also almost perfectly reproduced in a speech by Peter Mandelson (then a man of some significance in the Blair government) to the Fabian Society, which launched the Social Exclusion Unit.

> We are people who are used to being represented as problematic. We are the long-term, benefit-claiming, working-class poor, living through another period of cultural contempt. We are losers, no hopers, low life, scroungers. Our culture is yob culture. The importance of welfare provisions to our lives has been denigrated and turned against us: we are welfare dependent and our problems won't be solved by giving us higher benefits. We are perverse in our failure to succeed, dragging our feet over social change, wanting the old jobs back, still having babies instead of careers, stuck in outdated class and gender moulds. We are the 'challenge' that stands out above all others, the 'greatest social crisis of our times'.
>
> (Mandelson 1997, in Haylett 2000:6–9)

In attempting to identify the 'problem' for the audience, Mandelson re-produces and re-circulates the pathology that has been historically associated with the term 'class'. Here it becomes translated into policy, emblematic of the 'mission' of the Social Exclusion Unit to both identify and deal with these problems. The rhetoric is powerful because it produces the potential for identification. It is a form of representation, enabling the visualization of the working-class so that they can be recognized, whilst also trying to render them responsible for their own representation. It should not surprise us that, again, repeating a long historical tradition, a huge number of middle-class professionals have been created to enable them to define, quantify, observe, control and reform those who are so different from themselves (Hughes *et al.* 2001).[2] The maintenance of the division between those who 'reform' and those who are seen to be in need of 'reform' is central to the institutionalization of class divisions.

As in the historical development of the term, class divisions are also drawn on the basis of respectability. Those receiving benefit are separated into the deserving and the undeserving poor. Benefits are seen to be bad for the recipients, trapping them in a culture of dependency. There is a growing tendency to describe and explain poverty in cultural terms: for example, blaming the poor for their own circumstances. The main characteristics of this discourse, Levitas (1998) demonstrates, is that it presents those excluded as culturally different from the mainstream; that is, it focuses on the behaviour of the poor rather than the structure of the whole society. By implying that benefits encourage dependency, it figures not the optimizing 'subject of value', but the value-less, passive, use-less subject. This is not the subject with potential to enterprise, but one that only constitutes a burden; its own culture is held responsible for the lack of value.

The sign of the 'single mother' once operated as that onto which all dependency, fecundity and disorder was crystallized. It was used consistently throughout the Thatcher years and had its US equivalent in the 'benefit mother' (which was racialized in a way that the UK version was not. But 'New Labour' rhetoric also deployed it, both to justify state welfare cuts and to promote the normative white heterosexual bourgeois family (Standing 1999). However, the rhetoric seems to have diversified, so whilst the single mother is still shorthand for the undeserving, it has also produced some resistance amongst middle-class single parents, who can access circuits of symbolic representation to challenge their pathologizing by association. The pathological crystallization process has been spread into other signifiers, and women's bodies are less central. For instance, Diane Reay (1998) describes how educational euphemisms, such as 'inner city schools' and 'good enough children' (particularly pertinent in Australia where class is often absent from educational debate as emphasis is put on individual performance), denote class across a range of educational spaces; in the same way 'job seeker' places responsibility on the recipient of structural inequality in a way that 'unemployed' did not.

However, what is particularly pertinent to this range of euphemistic transferences is how attention is given in 'social exclusion' discourse to geographical and spatial differences. The highlighting, identifying and naming of 'sink estates' as the 'worst housing estates' produces evidence of an actual physical difference between the respectable and unrespectable, the deserving and undeserving. Stolcke (1995) charts how this spatializing of difference draws boundaries around those who need policing and containing, so that the rest of respectable society can be protected from their potentially disruptive, contagious and dangerous impact.

In a detailed study of Europe, Stolke details how significant changes in the rhetoric of exclusion can now be detected. From what were once assertions of the differing endowment of human races, there has risen, since the 1970s, a rhetoric of inclusion and exclusion that emphasizes the *distinctiveness of cultural identity*, traditions and heritage among groups and that assumes the closure of culture by territory (Soysal 1993). A similar shift in the rhetoric of exclusion has also been identified within the French political right: Taguieff (1981) documents how, rather than interiorizing the 'other', the New Right exalts the absolute, irreducible difference of the 'self' and the incommensurability of different cultural identities. This culturalist rhetoric, Stolke reveals, is distinct from racism that reifies culture as a compact, bounded, located and historically rooted set of traditions and value. This incommensurability Stolke names as 'cultural fundamentalism', which assumes a set of symmetric counter concepts, that of the foreigner, the stranger and the alien, as opposed to the national and the citizen. Instead of ordering different cultures hierarchically, cultural fundamentalism segregates them *spatially*, each culture in its place. The fact that nation states are by no means culturally uniform is ignored. Local cultural fundamentalism invokes a conception of culture contradictorily inspired both by the universalist Enlightenment tradition and by the German Romanticism that marked much of the nineteenth-century nationalist discourse. Cultural fundamentalism as the contemporary rhetoric of exclusion thematizes, instead, relations between cultures by defining cultural boundaries and difference. This general shift towards spatial differentiation can be identified in much more detail in the contemporary rhetoric of multiculturalism.

Using multiculturalism

Alongside Taylor (1994) and Zizek (1997), Bourdieu and Waquant (2001) link the development of 'planatary vulgate' (global inevitability) to the locution of 'multicultural':

> By artificially restricting it to the university microcosm and by expressing it as an ostensibly 'ethnic' register, when what is really at stake is not the incorporation of marginalized cultures in the academic canon, but access to the instruments of (re)production of the middle and upper classes ... in the context of active and massive disengagement by the state.
>
> (Bourdieu and Waquant 2001:2)

North American 'multiculturalism', Bourdieu and Waquant maintain, is neither a concept nor a theory, nor a social or political movement – even though it claims to be all those things at the same time. They identify it as a *screen discourse*, whose intellectual status is the product of a gigantic effect of national and international allodoxia, which deceives both those who are party to it, and those who are not. They also argue (again alongside Zizek) that, although it presents itself as a universal discourse, it is in fact a particularly North American imperialist discourse.

Multiculturalism has been adopted to a lesser extent in the UK to demarcate differences between groups. Haylett (2001), for instance, demonstrates, through a study of UK welfare rhetoric, policy and practice, that the working-class have to become racialized. This, she argues, is a re-positioning, a stage in the reconstruction of nation through the reconstruction of white working-class identities. It is the middle-class that does the work of nation-building, whilst the political rhetoric of underclass and global power legitimate through inevitability. As Haylett maintains:

> The shift from naming the working-class poor as 'underclass', a racialised and irredeemable 'other', to naming them 'the excluded', a culturally determined but recuperable 'other', is pivotal to the recasting of Britain as a postimperial, modern nation.
>
> (Haylett 2001:352)

Haylett documents how on 3 June 1997, the British Prime Minister, Tony Blair, chose the Aylesbury estate in South London as the backdrop for an announcement. This announcement was about a mass of people, in mass housing, people and places who were somehow falling out of the Nation, losing the material wherewithal and symbolic dignity traditionally associated with their colour and their class, becoming an ugly contradiction: abject and white. This announcement used the white working-class poor as symbols of a generalized 'backwardness' and, specifically, a culturally burdensome whiteness; they were the blockage, not just to inclusion, but to the development of a modern nation that could play on a global stage.

Here the discourse of racialization is used to mark both the physical, spatial and representational differences within the working-class. This presents a new development, as it is usually blackness, in particular 'black youth', that is rhetorically positioned in British political discourse as representing the atavistic and backward. Haylett argues that the mutability of these processes means that gaps occur between whiteness and whites, so that white groups sharing the same skin colour are not equally white, in the same way as strangers are not equally strange (Bonnett 1998). The discourse of multiculturalism brings into effect a form of 'culturespeak', a kind of UK cultural fundamentalism that constitutes the rhetorical promotion of a generalized alterity.

Historically, white working-class women were frequently ethnicized through assumed sexual profligacy and geographical association with diverse ethnic groups (see Gilman 1992), yet the consolidation of whiteness as a homogeneity, in opposition to black, led to them being incorporated into whiteness. Cecily Forde-Jones (1998), for instance, documents how, in Barbados in the 1800s, attempts were made through rhetoric and the administration of poor relief to incorporate poor white women into dominant definitions of whiteness. This, she argues, is because race, rather than class, was the primary marking of social superiority, and the lumping together of black and white women was a threat to the ruling white class, who legitimated themselves through 'white superiority'. A significant shift has occurred, from attempts to incorporate the white working-class into the nation, and the more recent attempts to delineate them as the hazard to modernity. Political rhetoric now distinguishes between different types of whiteness: the respectable who can be incorporated, and the non-respectable who represent a threat to civilization, citizenship and, ultimately, global capitalism.

When whiteness becomes a marker of excess, such as through white trash or through association of white estates, the working-class become offensively and embarrassingly racially marked as white (Balibar 1999; Wray and Newitz 1997). There is pure white and dirty white. This is made evident, as Haylett shows, in contemporary journalism:

> This self-loathing, self-destructive tranche of the population is far less assimilable into morally constructive social life than any immigrant group ... Those ethnic minorities which bring with them religion, cultural dignity and a sense of family will find a way. The only bar to their steady progress will be the mindless hatred of indigenous working-classes, who loathe them precisely for their cultural integrity ... I fear that long after Britain has become a successful multi-racial society it will be plagued by this diminishing (but increasingly alienated) detritus of the Industrial Revolution.
>
> (Daley 1994:16)

Here the white working-class are represented as simultaneously not part of the British state but indigenous to it. They are completely lacking in morals (integrity, beyond moral life), they are waste, detritus, their labour has no value and they have no positive agency (although they are able to hate and destroy themselves). Haylett argues that the identification of the white working-class poor as a barrier to the progress of 'multicultural modernization' is pivotal to the contemporary process of national welfare reform.

She maintains that poor whites reveal a contradiction that threatens to unsettle dominant social systems of class-based and race-based privilege, most especially the symbolic order of those systems; that is, the way they are visibly marked. First, they illustrate that whiteness does not naturally predispose people to social privilege and success. Second, they show that poverty has to maintain an appearance, an order of things to justify its existence. When large numbers of people are poor, and they are white, then the legitimacy of the symbolic order starts to creak. Poor whites, she argues, thereby come to reveal the symbolically 'worked at', socially produced nature of the order of things (Haylett 2001:361). Inclusion becomes cultural: it is inclusion of the culture of the nation; that is, the values, aspirations, and ways of living of the rest of 'us', those identified as respectable, worthy and not spatially and fundamentally different as a result of their culture.

In opposition to the working-classes' role as the constitutive limits to modernization, not surprisingly, a representative middle-class is positioned at the vanguard of 'the modern'. They figure as a moral category, referring to liberal, cosmopolitan, work- and consumption-based lifestyles and values; and thus 'the unmodern' on which this category depends is the white working-class 'other', emblematically a throwback to other times and other places (Haylett 2001).

Seepage and effects

The analysis above illustrates that political rhetoric is one of the central means by which symbolic value is attributed, institutionalized and legitimated. But it is not only at the level of the political that such rhetoric works. Its combination with economic restructuring is one of the main means by which attempts are made to eradicate the working-class from the national agenda.

Beynon (1999) documents how, in the UK in the 1980s, the Tory party under the leadership of Margaret Thatcher attempted to arrest economic decline through a radical strategy that incorporated a mixed strategy of discursive *and* economic engineering. The most important of these involved the linked deregulation of international capital markets and local labour markets. In this strategy the trade unions and British working-class were together seen as a major obstacle to renewal.

Beynon shows how the political rhetoric was translated through the popular with the state use of advertising that drew on elements of the iconography of the left. In these, while the past was being parodied, other physical symbols of the old order were being torn down. Alongside this was the generation of 'heritage'. Numerous museums were opened and many authors have pointed to the ways in which these and other cultural enterprises both re-order the nation (obliterating issues of class) and re-affirm a particular kind of national English heritage that, among other things, excludes ethnic minorities (see Gilroy 1987; Hall 1992). There were also attempts to re-signify and re-moralize through a direct use of the term 'new', so everything good became 'new', and everything bad was associated with the old. The attempt to brand 'new' Britain as a modern multicultural global player was part of this political strategy.

The use of left iconography can be seen even more clearly in the management, advertising and business literatures studied by Frank (2001). He documents how the corporate community went about winning legitimacy for the market. He charts the development of a discourse of 'market populism', whereby the political is represented as a realm of hopeless and unavoidable corruption, in contrast to the market and corporate world where the 'people's work' is done. This involves shifting the values that were once attached to certain groups and re-applying them to others:

> It was lovable outcasts like Bill Gates and his legion of tattooed-casual disciples who stood up for law and order, and it was union workers, once the rock-solid middle-class, hailed by Nixon and Reagan, who were the deluded, racist foot soldiers of protectionism.
>
> (Frank 2001:xii)

The shift here is from the workers previously designated as left wing, as nation-threatening 'communists' or 'philistines', into automatons, people lacking agency of their own, empty vessels filled with the will of others, but also racist. Unionized workers, he illustrates, are represented as automatons because they act *outside* the market. Only when people act within the marketplace, the literatures suggest, do they act rationally, choose rightly, make their wishes known and transparent and have freely expressed choices. Markets are therefore proposed as the space where we are most fully human; where we show that we have a soul and a self. The logic of this argument, Frank maintains, is that 'to protest against markets is to surrender one's very personhood, to put oneself outside the family of mankind' (2001:xiii); therefore:

> In addition to being mediums of exchange, markets were mediums of consent. Markets expressed the popular will more articulately and more meaningfully than did mere elections. Markets conferred democratic legitimacy; markets were a friend of the little guy; markets brought down the pompous and the snooty; markets gave us what we wanted; markets looked out for our interests.
>
> (Frank 2001:xiv)

So, whilst we have political rhetoric transferring responsibility for its actions onto the powerless, the powerless are also figured as unable to participate fully in the new market order (what Frank calls the discourse of the 'New Economy' of market rule), because they do not have the requisite agency. But, moreover, the language of class is used by the powerful to position themselves against the controls of the state, as victims of a corrupt political order. The fantasy of the market as an anti-elitist machine made the most sense, he shows, when couched in the dynamite language of social class. Businessmen and Republican politicians have always protested against the use of 'class war' by their critics on the left; during the 1990s, though, they happily used the tactic themselves.

> The real class war was between righteous new money, the entrepreneurs who created wealth, and bitter frustrated old money, the resentful heirs of the great fortunes who, having 'mastered the art of communication' proceeded to manipulate the single-parent, slum-dwelling poor.
>
> (Frank 2001:35)

This revival of the use of the language of class, in the US in the 1990s, Frank identifies as part of a new moral climate against elitism, in which politics becomes spoken through the morality of white middle-class righteousness.

What I'd argue is significant here, is the working of political rhetoric through the popular, of management literatures, advertising and business discourse. This translation of economic restructuring through different discursive space enables moments in class articulation to co-exist. The re-combination of elements, the folding of the old into the new, the translation through poverty, global inevitability, the disruption and constitution through other discourses of race and sexuality, all go to make up what we know as class.

Conclusion

The working-classes are being spoken of in many different ways: as underclass, as white blockage to modernity and global prosperity, as irresponsible selves to blame for structural inequality, as passive non-market competitors, as lacking in agency and culture, whilst the middle-classes are represented as at the vanguard of the modern, as a national identity and a cultural resource. In this symbolic identification and evaluation we see class divisions being made. The rhetorical positioning of the working-class is a powerful moral formulation, presented as literally use-less, as a group as inept as they are dysfunctional. This is rhetoric designed, not to enhance mobility and opportunity, but to fix firmly in place, metaphorically and physically. By setting the parameters between being useful to the nation and/or having valuable cultural diversity, those whose culture is defined as lacking are unable to participate in political claims-making. This reinforces not only the culturally fundamental difference between the optimizing selves, who can use their culture to enhance their value, and the redundant individual whose culture has little value, but it also forces the working-class to the borders of national (and global) space. They are represented as having nothing to offer; their culture is not worth having; they only represent a burden. What is also powerful here is how the national state rhetoric combines with that of corporate capitalism across a range of sites, even though the latter defines itself against the former.

In a study of how Whitehall (the UK civil service) understands its regions, Simon Marvin (2002) found that bureaucrats who are responsible for both formulating policy and putting it into effect work with what he terms 'Assumptive Worlds', relying on 'Imaginary Simplifications', allowing them to short-hand issues and problems by drawing on historical and popular representations in their understandings of that for which they have no knowledge. We can see this through the political rhetoric that is being circulated about the working-class, which relies on imaginary simplifications and assumptive worlds. These are not innocent representations, but are produced in the interests of particular groups. This becomes most apparent when we see how the language of class is deployed by the corporate class: to legitimate their own interests, to make moral claims and to position themselves against imaginary elites and powers.[3] The powerless are positioned by the symbolic evaluation of immorality, whilst the powerful claim morality for themselves. This is a display of cunning rhetoric, which has very powerful effects, not least by its repetition and in its institutionalization.

The next chapter further charts the process of devaluing the culture of the powerless, whilst claiming moral high ground for the corporate or cosmopolitan culture of the powerful, which is consolidated even further through popular representations. The chapter details how class is represented across different sites with incredible similarities, or maybe imaginary simplifications.

6 Representing the working-class

So far I have demonstrated how various sites of the symbolic attach negative value to working-class personhood and culture. This chapter, whilst continuing to track the ways in which this process works across the sites of the popular, also shows how, in a contradictory manner, certain aspects of working-class culture are being re-evaluated, so that they can be used to enhance middle-class personhood. Ehrenreich (1990), for instance, documents a shift in the US from the representation of the working-class as useless, tasteless and inarticulate, to its having a culture worth plundering. There is a long history of selective appropriation; the significance here is how what was once designated as immoral is now being re-valued, in order to open out new markets and new resources for producing particular selves. In this sense personhood becomes a matter of resourcing, and class becomes a matter of symbolic evaluation, which impacts upon movement through social space. Both resourcing and evaluation depend on the mechanisms and sites for the exchange of culture. The working-classes, who create their own culture (obviously in negotiation with the history of representations and positions), and not in conditions of their own choosing, have far less potential to generate exchange-value from their culture because of social circuits in which they operate. To convert their cultural resources into symbolic capital would require access to conversion mechanisms, and this is where representations are central, because they attribute value to different people, practices, objects and classifications, thereby enhancing or limiting the potential for exchange. One of the central issues in this evaluating process is how differentiation is made between culture worth having and knowing, and culture that is not. This chapter begins to chart these differentiating value attributions, exploring how attribution offers and/or blocks the potential for value.

Homi Bhabha (1996) uses Jacques Lacan's concept of 'camouflage' to suggest that the real problem of differentiation in the contemporary is not distance but proximity. The problem is of perceived similitude by those who feel too close: 'All the affect, anxiety, disavowal comes not at the point at which differences can be binarized or polarized. The problem of mistranslation – these happen because differences are, complexly, in some ways very small (Bhabha 1996:63).

In past formations of class, differentiation operated through drawing and maintaining distance between the progressive middle-class and the primitive, degenerate working-class (McClintock 1995). And, as Bourdieu (1986) maintains, distinction and distanciation produce the middle-class. The working-class have consistently been differentially cleaved into the respectable and unrespectable, but they have always remained classified as different. Now, we are in a period where the proliferation of difference through markets, advertising, and other sites of the popular, means that recognition of difference is a lot more difficult to maintain, to know and to see; boundaries are far more permeable than in the past. Political rhetoric (as the last chapter showed) exists to *make* difference; a difference that can be known and identified. Representations, however, are far more diffuse than rhetoric, as they enter and move between different circuits of distribution, and one of their central functions within capitalism is to be dynamic, open out new markets, sell new products (be it consumer goods, ideas or affects), and thereby create new associations between object and value.

Those with symbolic power devise representations that circulate through a variety of distribution systems, for a number of different interests: to sell TV space to advertisers and therefore use representations to gain high audience ratings; to generate 'truth' and 'authenticity' about the other; to identify and contain social problems; or sometimes just to fill the air/soundwaves. Yet these interests are not always straightforward; many of the reasons for these representations have nothing to do with intentionality, but are more about the ignorance of the producers and their *lack* of knowledge about the cultures they represent. Complacency is more likely than intention, because those who generate representations are often limited in their knowledge. They are the market version of the 'imaginary simplifications' and 'assumptive worlds', identified by Marvin (2002) (in the last chapter). The representations that we have of class often follow the method identified with rhetoric and discourse; that is, they are often old classifications, brought up to date and re-folded and re-cited with new aspects, to enable them to fit into and be known as contemporary.

This process is identified by Susan Douglas (1994) who details how time lags, fear, ignorance and deadlines inform representations just as much as interest and intentionality. She documents how, in the 1980s in the US, the media had a dilemma, struggling to incorporate feminism into its 'news' commentary. The media had to pay some attention to feminism, or it would be seen to be old-fashioned and out of date; yet those who had power in the media did not know or understand what was going on, nor did they care about accurate representations. Some, however, did intentionally want to maintain their own power and authority by trashing feminism. Douglas shows how all these different interests (and lack of) came together in institutional work conditions (such as meeting deadlines), producing a series of contradictory representations of feminism, until one dominant representation (an imaginary simplification: dungaree-wearing harridans) could emerge as a shorthand. This is the sort of confusion the media are now in, in terms of class representations. The prior shorthand image of class, namely that of the heroic industrial working-class man, can no longer operate to contain and condense all the changes and differences within class. Moreover, the fascination with the white working-class male in the 1960s and 1970s has declined. This fascination was double edged, though, producing the category of the heroic hard physical worker, a repository of everything the middle-class did and did not want to be: heroic but also potentially racist, fascist, authoritarian, undisciplined, ignorant[1] (see Ehrenreich 1990).

New representations are, therefore, being worked through. As so few media workers are recruited from the working-class, and their contact is read through prior similarly uniformed (mis-recognized) interpretative frameworks, it is unlikely that representations of the working-class can be in any way accurate.[2] This is also a familiar debate in relation to race. As this chapter will show, class representations (just like rhetorics of class) are alive, kicking and ubiquitous.

Smith (1994a) makes use of Derrida's notion of the logic of supplementarity to understand how homophobia is reproduced. She finds that homophobic discourse is organized not around a fear of otherness, but around an *obsession* with otherness. This is different to producing distance, and the fear and desire motive articulated by Fanon (1986) and Hall (1990). Smith illustrates how the obsession is structured symptomatically: homophobic representations condense a whole range of anxieties onto the queerness signifier. Queerness functioned as a supplement to Thatcherite discourse, so that it became one of the enemy elements that supported the phantasmatic construction of the family as the antagonism-free centre of the British nation. Class works in a similar way. The respectable middle-class are the phantasmic construction of the modern nation, hindered by the white working-class who represent the atavistic block to progress. This recent racializing of the working-class, as identified by Haylett (2001) (and described in the last chapter), enables divisions to be drawn between different aspects of the working-class, placing some without value, beyond assimilation. In a merging of political and popular representations the media coverage of recent reports into the 2001 race riots in the north of England clearly identified the white working-class in Oldham, Burnley and Bolton as responsible: they were the atavistic blockage to global progress, preventing the development of the nation; an enemy element, enabling the consolidation of anxieties about stable social order.

However, representations are not just about producing knowledge to enable distance to be drawn from proximity, but also about attributing value. Just as respectability can be used to divide classes for political purposes, aspects of working-class culture can be assigned a particular exchange-value. Rather than being designated simply as pathological, some parts of the working-class are represented as offering the potential for consumption. So the association of criminality and danger can be re-valued as glamorous, rather than threatening. The value attributed to different representations shifts; so what appears as dangerous in one discursive frame (violence as a social problem and social policy issue) becomes glamorized in others. This, of course, has a long history in the re-appropriation of black culture, in which black men have been criminalized for their perceived threat and danger, whilst simultaneously being used in popular music and film as dangerously glamorous and cool. The consequences of this, as Diawara (1998) shows (see Chapter 1), however, is to limit the mobility of black men across other social sites, reducing and reproducing them as *only* cool and dangerous.

This chapter explores the way in which these processes are now taking place.

This is not a history of popular class representations, which have very effectively been mapped by Hill (1986) and Laing (1986). Nor is it an analysis of contemporary TV and films, which have been extensively covered (Hill 2000; Hollows 2000; Hunt 1998; Jancovich 2001; Munt 2000; Roberts 1999b; Rowbotham and Beynon 2001; Tasker 1998). Rather, it is an attempt to identify the symbolic processes by which certain representations are attributed with value, thus being defined as good/ bad, having worth/being worthless, so that boundaries can be drawn, and culture can/or cannot be converted. This is a massive area, but some of the ways of representing the working-class, identified in this chapter, include: as excess, as waste, as authenticating, as entertainment, as lacking in taste, as unmodern, as escapist, as dangerous, as unruly and without shame, and always as spatialized. Each section examines these evaluations and concludes with a discussion of the shape of the contemporary class struggle, showing how some of these evaluations become unstuck. The chapter focuses on how class is made as a cultural property, a resource that can be used (or not) depending on the value attached to it and the markets in which it can realize value. These valuing processes are the ways in which certain forms of culture become fixed as a property of the person. Representations are powerful tools for both revealing and concealing the attribution of value to particular cultures and persons, giving us the frameworks by which we mis/recognize and interpret others in our encounters and relationships with them. Representations are central to inscription, positioning, embodiment of value, exchange and the perspectives we take.

Excess, waste, disgust

The working-class have a long history of being represented by excess, whilst the middle-class are represented by their distance from it, usually through associations with restraint, repression, reasonableness, modesty and denial. Leon Hunt (1998) charts how the working-class in the 1970s were consistently used as a cipher of embodied excess.[3] And Yvonne Tasker (1998) demonstrates how this legacy is still alive and kicking in contemporary Hollywood, where signifiers of obvious excessive attention to appearance denote low moral value and potential disruption. She maps a range of transformation narratives in which the visually excessive working-class woman is turned into the subtle and discreet middle-class woman, usually by a powerful man, (e.g. *Working Girl, Pretty Woman, Up Close and Personal*). In the British versions (*Pygmalion/My Fair Lady*), attention is given to language as well as appearance. The transformation is always enacted by the gradual loss of excessive style. Tasker argues that the attraction of these films is the tension and pleasure generated by the risk of the women being exposed, caught out and discovered, but then ultimate redemption and escape. This encodes working-classness, not only as something that has to be left behind, that which is fixed in order for mobility to proceed, but also as that which has no value. These films offer middle-class taste and positioning as the means by which being working-class can be overcome and eradicated, and as something to be aspired to, reproducing a definition of that which is valued as cultural capital is middle-class culture.

This transformation can only work as a narrative if femininity is read as a class-based property. As argued elsewhere (Skeggs 1997), the division between the sexual and the feminine was, historically, most carefully coded at the level of conduct, where *appearance became the signifier of conduct;* to look was to be. The construction of appearance became a cultural property of the person, the means by which women were categorized, known and placed by others. Appearance operated as *the* mechanism for authorization, legitimation and de-legitimation. Appearance worked as a sign of moral evaluation; and, as Lury (1993) and Nead (1988) show, too much attention to one's appearance was seen as a sign of sexual deviance, of sexuality in excess: it was morally reprehensible.[4] Anne Hollander (1988) documents how, accordingly, objects of clothing became invested with intangible and abstract elements of the moral and social order.

Modesty has been central to the formation of middle-class femininity. In an analysis of academic shoes, Brydon (1998) notes how any attempt to draw attention to the body in academia would be read as a sign of diminished intellectual capacity, an attack on the propriety of academic space. The outer appearance is, therefore, read as a sign of the inner character (or personality: see Chapter 7). She shows how the logic of the reading of the object (shoes) as a challenge to propriety depends on a fallacy: the meaning of things is assumed to be a property of the object itself, rather than the response to the feeling, or *the relationship* of the reader to the object. If projection is seen as one of the mechanisms by which splitting occurs, those aspects of self from which one wants to draw distance are projected onto another person, or another object. To then read the site of projection as the 'truth' of the person or object is to mis-recognize and mis-read one's self. To read something (a body or object) as excess is to render it beyond the bounds of propriety, to locate it within the inappropriate, the matter out of place, the tasteless. A reading of a body as excessive is therefore to display the investment the reader has in maintaining propriety in themselves.

Excessive sexuality, as Mercer and Julien (1988) detail, is the thing which, *par excellence*, is a threat to the moral order of Western civilization. Sexuality has long been codified in the representation of the working-class, often condensed into the figure of the prostitute who is represented as supplementary, in opposition to bourgeois femininity (Gilman 1990). In a study of Brazilian travesti, (Kulick 1998) and a study of Mexican transvestites (Prieur 1998) Kulick and Prieur show how the wo/men[5] they interviewed knew that, in order to work, they had to produce themselves through the excessive appearance of sexualized femininity. They understood the value of a strongly sexualized body; hence, the interest in silicone, which they defined against the elegant, cultured, pretty, well-dressed, cultivated women they knew. Doing gender by embodying sexualized femininity, in order to engage in sexual trade, they mark themselves beyond propriety, as a working-class version of women. By making this explicit to the sexual exchange the travesti force a direct recognition of different classed values attached to doing gender, and how these are generated through different relationships to sexuality.

For instance, excess has been particularly well documented in studies of hair. Excessively styled hair and dyed hair, or in the US 'big hair' (i.e. artificial), on white women is seen to be a sign of sexual proclivity, immorality and white trash (Ortner 1991).[6] It is making obvious the time and attention given to appearance that marks its worth; here labour is not hidden, as in the fetish of the natural, but is de-valued for being made visible. This is in direct opposition to the upper-middle-class French women studied by Bourdieu (1986) where the higher the social class of the women, the more likely they are to be thin and the more likely they are to pay for the labour of others to generate this thinness, hence the labour is concealed and worn on the body as 'natural'. So a classed difference can be seen in the value given to *labour* in the production of appearance. It is the appearance of natural, rather than artifice, that marks a higher cultural value. The binary between nature/artifice is mapped through hidden/apparent labour, read on the body through appearance. Some political struggles have attempted to reverse the dominant binary mapping; for instance, hair became a site of political struggle in black politics, where 'the natural' was used to demonstrate political rebellion, re-coded and re-valuing black hair, which had previously stood as a sign of sexuality and savagery (Mercer 1987).[7]

Frank (1997) documents how Love cosmetics in the 1960s were promoted as anti-cosmetics, make-up for a time and a generation at war with its pretence, artifice and falsehood. 'This is the way Love is in 1969', the premier adverts' headline announced: 'freer, more natural, more honest, more out there' (Frank 1997:129). Also, Love cosmetics generated their value through the equation that was made between the user, nature and individuality. Older brands were said to mask and conceal the user's selfhood, whereas Love enhanced her individuality. This branding made class difference through gender, by hiding labour; thereby associating appearance – labour – with the working-class.[8]

In a contemporary analysis of what he defines as 'transparent commodities' (clear liquid goods such as Crystal Pepsi or Ivory dishwashing liquid), Marc Kipniss (1993) argues that they further fill the empty commodity space – devoid of all specific social content (i.e. the condition of their production) – with a new meaning, that of transparency itself; they now appear as something clean and natural which enable consumers to purify their consumption spaces, expelling that which may pollute. As many different transparent products trade on their 'pure' essence, those that are not pure become even more marked. So as 'natural' becomes built into branding, enabling the product to be experienced as if pure, then the un-pure becomes even more negative by association. This is what occurs when bodies meet in contested space in which claims for its use draw on moral discourses about the purity of the area (Moran and Skeggs 2001a).

For instance, our recent research project on *Violence, Sexuality and Space* also demonstrates how working-class women are identified by particular attention to appearance, signified by distinctions between hair styles: permed, 'brassy blonde' and 'pineapple heads' (hair pulled back into a pony tail on top of the head which is then brushed out to resemble a pineapple). All these styles operated as condensed class signifiers.[9] The distinctions between the different shades of blonde was carefully coded and read alongside clothing, so that the appropriate value allocations can be calibrated in order that distance can be drawn and mis-recognition made.

I purposely use mis-recognition here because of the attribution of negative value. But to whom is this style negative? And why is it read as such? The process of valuing particular styles disguises how it is a specific class-based process. Only from a middle-class point of view do these hairstyles appear as excessive. Or, as Tyler (1991) notes, only from a middle-class point of view does Dolly Parton looks like a female impersonator. Only in a space that is trying to make itself 'pure' from the 'dregs' of society, as one of our informants explained, does the un-pure becomes so visible.[10]

Working-class excess is also represented through vulgarity, as Rowe (1995) has so clearly documented in her analysis of *Roseanne* or as we see in the UK TV programme *The Royle Family* (see later discussion) Drawing on Bakhtin (1984), Rowe demonstrates how working-class women have consistently and frequently been associated with the lower unruly order of bodily functions, such as expulsion and leakage (and reproduction), which are used to signify lack of discipline and self-control. This is substantiated by Barret-Ducrocq (1992) who notes middle-class condemnation of working-class style:

> Their style seemed to express a vulgarity and carelessness implying the worst sort of sensuality: women 'half-naked', without corsets; matrons with their breasts unrestrained, their armpits damp with sweat; women with 'their hair all over the place', blouses dirty or torn, stained skirts; girls in extravagant hats and loud-coloured bodices.
>
> (Barret-Ducrocq 1992:11)

'Letting go' was the term used by working-class women, in my previous research, to describe bodies that were not disciplined and respectable. The fat body displayed – literally inscribed – excess and enabled a reading of lack of self-governance. Fat was seen to be a cultural property of excess, as was fecundity, displaying irresponsibility and a lack of care of the self (Skeggs 1997). As Bourdieu puts it: it follows that the body is the most indisputable materialization of class taste. The body is 'sign-bearing, sign-wearing', the 'producer of signs which physically mark the relationship to the body' (1979:192).[11] Vulgarity is frequently associated with disgust. Elspeth Probyn (2000a), for instance, illustrates how Peter Greenaway's film, *The Cook, The Thief, His Wife and Her Lover*, strategically fuses food and sex, using the figure of the cannibal to carry the contempt for the lower middle-class rich. The disgust that is produced about class and read on the body is, Probyn argues, always a matter of proximity.

She uses Tomkins' (1995) research to show how disgust has 'evolved to protect the human being from coming too close' (p.15). Disgust is permanently distancing, whilst the combination of disgust and shame produces a back-and-forth movement, only shying away once we realize that we have been too close. So disgust with the working-class because of the association made with excess works to *maintain distance whilst in proximity*; it is metaphorical and physical. Yet disgust also relies on public acknowledgement. Expressions of disgust, Probyn maintains, operate by calling on public recognition. In other words, when something or someone is designated as disgusting, it provides reassurance that we are not alone in our judgement of the disgusting object, generating consensus for middle-class standards, to maintain symbolic order. Public statements, therefore, enable a distance to be drawn from uncomfortable proximity. The phrase 'that's disgusting' sounds more often than not like a plea to establish a common ground, generating comfort in the recognition that what offends me also offends you: to assuage doubts that *we* have not been contaminated, that *we* are not disgusting or shameful (Probyn 2000a).

The noise of working-class women is one way in which proximity is made apparent, in which the only way distance can be maintained is by middle-class public recognition that propriety has been disturbed. The unrestrained presence of the working-class generates the fears that expose the fragility of middle-class respectability. Hence, by describing and signalling their 'problems', the middle-classes maintain the boundary of propriety and respectability (see also Moran and Skeggs 2001a; Moran and Skeggs 2001b). Yet the value system of the middle-class is not wholly accepted, and respectability has long been a site of struggle (see Stansall 1986).We can perhaps see this more clearly in a critique made by Raphael Samuel of Reas' photographic book on the heritage industry, *Flogging a Dead Horse*, cited in Newbury (2001), which depicts the working-class in vivid spectacle, leading Samuel to comment:

> It is a sustained essay in disgust: it is not the teashop ladies, those ancient targets of macho abuse, but the spectacle of the Northern working-class – young and old, men and women – which excites sexual disgust. In the camera's eye they are no less repellent when smiling than when scowling, and it is difficult to imagine them doing anything which might make them appealing, or earn them a modicum of dignity and respect ... The idea that the masses, if left to their own devices, are moronic; that their pleasures are unthinking; their tastes cheapo and nasty, is a favourite conceit of the aesthete.
>
> (Samuel, in Newbury 2001:61)

Samuel evokes sexuality to maintain the power of the rhetoric, demonstrating outrage at the visual repetition of the association of the working-class with moral irresponsibility and waste; the working-class as useless rather than excessive, threatening or irresponsible. The discourses of disgust, excess and waste condense, combine and are visualized on certain bodies. Such discourses mark boundaries and constitutive limits. This leads Boyne (2002) to note how an aesthetic has been developed to depict the poorer circumstances of others (see also Cook 2000). What is central to this aesthetic, Boyne argues, is its lack of analysis, a critique he makes of Bourdieu's *The Weight of the World*, in which description in the 'social realist' mode replaces analysis of why the respondents live in poverty.

The term 'white trash' encompasses perfectly the association of the working-class with disgust and waste – it racializes the working-class so that distance can be drawn from other forms of whiteness (see Wray and Newitz 1997). Sally Munt (2000) suggests that working-class people have become discursively associated with 'waste', typified by the profligate spender and the feminized couch potato.

The danger of the working-class, Munt argues, emerges from boundaries being threatened, from a feminine excess which needs restraint, of fat, cigarette-smoking, beer-drinking men who have become a drain on the social body: 'they leak, they weep, they rage: excrescent and grotesque' (Munt 2000:8). This carries the long tradition of attributing dirt and danger to the working-class, as outlined in Chapter 2, yet shaping this tradition through a contemporary aesthetic, continuing to identify the working-class with waste, excrement, sewerage, that threatens to spill over and contaminate the order of the nation. However, it is because the working-class is beyond governance that it is presented as a potential threat.

For instance, Bhabha (1994) emphasizes the basic ambivalence at the heart of colonial discourse, which both fixes and assigns its place to the 'other', yet also strives to capture an otherness also conceptualized as wild, chimerical, excessive and unknowable. The representations of excess and waste point to bodies that cannot be normalized or disciplined. Walkerdine (1987) identifies this attack on 'reason' as potentially disruptive in these representations, as they will not allow the *conversion* of conflict into discourse. Paradoxically, by representing the working-classes as excess and waste, their incorporation cannot be guaranteed: they are positioned as that which both represents and resists moral governance. This illuminates a contradiction at the heart of what Fairclough (2000) defines as 'cultural governance'. If they are represented as beyond governance, how can they be contained? One way, of course, already identified, is to turn them into an identifiable 'social problem' in order to literally contain and control. Or, more specifically, as Waquant maintains, they will be criminalized and incarcerated, as has already occurred to a majority of young black, and a substantial proportion of white, working-class men.

Hunt (1998) charts a movement in the 1980s from hedonism associated with excess, irresponsibility and the working-class, to a shift where hedonism became harnessed and re-branded into the lifestyle of the middle-classes. This is respectable excess, what Featherstone (1982) describes as 'calculating hedonism', a precondition for 'the achievement of an acceptable appearance and the release of the body's expressive capacity (p.18). Or what Brooks (2001) identifies as 'utilitarian pleasure'. Contained 'excess' is acceptable within limits, if practiced by those who are seen to be capable of self-governance and restraint: it may even enhance their productivity. When a whole culture is represented by excess and lack of control, however, a 'problem' is seen to exist.

In fact, what was once identified as excessive sexuality, and associated with working-class women *against* the respectability of middle-class women, is now being re-worked, through TV output such as *Sex and the City*, where what was once decried as immoral is re-coded and re-valued as modern cutting-edge entertainment. The negative value attribution of excessive sexuality to working-class women has also been re-evaluated and used to spice up fashion campaigns. Fashion designers have long been attached to a white trash aesthetic as it gives them a way of doing sexuality with femininity, extending the type and range of femininity to open out new markets, offering something 'different' (see Skeggs 1997). This search for new audiences, hence new advertising markets, means boundaries have to be stretched, and what was projected onto one group (the working-class) as the site of the immoral and dangerous is now re-valued when it become attached to another group (the middle-class) as exciting, new and interesting. This re-evaluation through attachments to different groups brings with it a whole host of other valuing adjectives. So excess, waste and artifice combine to produce disgust at the working-class body, but radical avant-garde value when attached to middle-class bodies, where excess is done *with* constraint (because they are self-governing, rather than beyond governance).

Authenticating

Just as there is a long history in the UK and US of white working-class groups appropriating the symbols and practices of black groups for their own cultural distinctiveness (see Gilroy 1990), there is also a long history of white upper- and middle-class men using the cultural practices and symbols of black and white working-class men to shore up their masculine superiority. This is not just about creating entertainment value, which can be seen in the films of Guy Ritchie (e.g. *Snatch, Lock, Stock and Two Smoking Barrels*), a process with a long history (e.g. Mick Jagger), but it is also about attaching authenticity to the self through the appropriation of other cultures; cultures that have been evaluated as dangerous. The art-culture system of symbolic production, James Clifford (1988) argues, is a machine for making authenticity. (See Chapter 8 for a more sustained discussion.) This can be seen in particular through Diawara's (1998) earlier analysis of black masculinity (in Chapter 1) in which black male characters appear to be *not* acting; they just *are*. Hence, through essentializing, they are made authentic.

Back and Quaade (1993) show how Benetton employ a similar coding device when juxtaposing models of different skin colour against each other, in order to suggest that, just like the clothes they sell in a variety of different colours, race is an interchangeable value that can be sold to an audience, always addressed as white (see also Lury 2000). This ability to detach the characteristics associated with ethnicity, colour coding groups and attaching them to clothes, fixes the raced characteristics as authentic, essentialized and/or natural. These ethnic characteristics become a resource for the company to promote itself as diverse and its clothes as modern. Different combinations are put together to create the greatest value: the blackness that is figured as 'cool' is a particular (safe) version of working-class blackness ('of the street'). The hardness of white working-class men, the anti-authoritarian mafia 'Italianness' (e.g. the whole of Martin Scorsese's output and *The Sopranos*), and the authentic 'grit' of Irishness too, are marketable, offered as an experience, an affect, a partial practice, a commodified resource, offered for others to consume. All these racializing representations attribute value and configure a particular relation to class, gender and sexuality.

Paul Gilroy (1987) argues that attaching authenticity to particular groups is always racist because it continues to reproduce the association of blackness with nature, assuming a more 'primitive' state. Michelle Wallace (1979) traces how the definition of authenticity relies upon being over-layered by other binaries of value: serious/trivial, authentic/commodified, natural/artificial.

In recent studies of one of the main sites of symbolic production – advertising – researchers have drawn attention to the significance of marketing affect and experience. The whole process of contemporary branding is premised upon reading the experience of product use back into the product itself (for example, Pringles are branded as 100 per cent irresistible). This has subsequently produced a global search for finding, making and selling the 'authentic experience', frequently a search for the 'genuine'. Clearly, this has a long history (as the debate on primitivism in Chapter 2 shows) as a method by which the middle-classes distance themselves from artifice and materiality. As Frank (1997) notes, one of the greatest marketing achievements of contemporary capitalism is the ability to sell 'non-materialism' to consumers through material practice. This distaste for concern with status and appearance has long been promoted as a position for middle-class consumers by marketing strategies in the advertising industry. The Volvo advertising campaign in the 1970s adopted a strategy of 'anti-advertising' (Frank 1997), where it promoted Volvo cars for those who do not need to, or want to be, concerned with conspicuous consumption; an anti-material materialism. The disdain for those who were concerned about social status was a central part of the campaign.

Experience is the only thing left to buy for those who are materially sated. Jo Anne Pavletich (1998) describes the rise of a culture of restricted affect, in which the containment of emotional expressivity, accompanied by the search for intense experiences, is part of the emergence of new forms of corporate culture and state control in the US. Here the strategy of marketing and branding new experiences is so prevalent that it has even been identified as a specific economy, and has become absolutely central to the re-branding of different goods (Franklin *et al.* 2000). This strategy is an attempt to convert use-value (experience and affect) into exchange-value from which profit can be made.[12] But only some affects and experiences are marketable, and this relies on symbolic coding and value attribution.

The marketing of affect and authentic experience is a strategy strongly class and race inflected. Authenticity as a value is historically associated with those closer to nature, and has to be re-attached to people, products and practices with no prior associations. Travelling to 'exotic' destinations, for instance, becomes branded as an experience of the genuine, the authentic or the spiritual, rather than colonialism. But because authenticity has class and race associations, this has to be achieved by detaching experience from one group in order that it can be attached to another. But working-class experience cannot be fully detached from its origin, as it needs a source from which to replenish. So only aspects are transferred, transformed and re-evaluated. Other aspects of authenticity are held in place and offer only limited potential. For instance, some groups, practices and places are just 'too authentic'. The film *Fightclub* by director David Fincher plays with this desire by offering violence as the ultimate experience to escape the mundane nature of consumer culture, in which the alter ego of the bored service worker (played by Edward Norton) is the violent, unpredictable, ungovernable working-class white trash: however, the excessive violence is offset by the beauty of the actor Brad Pitt who makes the authenticity aesthetically palatable.

Hillbillies in the US are also considered to be 'too authentic'. Wray and Newitz (1997) shows how whiteness becomes a *distinct* and *visible* racial identity when it can be identified as somehow primitive or inhuman (this is in contrast to its normative invisible ubiquity). Relying on a reading of *Hillbillyland*, a study of representations of 'mountain people' in Hollywood film, Newitz documents how the hillbilly figure designates a white person who is racially visible, not just because they are poor, but because they are *monstrously* so. The white trash cultures that signify authentic and primitive are therefore a source of realistic and fantastical menace to the white middle-class, not just a resource. Just as primitivism was divided into primitive-phobia and primitive-mania, the working-class are likewise divided by their exchange-value to others who want to attach authenticity to themselves and to those who require boundary markers to signify their own propriety. Certain practices associated with the working-class are seen to confer authenticity upon their users. This is transference from a cultural property of the 'originary' practice to a cultural property of the user. This process both fixes those who are appropriated and demonstrates the cultural entitlements of the powerful. It is a mechanism by which working-class culture can be used as a cultural property for others and attributed with worth in a regime of value (Bennett *et al.* 1999). All this valuation and re-evaluation depends on whether the practices or objects can travel out of one field of exchange into another.

To claim authenticity, artifice, vulgarity and the frivolous must be expelled. So working-class women, associated with excessive artificial appearance, have less proximity to the value of authenticity. Artifice and pathology offer fewer possibilities for appropriation, so white working-class women's culture is therefore less attractive as a resource.

As tasteless

The association of the working-class with tastelessness has been extensively documented by Bourdieu (1986), who concludes that taste operates to commit symbolic violence:

> If there is any terrorism it is in the peremptory verdicts which, in the name of taste, condemn to ridicule, indignity, shame, silence ... men and women who simply fall short, in the eyes of their judges, of the right way of being and doing.
>
> (Bourdieu 1986:511)

For Bourdieu, taste is always defined by those who have the symbolic power to make their judgement and definitions legitimate (the conversion of cultural into symbolic capital). This enables properties and products associated with the working-class to be taken out of context, re-signified and re-valued by those with access to symbolic power. So terms like 'tacky' and 'kitsch' name this process, whereby that which was once associated with the working-class becomes re-coded and made into an exchange-value for the middle-classes. Giving the objects of this process a distinctive name, such as 'kitsch', means that a knowingness is inserted into it; the classifier knows of the prior negative signification and association of the object, a positioning which can be seen to give it authentic value. The social position of the person who is doing the naming is usually of significance (i.e. it has to be spoken from a position of distance, or through irony or positions associated with superior knowledge). This can be seen as part of the wider process of middle-class self-resourcing that will be discussed in more detail in Chapter 8.

In a case study of the introduction of new media technology in the UK, Charlotte Brundson (1997) documents the resistance displayed to satellite dishes by the middle-classes. This, she argues, was because prior media coding generated negative value by locating their use with the 'tasteless working-classes'. She gives the example of a London journalist:

> So far in London, take-up of Sky has been slow. If, however, you actually welcome round-the-clock rubbish being beamed out the problem is that you can't watch it discreetly. Under normal circumstances, if your tastes extend no further than *Neighbours*, Capital Radio and *Dynasty* at least you can indulge yourself without the whole street knowing about it.
>
> (Mark Edmonds, *London Evening Standard*, 12 July 1989)

In fact, a significant amount of 'alternative' comedy, across a range of media, was devoted to equating tasteless = use of satellite dishes = working-class. More recently, similar sentiments are still being repeated by middle-class cultural intermediaries: in a supposed architectural review of the Lovell Telescope at Jodrell Bank (a 1,500-ton, 76.2-meter bowl), in the local Manchester listings magazine, Phil Griffin notes: 'It is particularly touching that so many people in Wythenshawe appreciate it so much, they display little scale models of it on the outside of their houses' (Griffin 1999:6).

In this statement he manages to insult and insinuate that people from Wythenshaw (a large council house estate of the type identified by New Labour as a social problem) clearly have no taste. But his comment enables him to attribute taste to himself, because he is the clever knowing one, who can draw ironic distance and make distinctions; as Bourdieu (1986) comments, taste classifies the classifier. It's a subtle move but is one of the ways in which class is frequently played out, repeated and condensed as taste.

Another way in which class is marked and difference known is through drawing boundaries around certain practices and knowledge, in order that only some people can be seen to comfortably make use of them. By deriding those who step out of place, boundaries are maintained. Cook (2000) shows how the relationship between class and taste can often take two different forms: one, of the kind exemplified by Bourdieu above, which emphasizes the ways in which classes are distinguished one from another by their tastes. The other proposes an idea of taste as a way in which one class imagines itself *as* another. For instance, the UK TV programme *Keeping up Appearances* uses white trash as a device – the fixed lowest reference point of excess, waste and vulgarity – in which the main character, Hyacinth Bouquet,[13] is foiled in her aspirations. The programme also contains the 'real' middle-class who function to expose the futility and pretentiousness of her aspirations. In this programme, Cook (2000) argues, taste is both aspirational and mimetic, a way of imagining oneself as being in another class, even a class apart. The comedy of the series derives both from the central character's energetic obsession to maintain appearances and from the exposure of what those appearances are intended to conceal. Whereas Tasker (1998) earlier identified the audiences' pleasure in concealment and transformation, here pleasure is produced in the comedy of revealing, exposing and ridiculing. The joke, Cook (2000) explains, at least for one part of the audience, is that to be so preoccupied with questions of taste is itself tasteless.

In a debate on the popular UK TV programme *Blind Date* (31 March 2001) we can identify different ways of articulating class through taste, both directly and indirectly. A couple had been sent on a holiday date to Antigua and clearly did not get on:

Woman: I offered him a camera but he said I wouldn't be any good with it 'cos I came from a council estate.

Man: She had no class, no table manners, didn't know how to use a napkin.

Woman: He wouldn't know how to recognize class if it hit him in the face.

What is interesting here is the way in which class is first named – as education (using a camera), as manners and as a class location (estate) – but then disputed by the man accused of not having access to the right knowledge himself. How could he know? To directly name somebody as tasteless, immoral, irresponsible, excessive, is to open oneself out to the same accusations, unless one has access to the forms of cultural capital that can offer protection from the accusations.[14]

Cook (2000) also shows how academic theorizing about taste is itself structured through contradiction, as it attempts to represent that which is being coded as tasteful and tasteless, and hence is drawn into classification-making. In an analysis of the work of Richard Hoggart, Dick Hebdige and Pierre Bourdieu, Cook demonstrates how the analysis of the relation between class and taste always draws on and produces judgements of taste. This is because of the discourse through which authority, logic and cultural judgements of taste emerge:

> These arguments about good and bad taste are part of the emergence of something like a modern market in aesthetic commodities. From the outset they work as consumer guides. Yet this is also and necessarily an episode in self-fashioning or subject formation: the creation of the man or woman of taste, a process that continues through to the present day. The exercise of taste is constantly drawing and redrawing the boundaries between and within classes. It is a continuous and sublimated form of class struggle.
>
> (Cook 2000:100)

Taste as a mechanism of distinction is one way in which social positions become 'culturalized' and embodied; that is, they become known through the attitudes, practices or symptoms of those who occupy them. Social positions are read and recognized through symbolic inscription and its daily practice. Entertainment is one of the central sites where these symbolic struggles take place and are made visible.

Entertainment

Bromley (2000) documents how British class (both middle and working) is used as a branding mechanism to sell films to the US, in order to feed into prior knowledge and thus conform to already existing stereotypes: for example, *Four Weddings and a Funeral*, *Trainspotting* and *The Full Monty*. Even when class is not spoken directly in political rhetoric or academic theory, it can still be branded and marketed for a transnational audience. For instance, the new game for Sony Playstation, *Getaway*, enables the mimesis of the position of the London gangster. The dangers of the 'underworld' are made available to those who can only ever experience them virtually, a different technical take on the voyeurism that was previously provided by the entertainment media of radio, film and TV.[15] Also, in terms of entertainment, there is a long history of using the working-class not as a sign of danger, but also, as Sweet (2000) illustrates, a shorthand to emotional impact.

So the negative representations stuck to working-class bodies can be used to shorthand affectivity for others. There is a huge market in 'poverty' movies and novels whose main function is, perhaps, to maintain difference and draw boundaries to generate affect thorough mimesis. Using the working-class to speak emotions is central to British soap operas. Naturalistic styles to extremes to probe what cannot usually be expressed by middle-class codes of restraint and manners, crossing the border between public and private and reproducing everyday intimacies. What is significant about these, Rowbotham and Beynon (2001) maintain, is how they provide no way of understanding the representation being offered; no history, no analysis, no explanation. Soaps just stand as 'entertainment' and evidence, a 'shorthand', an imaginary simplification of 'authentic truth'.

However, the use of the working-class as entertainment is not straightforward; there is an established tradition of left-wing filmmakers who challenge these traditional representations. Haylett (2000), for instance, describes how two films – Mathieu Kassovitz's *Hate (La Haine)* (1995) and Ken Loach's *Ladybird, Ladybird* (1994) – contest dominant symbolic meanings by opening up different inter-pretations about the working-class. Unlike political rhetoric, she reveals how the discourse of 'underclass' is not reduced to 'one thing' that has negative 'effects'. Rather, it is also partly constituted by representations that make realistic subject positions available to the working-class poor, and hence new understandings available to mainstream audiences. She contends that these films offer a form of 'strategic defence'. In *Hate* and *Ladybird, Ladybird*, the main revelation is that whilst things are not all right for the protagonists, the reasons for this are to do with other social groups, *their* authority, *their* privilege, *their* values. A central part of the positive working-class affirmation offered by these films involves antipathy towards all 'things middle-class'. Power is exposed. So whilst other representations try to codify conflict as a problem of the pathological working-class, alternative representations challenge the allocations of responsibility, producing strong signals of antagonism.[16] Yet the overwhelming reproduction of the working-class with specific values across so many sites means that the struggle has to continually be fought by those with far less access and resources to the central sites of symbolic domination. Contestation is not easy. But what is significant is that representations are not dispositions; representations have to work on the body for them to be read as authentically belonging. When the different symbolic sites of representation coincide, such as political and popular, producing information and entertainment that generate the same representations and the same value allocation, a powerful symbolic conden- sation may occur, but it is in the gaps between symbolic sites and the translation onto the body that significant exposures of value attribution occur. For instance, the reproduction of the working-class as unmodern across the political and the popular generates a powerful *concentration* of negative value, one that cannot be used as a resource, but only to mark a constitutive limit that can be read on the body if coded consistently across a range of sites.

The unmodern

Hunt (1998) identifies how, in the UK during the 1970s, the white working-class became closely associated with the unmodern. They were attributed with a populism that was unredeemable: the tabloid newspaper *Sun* reader came to represent that which was not recuperable; consolidated by the urban myth that the *Sun* is written for a reading age of eight. So the working-class are represented as backwards and stupid, as well as unmodern.

In the US the white working-class became attributed with 'backwardness', not just through the hillbilly association, described earlier by Wray and Newitz (1997), but by being linked to racism (Ehrenreich 1990). The middle-class projected their responsibility for racism onto those who could not deflect it. Hunt (1998) traces the contradictory effects produced by trying to introduce 'progressive' takes on race on TV. By using working-class characters, such as Alf Garnett in *Till Death do us Part* in the UK or *Archie Bunker* in the US, as the 'sound' of racism, the TV becomes the only space where the un-sayable, unfashionable and anti-consensual are given space and thus come to be associated with racism and sexism in the working-class – not dissimilar to the association of pornography with a particular class profile (see Kipnis 1999). For, as Hartmann and Husband (1974) have shown, racist stereotypes are more readily accepted by those who have no contact and no knowledge of the group being represented/denigrated to challenge the representa- tions. In another attempt to introduce issues of race to the British public through comedy, Hunt demonstrates how the incredibly popular UK TV programme, *Rising Damp*, depended on the contrast between the white working-class bigot – Rigsby – and Philip, a black African prince, a character who was inscribed into the British class system by voice and education. The comic register of such comedy, Hall (1981/1990) argues, is that it protects and defends white middle-class viewers by locating racism with the working-class.

Wray and Newitz (1997) detail how, in the US, the term 'white trash' works as a racial epithet to mark out certain whites as a breed apart, a dysgenic race. They argue that this attribution of white with trash is because the US has an extremely impoverished political language of class, so certain racial representations are used as allegories for it. Race is therefore used to 'explain' class, but class stands out as the principal term, because whiteness is so rarely connected to poverty in the US imaginary. Ehrenreich (1990) details how this is a result of a long history of symbolic association which has generated 'the poor' with black and the working-class with white, as if the two are separable.

Another way of signifying unmodernity is through spatial fixity, through not being mobile. We have seen how, in political rhetoric, the word class is not mentioned, but alternative references such as 'council estates', 'projects', or even specific naming of areas occur, such as Wythenshawe above, or the 'Aylesbury Estate' in New Labour rhetoric (Haylett 2001). In our research project on 'Violence, Sexuality and Space' the term 'class' was rarely directly articulated, although reference to taste and its lack was ubiquitous; rather, local areas were continually used as shorthand to name those whose presence was seen to be potentially threatening (see Chapter 9 for a development of this argument). Often this combined a number of the features discussed above (clothing, hair, bodies, lack of taste) to make sure that the point and positioning could not be misinterpreted.

This geographical positioning is routinely cited within the media. The term 'Essex girl' is now a condensed signifier of the epitome of the white working-class woman in the UK. The feminist cultural commentator, Germaine Greer, describes Essex girls thus:

> She used to be conspicuous as she clacked along the pavements in her white plastic stilettos, her bare legs mottled patriot red, white and blue with cold, and her big bottom barely covered by a denim mini-skirt. Essex girls usually come in twos, both behind pushchairs. Sometimes you hear them before you see them, cackling shrilly or yelling to each other from one end of the street to the other, or berating those infants in blood-curdling fashion … The Essex girl is tough, loud, vulgar and unashamed. Her hair is badly dyed not because she can't afford a hairdresser, but because she wants to look brassy. Nobody makes her wear an ankle chain; she likes the message it sends … she is not ashamed to admit that what she puts behind her ears to make her more attractive is her ankles. She is anarchy on stilts, when she and her mates descend upon Southend for a rave, even the bouncers grow pale.[17]

(Greer 2001:2)

This characterization seems to contain nearly every item in the representational pathologizing register of working-class women. They have no taste (excessively short skirt, brassy hair, shoes), are physically excessive (big bottom), immoral, have no shame, are vulgar, fecund and without responsibility. They do not know how to rear children properly, are excessively loud and sexual, travelling in packs and terrifying in a group, they are local and located. The only thing missing from this list is the term 'estate' to make this location even more specific. This semiotic condensing is repeated across a range of genres, so that in the TV legal drama *Hot Money*, the judge's summation of a case notes: 'I have been moved to wonder during these proceedings whether anyone who hails from Essex is capable of telling the truth' (*Hot Money*, 12 December 2001). This produces the class challenge: 'People don't hail from Essex, your honour. It's just not the sort of county you can hail from.' This play on the aristocratic 'hailing', which both sustains and undercuts the condensation of class into Essex, is an example of how class is used across a range of sites.

The highly critically-praised TV programme *The Royle Family* represents the working-class as immobile. The family offer no threat, no challenge to the class barriers but reproduce all the stereotypes with ease (an incredible discomfort and painful humour for those with resonant experiences). They are so fixed in their place that they rarely leave the front room of their house. They are supposed to be an ironic commentary on the working-class; however, as Medhurst (1999) has pointed out, when viewing the programme with a group of middle-class university students, some thought that this was exactly how the working-class lived. As with the workings of racism, lack of alternative perspective, knowledge and experience means the representations, continually repeated with few alternatives, offer a potential 'truth', often the only possible interpretation to which the middle-class have access.

What is central to all these representations of the working-class is how they demonstrate a shift from class as being defined by economic classification, which was dominant from the 1950s to the 1980s (see Savage 2000), to a return to strongly moralized positions. Representations illustrate both confusion and ambivalence at the heart of understanding contemporary social class positioning.

Class as a cultural property

This is made most explicit in a spoof survey in the *Sunday Mirror* (9 February 1997), entitled 'Social Brackets have New Names But Everyone in Britain Still Belongs in One of Them'.[18] The survey invites readers to tick the cultural activity in which they participate in order to assign themselves to a category. The working-class are described in categories C2 ('Essex Man' – note geography), D ('Mass of Contradictions') and E ('Trap with No Way Out' – note fixity, on this scale), and are all identifiable by cultural activities:

> I have more than one pet
> I do not drive a car
> I smoke cigarettes
> I live mainly on state benefits
> My sex life would be improved by having less sex
> I rent my home from the council
> I support the monarchy
> I never finish a book for pleasure

(Sunday Mirror, 9 February 1997)

Apart from renting the council house, and state benefits, every other category of identification is based on attitude and cultural practice, and has a strong connection to the representations outlined above. Similar recognition exercises are undertaken every day, whereby people are identified by their cultural attitudes. It could be argued that the site of the popular can only deal with class as a cultural product, since it is, by definition, symbolic; it represents 'lives'. Yet the judgements and moral attribution to practices, accompanied by lack of attention to circumstances, enable attention to be deflected away from cause and positioned onto the irresponsible individual. The site of the popular replicates the same forms of moral attribution as the political and academic, but also provides visualization, enabling inscription to be condensed and embodied more quickly and effectively. As class comes to be defined as a cultural property, it becomes more easily accessible for others to know and use it, touristically travelling in and out to see if it fits or suits.

However, in the heavy artillery of class representations where the moral attributes of excess, waste, fecundity, fixity, tastelessness and authenticity are continually reproduced and attached to the working-class, there is one significant challenging response, that of accusations of middle-class pretentiousness.

Anti-pretentiousness

Vicinus (1974) identifies the critique of pretension as a central part of music hall entertainment in the nineteenth century, which provided a humorous critique of the uptight restrained middle-classes, who attempted to make moral judgements of the working-class. The tradition of attacking through humour those who are supposed to be not only economically superior but also morally better has a long history. Similarly, Butsch (2001) shows how movie audiences in the 1920s and 1930s expressed equal derision at representations. We can also see how this attempt to de-value the valuers also occurs across a range of sites in the contemporary.[19] But the downside of this is that it also operates as a mechanism to keep the working-class in place. Vicinus details how scorn was also heaped on those with pretensions to gentility: 'putting on airs was the greatest sin anyone could commit' (pp.262–3). Hence, the bulk of music hall entertainment reminded the working-class 'to keep its place, to enjoy what it had and to stop others from stepping out of line' (pp.262–3). Walkerdine and Lucey (1989) document how clichés such as 'must wants more' and attacks on any pretension keep the working-class alert to their social positioning and wary of any attempts to move from it.

Not only is anti-pretentious humour a form of surveillance and a critique of the middle-class by the working-class, it also operates as a form of surveillance within the middle-class. Again, this can be charted historically, through, for instance, the novels of Charles Dickens, such as *Great Expectations*, which carefully charts the pitfalls of becoming a snob. Thus, what was once a critique of the aristocracy by the newly forming middle-class becomes reflected upon themselves, as they too must not step outside of their social position.

This is made explicit in the contemporary, again in alternative comedy. So Adam Buxton and Joe Cornish (of the cult *Adam and Joe Show*) when interviewed in the *Guardian* (15 September 2001, p.11), reflect on their fan base and argue that they were categorized (unfairly, they thought) as 'unfashionably middle-class and too posh … It's just because we are this sort of nebulous item, so people fixate on the school we went to and think "Oh they're not northern, they're not stand-up, they're not anything really, so let's make them slacker toffs".' To make sure that the reader and interviewer understand their ironic take on such matters they add: 'Fair enough really'.

Aware of how they are read and positioned, the pair justify it by accepting their privileged position. This is a defence against ridicule, and subsequent lack of credibility attached to those who try to deny their middle-class origins. The term 'mockney' (mock cockney) is used to apply to people like Jamie Oliver, Guy Ritchie (Mr Madonna), Nigel Kennedy and Mick Jagger, who speak a form of working-class language, whilst clearly embodying every other cultural aspect of the middle-class. In a similar move to those who aspire to be 'above their station', these people become an object of ridicule because their dispositions and positions do not fit. However, rather than just acknowledging that they are middle-class, Adam and Joe, above, create distance by using the US term 'slacker' to displace UK class associations and to forge a generational identification. Popstar Sophie Ellis Bextor points to the difficulties of being both cool and middle-class: 'It's virtually impossible to be middle-class in pop these days … Now it's really unpopular to be middle-class. It's worse than being upper class or lower class. Middle-class is worst' (*Guardian*, 28 October 2002:4).

The Royle Family, referenced above as representative of immobility, simultaneously present a continuing critique of the middle-class pretensions shown on TV. The programme provides armchair critiques of the TV programmes they watch in their front room. In fact, the watching of TV is used as a temporal structuring device for each episode. In a discussion about Richard Branson, Virgin Corporation boss (held up as the icon of economic success in Britain, and middle-class):

Jim:	I know, you don't read about crashes because they keep it all covered up, but you can't tell me the likes of Richard Branson, whose got his own bloody airline, goes everywhere by balloon, he is not bloody soft is he?
Anthony:	Hey, he's loaded, he is. He is worth over a billion.
Dave:	D'you know how he started off his business that Branson? From a little record shop.
Barbara:	Ooh, can't imagine him behind a record shop can you? With his beard.
Jim:	What's his beard got to do with it?
Barbara:	Ey, imagine what it must be like to be him. All that money.
Jim:	Can't get that rich without being as tight as a camel's arse in a sandstorm, can ya? He wouldn't give you the steam off his piss that fella.

(Aherne and Cash 2000:45)

This extract cannot convey the extent of the subtle and continual nature of the critique that is woven into each programme. The whole series is a sustained attack on pretensions. When the girlfriend of the young son is revealed to be middle-class, the show completely derides potential pretensions, but this is not easily recognizable as antagonism. The middle-class are likely to mis-recognize the nature of the class hatred the show contains; they must, since it has won so many art-culture system awards. It therefore offers different forms of address to different viewers. To capture the subtlety of the continual swingeing critique of the middle-class by this programme is difficult; but it is unremitting and often painful. The 'piss-take', as Paul Willis (2002) documents, endures in working-class labour; it was used to make the day more bearable. Moreover, to 'have a laugh' has been a significant way to stage resistance to authority, as studies of working-class schooling and youth culture have extensively detailed (Wolpe 1988; Willis 1977). Willis argues, however, that the function of the piss-take is not just resistance to dull compulsion, but rather, a way of doubling; what is taken to be real is simultaneously maintained as fictitious, but also as a practical cultural form, in which the variable and ambiguous nature of labour power is articulated. So from his argument, which is used to explore how factory workers maintain a perspective on the constructedness of their reality, as well as on understanding the nature of their exploitation, we can see how, when applied to the symbolic realm of representations, *The Royle Family* works to expose the ambiguous nature of symbolic representation.

The power of the anti-pretension critique is, I'd argue, about *not authorizing* those who have been positioned with more moral authority; it is about blocking their ability to apply moral judgement. *The Royle Family* offers simultaneously a temporary respite from the pervasiveness of middle-class judgements, but also a reproduction of fixity, waste, excess, authenticity and being unmodern. How it is read and mis/understood clearly depends upon the social positioning of the audience, their discursive access, their knowledge and investments.[20]

The ubiquitous critique of pretensions in European culture may be part of the reason why the middle-class respondents of Savage *et al.* (1999) expressed such a strong desire to be read as 'ordinary'. This suggests a desire not to be read as pretentious, demonstrating awareness of, and a way of evading, hierarchy and privilege in *relationships* to others.

This could also be why in responses to the 1997 MORI poll for the TV pro-gramme *World In Action*, of those surveyed, 75 per cent said they were conscious of living in a society divided by class. And why in 2002 in a MORI poll, 66 per cent of people surveyed claimed to feel 'working-class and proud of it'. Nearly 50 per cent believed that Britain was more divided by class today than it was in 1979, and 70 per cent said they believed 'the class system is harmful to us and those around us'. More bizarrely, the 2002 poll also found that 55 per cent of those who would be categorized as middle-class by occupation, claimed to have 'working-class feelings'. Sayer (2001) maintains that people want to be ordinary (without preten-sions, being read as superior) because they do not want to be held as responsible for perpetuating or agreeing with inequality. Yet to evade acknowledgement of social position, and responsibility for the privileges (or not) that come with it, is what Bourdieu (1986) regards as a hopeless illusion; it is to attempt to escape the gravitational pull of the social field. No doubt this is why so many concepts – such as mobility, reflexivity and individualization – are generated by academics to enable mis-recognition and evade responsibility for their privilege and position.

Conclusion

This chapter has identified some of the ways in which 'working-class' is inscribed as a moral value and cultural property in the contemporary. The continual negative moral evaluation and positioning of the working-class, however, challenges the workings of performativity (see M. Fraser 1999). The representations are *not* taken up by those for whom they are intended; this is because of the negative evaluation, which is also a strongly gendered process. Who would want to be seen as lacking in worth? One challenge to negative evaluation is to devalue the authority of those who are in a position to judge through a critique of pretensions, but this is double-edged. It also works to contain and keep the working-class in their place, as they, too, become subject to their own critique.

Whilst academic representations and political rhetoric intervene and inform popular representations, it is the site of the popular media where the symbolic battle can be demonstrated most visibly. Understanding representation is central to any analysis of class. Representation works with a logic of supplementarity, condensing many fears and anxieties into one classed symbol. It is the central mechanism for attributing value to categorizations. Within this process we can see the same old representations being re-folded and reinforced through continual citation. However, others are being re-combined in different ways and point to wider political changes; namely, the shift from simply drawing distance, to drawing distance from others *from* proximity. But there is also an opening up of new markets with working-class culture to enable appropriation of that which can be used as a resource for the re-formation of the middle-class self (see Chapter 8).

The proliferation and reproduction of classed representations over such a long period of time demonstrates the understated ubiquity of class, showing how it is continually referenced, even when not directly spoken. Proliferation and repetition also point to the fragility of the authority of the middle-class. If they were secure, difference would not need to be continually drawn, values established, legitimated and institutionalized. So when some people chart the disappearance of class, because it is not obvious in discourse, they ignore the many different ways in which class is produced. Moreover, as representations have such a long history as a resource that can be mobilized by those with access to circuits of symbolic domination, we need to think about how they represent significant artillery in class struggles and how absolutely central the symbolic is to any understanding of class.

Frow (1995b) proposes that in the contemporary climate it is productive to think of 'processes of class formation ... played out through particular institutional forms and balances of power ... through desires, and fears, and fantasies' (p.111). Class, for Frow, is not a pre-existing slot to which we are assigned, but a set of contestable relations; it is not a given, but a process. It is the process of evaluation, moral attribution and authorization that, I'd argue, is central to understanding contemporary class relations. The significance of representations lies in the way in which they become authorized and institutionalized through policy and administration, how they produce the normative, how they designate moral value and how those who are positioned by negative and pathological representations are both aware and resistant. A daily class-struggle is waged through challenging the values generated through representation, precisely because representation constitutes what can be known as persons.

To understand this requires a shift in attention from an analysis that assumes that the meaning of things is a property of the object itself (i.e. the working-class are pathological), rather than the *response to*, or the *relationship to*, the object (i.e. it is how they are being defined through the responses and power of others). If the projection of negative value onto others is established as a central way in which class divisions are drawn, then to read the site of projection as the 'truth' of the person or object is to mis-recognize and mis-read one's self. Attributing negative value to the working-class is a mechanism for attributing value to the middle-class self (such as making oneself tasteful through judging others to be tasteless). So, it is not just a matter of using some aspects of the culture of the working-class to enhance one's value, but also having the authority to attribute value, which assigns the other as negative, thus maintaining class divisions. What we read as objective class divisions are produced and maintained by the middle-class in the minutiae of everyday practice, as judgements of culture are put into effect. Any judgement of the working-class as negative (waste, excess, vulgar, unmodern, authentic, etc.) is an attempt by the middle-class to accrue value. This is what the representations of the working-class should be seen to be about; they have absolutely nothing to do with the working-class themselves, but are about the middle-class creating value for themselves in a myriad of ways, through distance, denigration and disgust as well as appropriation and affect of attribution. To deny the existence of class, or to deny that one is middle-class, is to abdicate responsibility for the relationships in which one is repeatedly reproducing power.

7 The methods that make classed selves

So far I have emphasized rhetoric, representations and theoretical understandings of class. This has demonstrated how terms such as 'economy', 'reflexivity' and 'subject of value' have a classed epistemology, assuming and constituting a particular personhood, a particular self. This chapter makes a more detailed interrogation of the concept of 'self'. Often used as a neutral term, this chapter describes how it is the methods for *telling and knowing* that make the self and produce class difference. And just as previous chapters have shown how this process is about the attribution of value, the particular focus here is on how moral value systems inform the differences that are drawn between different types of self.

The concept of the self (in particular, the reflexive, knowing, inner self) is a specific historical production, enabled through particular methodologies: forced telling for welfare for the working-class, and authorial exhibitionism for the middle-class. However, this is not a straightforward story, for feminism and gay and lesbian politics have employed similar methods of telling in order to make political claims. Notwithstanding this dissident divergence, I demonstrate how the techniques of telling for the middle-class rely on accruing the stories of others, in order to make them into property for one's self. *Method makes the self.*[1]

The chapter is divided into four sections. The first explores the historical conditions of possibility for the making of particular 'selves', paying close attention to the development of the confessional as a method still used in the contemporary. The second links the confessional to recent forms of testimony, detailing how gender is produced through this process. The third explores how reflexivity, as a particular methodological technique, became a mechanism of classed self-possession and a form of self-authorizing, drawing attention to the difference between claiming reflexivity as a resource for authorizing oneself (*being*), and *doing* reflexivity in practice. Finally, the fourth section draws attention to how difference is made between fixed and mobile selves, and thus further develops a central theme of the book.

Forcing the working-class to tell themselves

This section begins with a brief analysis of how contemporary telling techniques have been shaped by the confessional. It is through the telling of the self that social processes of positioning, of value, of moral attribution, are put into effect as a manifestation and maintenance of difference and distinction. Berlant (2000) maintains that the telling of the self through particular techniques enables the re-formation of the nation in the US. The centrality of the self to national formation emerges from specific legacies, as this chapter will now show.

Abercrombie *et al.* (1986) argue that the confessional, like Christianity as a whole, preceded the emergence of feudalism, having its modern origins in the thirteenth century. The confessional survived the onslaught of competitive capitalism to flourish in a capitalist system. The confessional played an important role in the historic emergence of the individual, self-conscious person equipped with subjectivity and moral standards. Abercrombie *et al.* distinguish between the role of the confessional in guilt cultures and shame cultures. In guilt cultures social control is exercised as if it were internally in the conscience of the individual, and behaviour is monitored by these forms of guilt reaction. By contrast, in shame cultures, social control is exercised through mechanisms such as public confronta-tion of the sinner, gossip, and more public and overt forms of moral restraint. The institution of confession presupposes the existence of a doctrine of personal guilt, a moral order against which an individual can sin, with a variety of techniques for speaking about and hearing confessional statements.

There are strong reasons, Abercrombie *et al.* (1986) maintain, for believing that a system of control by the inner cause of conscience was a very peculiar develop-ment in Western society, leading to uniqueness in the development of the modern personality, in which the private and interior nature distinguishes it from other forms of confessional, in particular in the emergence of the concept of conscience. The confession was part of a new logic of personhood, organized around the key concepts of conscience, consciousness, feeling and sentiment (Huff 1981). It was the method by which the dual self – the one that views its interiority from an external standpoint – identified in Chapter 2, could be performed.

Feminist theorists such as Pateman (1988) have drawn attention to the historical impossibility of women becoming persons of conscience, yet Goody (1983) argues that the influence of Christianity did actually enable some women to be seen as worthy of personhood, because the Church needed converts and bequests. Thus, upper-class women could be part of the property settlement of families, so they were treated as individuals endowed with reason, will and independence. As social control became a significant social issue in the eighteenth and nineteenth centuries, the attribution of moral worth to some women (not just upper-class) was enabled and extended through the representations of the 'angel at the hearth' and the 'recuperable working-class woman', dividing the worthy from the non-worthy. As David (1980) and Donzelot (1979) illustrate, working-class women were recruited by the state to take control of, and responsibility for, their potentially disruptive and disreputable men-folk and children.

Foucault (1974) notes how the confessional became employed for a variety of different forms of social control, including the intimate and the legislative, practices which always express power and knowledge:

It plays a part in justice, medicine, education, family relationships and love relations, in the most ordinary affairs of everyday life, and in most solemn rites; one confesses one's crimes, one's sins, one's thoughts and desires, one's illnesses and troubles; one goes about telling, with the greatest precision, whatever is most difficult to tell.

(Foucault 1976:59)

In Foucault's work the confessional shifts from what people consciously hide from themselves to become concerned with what is disguised from them in the unconscious. Foucault's interest in confession is in the impersonality of the scene by which personal subjectivities become formed and taxonomies become rationalized, to mark the subject's place within a categorical typification. Abercrombie *et al.* (1986) document how the traditional Roman Catholic confessional was appropriated by Protestant biography, then re-deployed in the modern psychoanalytic confessional and, finally, re-constituted in bureaucratic forms of inquiry. The confessional mode became part of the bureaucratic apparatus of the modern state. This is a story of a technique expanding and being deployed in different ways, but always producing distinctions between groups. The form of individualism that developed from the confessional can thus be seen as a consequence of intellectual conflicts, competition between groups and classes, and legal and institutional changes.

The struggle to shape personhood has a long and dispersed history intricately tied up with relations of classification, namely *who could be a self*. The self that could be *told* also had to be *seen* in order to be *known* fully. The struggle around representation became a significant arena in which different technologies (such as the printing press, art and, eventually, TV and the Internet), enable different forms of narration *and* visuality.

Abercrombie *et al.* (1986) trace how the self became a resource that could be mobilized for the display of cleverness, as a form of intellectual property. For instance, in representations of the face in the pre-modern period, the artist's purpose was not to convey a likeness of the individual, but to make visual their status and authority (for example, depiction of office, patriarchal and religious status, and so on).

Ian Hunter (1992) maintains that the self-reflexive self became consolidated in the nineteenth century as a principle of Romantic aesthetics, namely that of overcoming incompleteness and aspiring to full humanity by using techniques of self-cultivation, which aimed to harmonize and reconcile the different, fractured, divisive aspects of personhood. The introduction and repetition of the chronological form is linked to this desire (Evans 1999).

Tony Bennett (1998) takes this a step further by showing how certain intellectual agendas, such as the aspiration to reflexivity, translate the dialectical technique of person-formation into a dialectical-historical method, enabling the intellectual call to self-reflexivity to become translated as a normative requirement of rigorous methodology, when really it is merely a mechanism by which the Romantic aesthetics of the whole and coherent self are put into place in the name of intellectual practice. He also points out how the concern with the technique of the coherent self, as methodological practice, always produces a present 'self'; that is, a self that is always reliant on history and memory.

This directs our attention to the ways in which the relations between persons and cultural resources are organized by particular cultural technologies, and to the variable forms of work on the self or practices of subjectification, which such relations support. These practices display not so much a particular form of (self) consciousness or interiority, but rather the cultural resources and the social positions on which the person can draw, and by which they are located. It is therefore a matter of positioning and access to the means of telling, but also the ability to be heard when telling.

Carolyn Steedman (2000) documents how histories of the modern self are inextricably bound up with particular techniques of writing and telling the self – more specifically, with histories of narrative. Giddens (1991), for instance, notes how through a three-hundred-year development period in the West, personhood and self-identity have come to be understood as 'the self ... reflexively understood by the person in terms of his or her biography' (pp.52–4). He interprets the telling of the self, not so much as a form of writing, but rather as a form of cognition: 'the core of self-identity in modern life' (p.53).

Charles Taylor (1989), surveying the whole of Western philosophy, argues that the significant feature in regard to the self is the movement of the self from *outside to inside*. The self gained an *interiority* that could be told through particular techniques.[2] Like Bennett, Taylor adds memory to the self-formulae, whereby remembering the self is a necessary requirement to knowing, telling and writing interiority.

David Vincent (1981), in a study of working-class autobiography in the nineteenth century, describes how experience is coded through particular techniques, especially literary forms. In this sense we can talk of 'textually-mediated class'.[3] He documents how almost the only working people to write their life histories were Puritans and later Methodists. What came to be known as 'the working-class autobiography' drew on two traditions: spiritual autobiography and story-telling. The first developed during a political crisis of the civil war period and continued as a recognized literary form throughout the eighteenth and nineteenth centuries – a significant number of the tellers were members of the Temperance movement. The main impetus behind autobiographical productions, Vincent argues, was to display respectability and write morally inspiring pieces of work.

Steedman (2000) develops this further by pointing to the significance of the tradition of the 'great European novel' to show that what we tell and how we tell it was part of the technique of literary production. That is, certain forms of subjectivity, 'the knowing self', were attributed to the bourgeois subject. The working-class, she argues, were only offered the position of self to occupy if they could fit into a particular mode of telling, such as the morally redemptive narratives of Puritanism. Both her detailed historical studies of the concept of childhood, and the analysis of the development of 'creative writing' as a form of educational practice, describe how the concept of a recuperative self was developed in working-class children, making morality central to self-production and child development.[4] Different techniques of telling enable the attribution of the 'self' to different groups; for the working-class, it always had to be a way of displaying respectability.

Moreover, Steedman traces how certain forms of subjectivity became related through self-narration to the administration and distribution of poor relief, making subjectivity a matter of *legal decisions about social worthiness*. The most well known of these is the narrative of the deserving poor; in particular, the gendered variant of the recuperable fallen woman, who reiterates the narrative of seduction, betrayal and redemption.[5] In these characterizations, legally required questions structure the forms of telling and thereby the conditions of possibility for the narration of the self. The accounts produced and recorded are forms in which the interlocutor has been removed and are structured through answers. Steedman notes:

> By these means, multitudes of labouring men and women surveyed a life from a fixed standpoint, told it in chronological sequence, gave an account of what it was that brought them to this place, this circumstance now, telling the familiar tale for the justices clerk to transcribe.
>
> (Steedman 1998:17–18)

She also lists other forms of enforced self-narration: literary Grub Street; philanthropic societies; criminal tales; and working-class histories. In particular, 'the plebeian, subaltern and female' were sources of interest.[6] Vincent (1981) also documents how, in the 1830s and 1840s, a new genre of 'Newgate novels' emerged which provided graphic details of criminal lifestyles. This was also paralleled by the 'Condition of England' question, a middle-class response to the threat of the urban mass, which entailed 'reporting' on working-class lifestyles, establishing another profitable vein of low-life reporting.[7] (See also Chapter 2.) In most of these 'reports' the life of these pre-constituted selves are structured in a way in which events *happen to* the protagonist. Vincent (1991) describes how families came to be seen as poor when they could no longer keep their stories private. The state, he argues, had the most sophisticated repertoire of devices, from reading the marks of poverty inscribed on bodies, on clothes, and on moving through the streets. All these mechanisms assume that the dispossessed could come to an understanding of their own story, which Vincent maintains they did, producing a major change in the way working men viewed their past. The shift in perception and production of the working-class as selves is a moral shift, one that has to be displayed to demonstrate respectability.

Ana Svensson (1997), in a contemporary study, shows how this model of forced telling is employed in Swedish prisons, where the biographical project of the state frames prisoner identity and the morality that is attached to it via the distinction between good and bad selves. She argues that this is a form of symbolic violence that seems to almost erase the possibilities for any form of radical auto-ethnography. How can you be radical if your self is named and organized for you?

This forced telling is in contrast to the stories of 'great individuals' who were agents of their own subjectivity, who produced themselves and were not positioned by legal interlocutors, educationalists, middle-class social observers and reformers. Rather, they conducted their selves through their own narration. Paul Ricoeur (1990) argues that the process of fictionalizing enables a permanence of the self. It is marked, he explains, by key phrases, such as 'I had to', 'I did', 'I refused'. The significant difference between those whose key phrases were given to them to tell and those who produced their own is the marking of the class difference of telling. Interestingly, Marie-Françoise Chanfrault-Duchet (2000) maintains that this process is not marked by gender.

Robbins (1986) demonstrates how self-narration was also strongly related to the construction of 'character' and 'personhood', whereby only the bourgeoisie were seen to be capable of being individuals. Character, he shows, was the 'mask that people were expected to don in the face of power' or 'character was a statement in which one employer described to another ... the habits and qualities of a servant' (1986:35). Liz Stanley (2000) draws attention to the 'currency' of character so that domestic servants needed a 'character statement' to show what kind of person they were as well as what sort of labour they could exchange:

> The 'character' was not only a moral statement but also a highly constitutive practice that could and did have repercussions for people's places within the labour market, within 'respectable society' and also as moral beings: it indicated what someone's status and worth should be taken to be, and the giving and withholding of 'characters' was highly consequential for people's positions within class, status and other hierarchies.
>
> (Stanley 2000:42)

The contemporary link made between appearance and character as a requirement of the middle-class service sector of the labour market (e.g. du Gay's (1996) 'enterprising self'), therefore, is not a new phenomenon. Moreover, as the next chapter will show, class distinctions were drawn between character and personality. The character one had was something fixed, whereas personality was something to be created through access to the 'right' resources (see Susman 1979).

The other significant feature of this process is that the working-class did *not* write themselves; they told the story as proscribed and were themselves transcribed. So access to the self is limited by the means and techniques of telling and knowing. Laura Marcus (1994) illustrates how the autobiographical form historically came to mark – and be marked – by the privilege of self-possession. Being the author of one's life, rather than the respondent to another's interlocutions, generated different sorts of personhood; a class difference that is being reproduced in contemporary forms of telling. The similarities to Giddens' and Beck's imperatives to narrate one's biography should be noted (see Chapter 3), as should the way in which the methods of the middle-class are proposed as a universal experience.

Class divided techniques for telling the self: the legislated often invisible interlocutor who framed particular ways of producing the working-class self, and the individualized unique self of the bourgeoisie, generated the ways of telling and hearing the self that are now incorporated into a variety of contemporary sites, as we shall see in the next section, which explores the gendering of the testimonial self (a more contemporary form of reflexivity).

The historical development of techniques of telling established certain processes:

- Telling was a technique of self-cultivation for some that harmonized fractured and diverse aspects of self.
- Only certain people's stories were considered worthy of telling.
- Self-telling required an interiority for some; for others it depended on legislated narratives.
- Moral attribution was only given to particular selves who displayed self-governance.

The centrality of legislation for the materialization of the self can be seen in the recent moves towards telling as testimony. The concept of testimony comes from, firstly, a legal framework whereby witnesses in court bear testimony. As Cosslett *et al.* (2000) demonstrate, testimony connects the first-person narrative to truth-telling. Secondly, testimony has a religious connotation, closely related to the confessional, whereby testifiers bear witness to their conversion or beliefs. Testimony, they note, is an occurrence in the present to do with the meaning of the past now facilitated by specific situations and interchanges. The testimonial also demands a witness. Ahmed and Stacey (2001) reveal how recent testimonial moves, such as the South African Truth and Reconciliation Commission and the Stolen Generation testimony in Australia, enable the position of the witness and the victim to become aligned, because both are presented as the site from which justice can be delivered (see Probyn 2000b). But, they argue, if testimony is bound up with truth and justice, then its coming into being also registers the crisis in both of these concepts; for one testifies when the truth is in doubt. Therefore 'truth' can be seen to be subject to appeal, the result of political claims, the result of power struggles between competing groups. Who can tell and how becomes central to this process.[8]

This, Cosslett *et al.* (2000) contend, shows that the telling of the self is neither simply externally required or internally generated, that subjectivity is an effect *produced by* forms of autobiographical practice and does not precede it. They maintain this means that gender itself is therefore also produced in autobiographical practice. The method re-produces the performative power of the categories that are brought into effect.

Paradoxically, it was dissident movements that argued for the contemporary telling of oneself as a public gesture of personhood, such as feminists, who insisted on putting one's self into the research process. This methodological technique often merged with confessional and testimonial techniques used to make political and moral claims on the dominant order. The demand to put one's self in the research was ironically a technique to expose the power, positioning, privilege and complacency of those (usually male) researchers who claimed objectivity, and played the 'God Trick' of evading responsibility for their work (Haraway 1991). Specifically, its aim was to question the exchange system by which women could be, and were, put to use for voyeurism, surveillance and appropriation in research (Walkerdine 1990).

Mary Evans (1999) also shows how testimonial practices associated with bourgeois individualism were used to tell 'sexual stories', in which the 'coming out' narrative operates almost as a form of redemption. This should not surprise us, for as David Evans (1993) illustrates, individualism was central to the formation of the dissident sexual movements that developed in the 1960s. Mary Evans (1999) also details how the telling of the self became explicitly gendered from the early 1960s: women's autobiographies became more prolific, more radical and more innovative, whilst men's autobiographies reproduced the traditional definition between the public and the private. However, by the 1990s, she notes, accounts by men were beginning to identify their vulnerability: the men's magazine *Achilles Heel* in the 1980s could be seen as an example of this trend, as could the stories by gay men, who were beginning to become more public with their sexual stories. The confessional guilt scenario has been repeatedly reproduced and also repudiated by popular male self-telling (Hollywood films such as *American Beauty* and *Tumbling Down*), representative of male revenge stories in which women are pathologized as the emasculating force.[9] This is not dissimilar to the political rhetoric in the US, identified by Rouse (1995) in Chapter 5, which also attempts to consolidate white middle-class men into the nation-formation.

The aim of telling of dissident stories was to re-signify identity with value (such as lesbian, gay, black) or generate new identities (queer), rather than accept the value and categorization of those imposed. These processes rely on cultural resources, as Ken Plummer (1996) shows. By generating identifiable categories, stories of identity (I am a man/woman/lesbian/gay/disabled researcher) can be told in which political claims rely on location, narrative and a sense of self: 'By telling a story about myself, I redefine myself as a subject with a specific history and seek to persuade others of the importance of that history' (Felski 2000:132).

Only from the position of, and with access to, the resources of the middle-class, can a presumption be made that there is a possibility first, to tell a story, second, to assume the power to re-define and, third, to assume a significance to the story. The institutional interlocutor who frames the self of the subaltern is not present here, and even though this statement is written to persuade others of its politics and moral purpose, it assumes that telling is possible. This is very different to those who have been forcibly made public through the extraction of their stories. Thus narrativization of one's experience is a resource; some are unable to present themselves as the subject of narrative. Bridget Byrne (2003) details how women, from different classes in London, are able to differentially resource the telling of themselves. Some cannot draw on narrative tropes of transformation and agency in accounting for their experiences.

Being positioned by structural relations (sexuality, gender, race, class) does not necessarily give access to ways of knowing (although some standpoint theorists would argue that it helps: see Maynard 1998; Skeggs 1995).[10] Positioning, however, does provide access to discourse, forms of articulation and resources. The 'self' is implicated in debates on identity, in which political claims are made for superior epistemological authority on the basis of where one is located within categorical positions (Bar On 1993). The debates over identity and epistemological justification, therefore, are about the claim and *right to know*. This is a moral articulation. It is also a naïve formulation of 'position must equal truth must produce authority and legitimation'. Identity politics has created particular problems in claims for authority as a property relation (see Berlant 2000; Brown 1995).

These debates assume there is an identity that can be used as a resource, and that people want to tell their stories in order to produce a moral claim from the telling. I was struck by Lilian Rubin's (1972/1992) research with working-class families in the US, which painstakingly details why the working-class may not want to tell their stories:

> Children in all families frequently are lonely or scared or both. But the child in the working-class family understands that often there's nothing his parents can do about it. They're stuck, just stuck with a life over which they have relatively little control. How can poor children justify or rationalize those feelings when they know that father works two jobs to keep a roof over their heads and food on the table; that mother does dull, demeaning, and exhausting work just to help make ends meet? Their own hurt notwithstanding, assigning blame to parents makes little sense to these children. Their anger either is turned inward and directed against self in childhood, or *the source of their anger is kept distant from consciousness*.
>
> (Rubin 1972/1992:27) (my emphasis)

This is not a matter of using experience but of denying it. As one of her participants notes:

> I tell my kids all the time 'It's better to forget about things that bother you; just put them out of your mind, otherwise you'll just be sitting around feeling sorry for yourself all the time. Just put those things out of your mind is what I tell them, just like I did; then they won't get to you'.
>
> (Rubin 1972/1992:29)

What does it mean to generate a politics around telling experience when experience is precisely what the person may want to forget?

Having established the terrain by which the self can be known (or not) and told, but also used to articulate dissident categorizations and claim moral authority, the next section explores how the self is extended through the telling of the stories of others for self-fashioning.

Self-authorizing

The process of telling the stories of the subaltern has been institutionalized in anthropology and sociology as a mechanism by which the self of the writer or researcher is known. So those excluded from selfhood, personhood, individuality, become the object – often objectified – by those who have access to the subject positions of researcher/writer. The lives of others can be used as extensions of the self – a temporary possession – in which they are brought into self-reflection and then discarded when unnecessary. The use of 'others' to know and constitute the self has a long history in colonialism (Ahmed 2000). Ethnography has been one of the main methodologies by which the possessive individual could be constituted, by using the relational capacity to draw to her or himself objects waiting to be personalized through acts of appropriation or consumption (Strathern 1999).

Nast and Pile (1998) explore how this privileged self-concern has been used in anthropology to *define* difference, to *make* difference. In this process, telling one's self (reflexivity) becomes a property of the researcher's self *rather than* of the practice of the participants. Rendering of difference becomes translated into properties of the self (or, in the case of copyright, properties of the self – writing the self – become properties of multinational publishing companies). The possibilities for the reflexive self are framed by processes of exchange and techniques of telling and knowing, which have to be legitimated and authorized.

This is why those who advocate the telling of the self do not always practice what they preach; their research is not informed by reflexive practice. Rather, they make direct claims to know via their own positioning (and/or, more recently, their textual style). I'd even argue that the centring of the self is a particular technique for eclipsing and de-authorizing the articulations of others. It is a matter of what the researcher designates as important. So the dictum to be reflexive can be interpreted in a banal way, whereby the experience of the research is one of the researcher's story, based on their identity, usually articulated as a singularity. This self-story rarely takes account of movement in and out of space, cultural resources, place, bodies and others, but nonetheless authorizes its self to speak. As Probyn (1993) notes: 'It is not the process of being reflexive about one's research practices that is the problem ... it is the conception of the self at work within this reflexivity that is at fault' (p.80). This formula of self narration often presupposes that the problems of power, privilege and perspective can be dissolved by inserting one's self into the account and proclaiming therefore that reflexivity was practiced; where, in fact, it was just about talking about one's own experiences from one's own perspective. Telling and doing are two very different forms of activity.

Strathern (1999) shows how not only is the self crafted from reified, objectified relations, but also that property claims are then made from these. She argues that where things already appear to exist in the world, establishing 'property' is a question of creating personal claims in them:

> When the 'thing' that becomes property through the claims that people make on it is then perceived as the product of social relations in the first place, that fresh perception may itself be perceived as a produce of social effort for it requires and constitutes knowledge.
>
> (Strathern 1999:18)

When Bourdieu (1992) uses the concept of reflexivity he does not mean direct self-examination. As Griller (1996) notes, he is particularly disdainful of tales of the self: 'Objectivation of any cultural producer involves more than pointing to – and bemoaning – his (sic) class background and location, his race or his gender' (Waquant 1989:155). Instead, we need to explore: '[t]he relationship between the properties of discourses, the properties of the person who pronounces them and the properties of the institution which authorises him (sic) to pronounce them' (Bourdieu 1992:111).[11]

Just as the middle-class have always been able to use and access the bodies of the working-class for labour, now knowledge of and experience of others are used to shore up the composite of the academic reflexive self. The skills which are accessed through research, produced through reflexivity and authorized through writing, are the means by which the research self comes to be formed and known. Strathern (1999) takes this one stage further, arguing that the logic is manifest through intellectual property rights in which property is culturally validated as extensions of person in the appeal to the moral right of creators to their creations. The creation comes from others who are given no property right at all. So the use of others as resources through the reflexive writing self becomes the means by which political claims are made and authority transferred. Bell hooks (1990) contemplates the continued use of other people's suffering to make the modern suffering, reflexive, bourgeois self:

> No need to heed your voice when I can talk about you better than you can speak about yourself. No need to hear your voice. Only tell me about your pain. I want to know your story. And then I will tell it back to you in a new way. Tell it back to you in such a way that it has become my own. Re-writing you I rewrite myself anew. I am still author, authority. I am still coloniser, the speaking subject, and you are now at the centre of my tale.
>
> (hooks 1990:345)

The ability to be reflexive via the experience of others is a privilege, a position of mobility and power, a mobilization of cultural resources. Paul Rabinow (1977), in reflections on his fieldwork in Morocco, explicitly defines his goal in the inter-pretation of his fieldwork as 'the comprehension of the self by the detour of the comprehension of the other' (p.5). But he also argues that this is unavoidable, as some form of symbolic violence is always inherent in the structure of the situation (see also Killick 1995).

What is at stake in the translation/interpretation attachment and use of the experiences of 'others' by ethnographers is made explicit in The Bell Debate. This was generated after white feminist ethnographer, Diane Bell, and her 'collaborator' Aboriginal woman, Topsy Nelson (Bell and Nelson 1989), published an article in *Women's Studies International Forum* on the rape of Aboriginal women by Aboriginal men. A letter to the journal in February 1990 accused Bell of: 'Creating divisions within the "Aboriginal community", appropriating Topsy Nelson's voice by citing her as a co-author rather than as an "informant", of exhibiting white imperialism, of exercising middle-class privilege' (Bell 1993:108).

Ahmed (2000) contends that what is at stake in this debate is not just a question about who is speaking and who is being spoken for, rather it is about the relations of production that surround the text: how was it that Bell came close enough to Topsy Nelson to enable this debate to be aired in public? The ethical problems of ventriloquism (Visweswaran 1994), of producing the 'native' as authentic and as truth (Spivak 1990; Narayan 1993), of spuriously 'giving voice', of accountability and responsibility and 'sheer arrogance' (Agar 1980), are part of the post-colonial critique which forefronts the ethics of merging the voices of others.

Both Nelson and Bell argue that their article was produced as a result of friendship. Yet Bell constantly frames her work and her ethnography in an academic mode of production. Nelson was not passively appropriated in this situation and claims that she used Bell 'to write it all down for her'. Yet, as Ahmed notes, their friendship was strategically framed; their friendship was a technique of knowledge. She proposes that the need to make friends with strangers (the basis of most ethnography) works, in terms of relationality and dialogue, to conceal the operation of an epistemic division within the process of becoming more intimate with one who has already been designated as strange. Centuries of colonialism designate some people as knowers and some as strangers (sometimes with some stories worth telling, but only in particular ways, as Steedman earlier noted) and we are positioned by these relations and techniques. Therefore, acknowledgement of the unequal forms of exchange they reproduce is not about telling the self, but being aware of positioning or systems of exchange-value and the limits on the mobility of some groups.

To support her argument further, Ahmed (2000) draws on Bell's (1983) earlier ethnography *Daughters in the Dreaming*, to demonstrate how Bell again authorizes her ethnography. In other words, Ahmed contends, Aboriginal women are present in the ethnography only insofar as they establish a term in an argument that has its terms of reference in anthropology. They are authorized through the interlocutor of academic anthropology, by which their words are translated and interpreted. Not dissimilar then from the methods of forced telling applied to the working-class. But is this so straight forward?

We need to ask, if the subaltern speaks, how is it that we can hear her? Can the subaltern authorize herself if she cannot speak or only be heard through the self/ words of others? Gayatri Spivak (2000) argues no. But unless researchers like Bell make subaltern stories available how would most people know about the subaltern at all? If subaltern groups have no access to the mechanisms and circuits for telling and distributing their knowledge, how do others even know they exist? It is surely a matter of how we do the research rather than abdicate responsibility entirely. It is interesting that Ahmed, the vociferous critic of subaltern ventriloquism, is a literary textual critic who has not delved into the difficult, messy world of empirical work. How do textual critics access subaltern texts? Where do subaltern texts come from? They are usually also a product of relations of appropriation (publishing is, after all, a capitalist industry designed for profit). As Rabinow (1977) earlier argued, we are always implicated in the circuits of symbolic violence.

How we play these circuits is what counts, as Bourdieu (1993) would argue. Certainly it is not by re-authorizing our selves through telling and confession but, I would argue, through *practice*. This is practice that understands the relations of production and is aware of the possibilities for appropriation; a practice with an awareness of the constraints of disciplinary techniques and the power relations of location and position, one that does not reify and reproduce the categorizations of exploitation and symbolic violence. A practice aware that self-constitution is about access to resources.

In Ahmed's arguments there is a risk of assuming that epistemological authority (e.g. inequality of knowledge about culture) must necessarily entail a social/moral inequality of worth between the researcher and the researched. Yet I know some things about the women whom I studied that they don't know, just as they know things about me of which I'm not aware. Often other people know things about us that we do not see or understand. Also, by virtue of my training, experience, ethnographic labours and time, I have access to explanations and interpretations with epistemological authority, but this need not contradict the moral equality between us.[12] The merging between my knowledge and the women's own knowledge produced the explanations in my earlier ethnographic *Formations* research. Most of us do empirical research to learn from others, not to exploit and use them. It is therefore important not to confuse positioning with morality, or we become complicit in the reproduction of passive pathologies. To add another angle, in which the middle-class self becomes authorized through research methods, I will now explore the 'new' reflexivity.

Mobile and fixed selves

Rather than explicitly telling the self, new forms of textual technique have been invented which de- and re-centre the self simultaneously. These new techniques, such as those developed by Woolgar and Ashmore (1991), and named 'the reflexive project', critically exemplified in Adkins (2002a), de-centre the singular voice of the researcher by using a variety of literary techniques of dialogism. Just like the face in the pre-modern period, these techniques are a mechanism of display, showing the copious amounts of cultural capital that in turn provide access to the requisite resources necessary for engagement in textual play. Textual demonstration displays the cleverness of the writer, whilst also supposedly de-centering the author at the same time. This is not just a matter of the powerful claiming marginality. Rather it is about the powerful showing how well they understand power by playing with it. It is a matter of having your authority and eating it. The new 'reflexive' theorists authorize themselves through their own cultural resources. For, as Rabinow (1986) notes, groups long excluded from positions of institutional power have less concrete freedom to engage in textual experimentation.

Consider also which forms of research are open to reflexive techniques. The 'new reflexive' theorists are not playing with subaltern research participants. They are not using the lives of others to shore up their displays of clever play with disciplinary technique. They use their own cultural capital via texts. This is quite a different matter for ethnographers who do have research participants to whom they are (supposedly, if they are ethical) answerable.

Yet telling personal stories and textual play can be seductive. They seduce us in the game, often operating as a form of rhetoric, whereby we become seduced by the confession, the immediacy of the experience of being there and the personal information. The telling of research stories not only enables the researcher to be identified as 'real', but also grants the spurious authority of authenticity, as Paul Atkinson (1990) documents so well. He demonstrates how two techniques in particular – the interspersal of 'authentic' voices from research participants and the confessional account of the researcher – operate as forms of textual seduction, leaving us less likely to question the authority of the researcher and more likely to attribute value to the spatial 'being there' nature of their experience. Nobody, for instance, can read Renato Rosaldo's (1989) account of his partner's death and not be moved. However, these rhetorical ploys do not always work. The accounts of men's confessions of sexual relationships in the field can have the opposite effect. Rather than displaying their reflexive awareness of power relationships, they can betray their complete ignorance (see Warren 1988), and the collection by Kulick and Willson (1995). The ways in which the self is made reflexive in these accounts depends upon the power and ethics by which the self/other relationship is read and formed in practice and upon the systems of exchange in which practice take place.

For instance, Adkins (2002a) exposes how, in a comparative review of her book *Gendered Work, Sexuality, Family and the Labour Market* with that of Roper on *Masculinity and the British Organization Man*, the reviewer, Williams (1997), attributes more authority to the writing of the self-reflexive account, which solidly places the male author at the centre of the research experience. Less authority is given to Adkins' *reflexive practice* that informed every stage of the research, because it is not told from the point of self-narration and confession. So the narration of the self is given more authority than reflexivity in the research practice itself. The researcher self becomes the site of authority, rather than the participants' accounts and explanations (as in Adkins' research project). It is as if the researcher is the only source of knowledge, hence the only source of self-reflection. This enables the authority in the empirical research to be located in the researcher rather than the research participants; in the textual resourcing of the self, not the practice.

Tracing the development of the modernist literary avant-garde in the late nineteenth century through to the post-modern writings of the contemporary, Felski (1995) illustrates how men have used a form of self-conscious textualism, via an imaginary identification with femininity, to produce a decadent aesthetic of surface, style and parody. The ability, she argues, to use the 'imaginary feminine', which has absolutely no bearing on the reality of women's lives, is being reproduced today at the expense of women. This leads her to contend that the technique of literary self-reflexivity may produce new gender hierarchies, in which those once marginalized by feminism in the academia re-claim their space through the imaginary positioning of themselves as sensitive textual and reflexive researchers. But it is not just gender that is being re-hierarchized; by using these particular resources, class also comes to be re-produced. It is no coincidence, Adkins (2002b) maintains, that the 'reflexive self' is promoted as the new ideal figure of late modernity (see Beck *et al.* 1994), because what it offers is a re-traditionalization of gender, class and sexual relations. Reflexivity does not simply reproduce pre-existing divisions and differences; rather, reflexivity 're-works such differences and is a technique of categorization, classification, difference, division and hierarchy' (p.129). She observes how adopting a mobile, reflexive position towards others is a privileged position of late modernity. Experimentation is, therefore, not inherently liberatory; rather it needs to be recognized as a technique central to the constitution of class, gender and sexuality. Experimentation reconstitutes differences differently (Ahmed 1998a).

We need to ask, then, who is representing themself as reflexive, as having a self worth knowing, a voice worth hearing. Zizek (1997) details how fixing, appropriating and re-figuring are central to the constitution and development of late capitalism, embedding gender and class in circuits and networks that provide advantages for certain groups of men. In earlier work, Adkins (2000b) and Cronin (2000a) demonstrate how new forms of de-traditionalization, the 'freeing of agency from structure' and the 'mobile self' are exactly that: mechanisms *for* re-traditionalization, the fixing of the feminine, the authorizing of masculine privilege and a distraction from pernicious and ubiquitous class and race inequalities. So just as sociological theory has reproduced these distinctions (see Chapter 3), so has sociological method.

Spivak (2000) also demonstrates how subaltern knowledge can be converted into property and capital through processes of labour market reflexivity, in a way in which global feminism itself may be complicit in the transformation of indigenous women's knowledge into property. Lury (1998) suggests that where structural classifications have been abandoned (because they are no longer seen to inhere in the individual but are instead seen to be the effect of technical prosthesis), what in fact may be happening is more intense forms of classification (see Chapter 8 for a development of this argument). These are the reflexivity losers who cannot access and utilize reflexivity as a cultural resource for either management strategy or narrating themselves. They are different from those who can utilize experimental individualism (the prosthetic self) in which reflexivity is a tool by which the resourceful self is produced. The logic of this experimental individualism (or the prosthetic self) for those who can tool themselves up is that disembedding, de-racination, de-gendering and de-classing is possible, even at a time when such classifications are becoming more acute for those at the extreme ends of the social scale.

Lois McNay (1999) maintains that reflexivity is an irregular manifestation dependent on a particular configuration of power relations. This makes it possible to see how some forms of reflexivity reproduce, repeat and reinforce existing power relations, whilst others may be challenging and disruptive. But we will only know this if we have some sense of the possibilities for action, access to resources and the fields, networks, or structural configurations in which the reflexivity takes place. For this we need to dislocate reflexivity from narrating the self, as a property of persons. Moreover, we also need to acknowledge the classical Weberian point that many forms of behaviour are not open to reflexivity; to attribute certain practices as reflexive may be to mis-recognize the limits of our and other's practices.

Conclusion

When people use the term 'self' they often think it is a neutral concept, but, as with all concepts, there is no neutrality. As this chapter has shown, the self is a classed term that produces difference through its utterance. It brings into effect particular forms of personhood. The techniques of the legal interlocutors historically defined how to tell a self, in order for the working-class to receive poor relief. This technique was very different from the heroic stories of bourgeois individuals, a matter not just of authorization and style. One had to learn to tell in a particular way if one did not have access to the resources and authority to produce a self. This telling has a long history of making some groups public, whilst establishing others with the option of being public or private. Because telling entered the public domain, it was used by dissident groups to tell of their selves and make political claims. But this political claims-making was framed through identity which, like the self, draws attention away from the resources that make identity possible in the first place. This was epitomized in the 'new' reflexivity whereby access to resources is what makes reflexivity, although this is rarely acknowledged in claims for the reflexive self. So, this constant denial of the class-resource-based nature of the self is continually produced and authorized, thereby making, constituting and producing difference and inequality, not challenging it. It is a modern-day form of self-fetishism, hiding the conditions of its production.

The self, therefore, is classed through the methods of its constitution. The resources and techniques necessary to self-formation and self-telling are not equally available. Yet, if research is being judged to be legitimate on the basis of self-telling, we can see how research methods themselves constitute class difference. We can see why those who are unaware or ignorant of their own class privilege universalize and cannot think beyond themselves. Significantly in the film *Trainspotting* the central character, Renton, refuses 'to tell' (Haylett, 2000). What has been defined as *the* condition of (post)modernity – that is, the reflexive self – is a very specific class formation, strongly resisted by those who are put under constant scrutiny and forced to tell in ways not of their own making.

8 Resourcing the entitled middle-class self

So far I have examined how class is valued, conceptualized, coded, re-signified, produced by rhetoric and representation, or displaced from academic and popular agendas. The previous chapters have shown that theories and methods are constitutive of what we know and understand to be class, but also that theories and methods of class always assume a particular self. Now I switch emphasis to consider how theories of the self also implicate particular class relations by examining the role that culture plays in self-formation, demonstrating that, underpinning many new theories of the self, is a particular model of exchange. Exchange, as Day (2001) notes (see Chapter 2), is always central to how class becomes known; it is therefore important to see how forms of exchange condition the possibilities for class formation. In most contemporary theories, including those that explicitly theorize class, and even those that aggressively deny the existence of class (such as mobility and reflexivity theorists: see Chapter 3), there exists a particular adherence to the historic ideal of the possessive individual; namely, that cultural properties, resources and/or assets can be accrued to the self, propertized and institutionalized to produce a specific form of personhood. The legacies of the possessive individual are institutionalized through contract law, predicated on the relational capacity to draw to her or himself objects waiting to be personalized through acts of appropriation or consumption. The 'individual' is defined through *his* capacity to own property in *his* person, with the capacity to stand outside of himself, to separate 'himself' from 'his body', and then to have a proprietal relation to himself as bodily property (Pateman 1988).This chapter will thus focus on how culture is exchanged to accrue value to the person, generating a contemporary version of possessive individualism, an exchange-value accumulative self, for the middle-classes.

The chapter is organized into four sections. The first outlines theories of the aestheticization of the self to understand the processes by which class, culture and self become intimately entwined. Developing this theme, the second section investigates theories of prosthetic culture and the experimental prosthetic self. The third compares aesthetic and prosthetic theories with the debates on middle-class culture and taste, also examining Bourdieu's concept of habitus. The final section shows that these different models of classed selves rely on an exchange-value model of self, which accumulates by making culture into a property of the middle-class self.

Aestheticization of the self

Developing Foucault's imperative to 'make one's life a work of art', Featherstone (1991) demonstrates how the middle-class are producing themselves by the 'aestheticization of the everyday'.[1] To do so, access to practices, objects and requisite knowledge is required in order to know what is worth having. Hirsch (1976) argues that the rate of production of new goods means that the struggle to obtain 'positional goods', ones which define social status in the upper reaches of society, is a relative one. The constant supply of new, fashionably desirable goods, or the usurpation of existing marker goods by lower-status groups, produces a paper-chase effect, so that investment in new informational goods is necessary for the maintenance of social distance. In this context knowledge becomes crucial: knowledge of new goods, their social and cultural value, and how to use them appropriately.

In an historical analysis of etiquette manuals, Arditi (1999) traces how the most important thing is not to learn the manners of the elite, but instead to master the logic instructing their manners. Therefore, requisite knowledge is not only about knowing a set of rules but also possessing the logic in order to reproduce them. Featherstone (1991) maintains that this process is not new, but rather is one of the ways in which the middle-class have always constituted themselves. Yet, what this assumes is that one group already has the right culture and others need to learn it. As Savage points out, the truly cultural never need manuals.[2]

It is therefore not just a question, for instance, of what clothes are worn, but *how* they are worn. The 'how' informs their exchange-value. The object does not wholly generate its value; it is the practice in which it is used. Manners manuals also provide the knowledge to spot imposters, because the newly arrived, the autodidact, will unavoidably give away signs of the burden of attainment and incompleteness of his/her cultural competence. Hence the new rich, who may adopt conspicuous consumption strategies, are recognizable because they have not been able to embody the disposition required. They do not know how to 'get it right' (Skeggs 1997; Kuhn 1995), opening up a gap between representation and disposition. The generation of an aesthetic self relies on the accrual of cultural capital in the right composition, of the right volume, with the right knowledge in the right way.

The competition to acquire particular goods and practices creates barriers and techniques of exclusion (Douglas and Isherwood 1980). The phasing, duration and intensity of time invested in acquiring competences for handling information, goods and services, as well as everyday practice, conservation and maintenance of these competences, is, as Featherstone (1991) notes, a useful criterion of social class. Time spent in consumption practices can convey an accurate idea of class position (Preteceille and Terrail 1985).

William Susman (1979) documents how aestheticization enabled the shift from character to personality. By 1800 the concept of character had come to define a particular modal type, seen as essential for the maintenance of the social order. The term character meant a group of traits believed to have social significance and moral quality (see Chapter 7). It was not that the culture of character died suddenly or that books and manuals stressing the 'character' vision of the self disappeared, but rather, starting somewhere in the middle of the first decade of the twentieth century, another vision of self rapidly evolved – one of self-development and mastery, based on aestheticization, thus interest grew in personality, individual idiosyncrasies, personal needs. Also, self-sacrifice yielded to that of self-realization. There was fascination with the very peculiarities of the self, especially the sick self. From the start personality was distinguished from character: 'Personality is the quality of being Somebody' (Susman 1979:9). This definition emphasized the importance of being different, special, unusual, and of standing out in a crowd, which required cultural resources. The new personality literature of the period stressed items that could be best developed in leisure time with emphasis on consumption. At the same time, clothing, personal appearance and 'good manners' were important, but there was little interest in their use as a display of moral value. Time, knowledge and access to resources – and what to do with them – were therefore central to the development of one's personality.

As Featherstone (1991) points out, many of the practices and lifestyles necessary to this new middle-class personality involve 'a controlled de-control of the emotions', requiring the mutual respect and self-restraint of the participants, as opposed to a narcissistic regression which could destroy the social bond (see Wouters, 1986). Featherstone suggests that the concern with lifestyle, with the stylization of life, shows that the practices of consumption, the planning, purchase and display of consumer goods and experiences in everyday life, cannot be understood merely via conceptions of exchange-value and instrumental rational calculation. Rather, they can be conceived as a balance of the instrumental and expressive which consumer culture brings together. He proposes a calculating hedonism, a calculus of the stylistic effect and an emotional economy, but also an aestheticization of the instrumental or functional rational dimension via the promotion of an aestheticizing distancing of the other. Consumption then, Featherstone (1991) argues, must not be understood as the consumption of use-values, a material utility, but primarily as the consumption of signs,[3] of exchange. These signs are the means by which value is known and attributed.

There are similarities between the movement towards aestheticizing the self and the more recent theorizing on prosthetic culture. The central differences are that prosthetic selves play rather than accrue culture, and are predicated upon a critique of how certain *perspectives* become legitimated. To explain in more detail, this next section will begin with a brief detour into recent perspectives on race and its legitimations.

Prosthetic legitimations

Debates on aestheticization assume a particular relation to culture as a resource, which is used to generate the self. A different relation to culture can be seen when we explore recent debates on race. The ambiguities surrounding the use of the concept 'culture' are, however, problematic, as culture is often used to mean everything. Bromley (2000), for instance, details how, even in the 'sedulous prose of academic political science' (p.2) and the preoccupations with the US foreign policy elite, race has now *become* culture. This enables race to be perceived in very particular ways. Soysal (1993) demonstrates how in European discourse on exclusion, what were once assertions of the differing endowments of human races have been replaced by a rhetoric of inclusion and exclusion, which emphasizes the distinctiveness of cultural identity, traditions and heritage among groups, and assumes the closure of culture by territory. This perspective uses culture to make the self of difference, segregating spatially, each culture in its place (Stolke 1995). The fact that nation states lack cultural uniformity is ignored, promoting a cultural fundamentalism premised on the belief that different groups have irreconcilably different cultures.

This shift from nature to culture, or what Lury (2000) and Strathern (1992a) identify as a shift from essentialism (predicated on biology/nature) to cultural essentialism, appears as the contemporary outcome of a long process of shifting authorizations. Whereas nature was used to legitimate racism, now cultural performs this role. Lury also notes how the rhetoric of culture difference has been used to 'open out' new markets, displayed recently in the successful Benetton advertising campaigns, which promote race as a cultural property, a resource that is available for use by all, a fashion item (see Chapter 6).

What is important to note at this stage is how class was never legitimated by nature in the same way. Although there were attempts at the beginning of the nineteenth century via eugenics to link together all subaltern groups as naturally primitive and degenerate (see Engels 1844/1958; Gilman 1990; McClintock 1995; Kahn 2001 and Chapter 2), the association between biology and nature was never sustained in the same way as it was for gender and race; this was due partly to the alignments around whiteness, particularly white masculinity, and also to the central role that labour came to play in legitimating the value, worth and positioning of the white working-class male. Working-class females were, of course, essentialized by gender, through their reproductive function, and their fecundity continues to be defined as a problem for the state (see Chapter 5).[4] But even so, the division of labour was much more crucial to establishing and legitimating class inequality than biology; gender was essentialized but not class. Different legitimations were applied to social positions, with culture coming to play a more central role in explaining and essentializing inequality and difference.

As Chapters 1 and 2 demonstrated, the development of the bourgeois possessive individual was predicated on the relational capacity to draw to her or himself objects, waiting to be personalized through acts of appropriation or consumption (Strathern 1999). This possessive self, Lury (1998) argues, is currently being renegotiated in a process of experimentation as a technique of the self, which makes possible a relation to the individual in which aspects that previously seemed (naturally or socially) fixed, immutable, beyond will or self-control, are increasingly made sites of strategic decision-making. The prosthesis – the experimental trying on, or attachment and detachment of cultural resources (which she defines as either perceptual or mechanical), makes this self-extension possible. In adopting/

adapting/attaching a prosthesis, the person creates (or is created by) a self-identity that is no longer defined by the edict 'I think therefore I am'; rather, he or she is constituted in the relation 'I can, therefore I am'. Access to resources is therefore central to this 'doing', experimental self. But, equally important, as (Strathern 1992a) contends, is knowledge and perspective.

Strathern insists that the shifting terrain of the possessive individual is specifically about the reformation of the middle-class. That is, many of the debates about the 'new' self are only applicable to the middle-classes, and do not have wider explanatory power. Her analysis is of English middle-class formation because, she maintains, this is the class concerned with creating perspectives, and converting and communicating them as knowledge. As we have already seen in Chapter 2, the nineteenth-century concept of social class came to embody the permanent representation of its own viewpoints.

For Strathern (1992a) the central feature of prosthesis is that it has forced choice out into the open. As a result of traditional sources of moral authority disappearing, the middle-classes continually have to make choices, of viewpoints, of resources, of what to attach to themselves. This proliferation of choice has flattened out perspective, she argues, leaving the middle-classes with *only* choice, making self-production or what Taylor (1989) and Cronin (2000b) call 'compulsory individuality', absolutely compulsory. Whereas theorists of individualization and reflexivity argue that we are all part of this choosing process, Strathern demonstrates how choosing is a particularly middle-class way of operating in the world, dependent on access to resources and senses of entitlement to others. But what about those who have no choice? Goldthorpe (1996) maintains that the rational capacity for making choices is a marker of class difference, in which the middle-class utilize their choices most effectively, assuming that the working-classes have choices which they utilize less adequately. We see in 'enterprise self' models a similar shift in perspective, from a position of inequality to one of choice (e.g. du Gay 1996). These perspectives presuppose a model of an agentic self that has access to choice, can choose, but also where class inequality emerges from this individual choice. Those who suggest that choice is universal betray the social position from which their perspective emerged. Choice is a resource, to which some lack access and which they cannot see as a possibility; it is not within their field of vision, their plausibility structure.

In her study of prosthesis, (Strathern 1991; 1992a) also points out that the opportunity for forms of extension comes not only from the choosing and putting on of parts (prosthesis), but from the notion of the part as dramatic, as performative (Munro 1996). The addition of a part (object) extends the possibilities for cultural performance as 'part' (subject). Her point is that the middle-classes move from figure to figure, attaching and detaching in their self- performance, and crucially, as Munro suggests, perception of the second figure involves forgetting parts of the first figure. There is never a whole, selves are always in extension.[5] Munro warns against reading this in a realist way, as if a core self appropriates a range of identities, assuming that there is a true self to which one can return. He argues that, in the process of extension, one never travels out of place (that is the core self), rather the only movement is circular, from one figure to another. One figure picks up on what the other excludes. This does not necessarily assume magnification and expansion; it may also shrink, hide, become anonymous. Thus, he maintains, we are always in extension: '*Indeed extension is all we are ever in*' (Munro 1996:264 (my emphasis)). The whole process is predicated on the power and ability to move, to *access* others, to *mobilize* resources. Yet we do not have equal access and ability to mobilize resources. Helmann (1988) suggests that in the new types of social relationships of post-plural society, the choices that resources afford constitute perspectives, and anything – relationships, institutions, persons – can be seen as a resource.

Lury (1998) develops the idea of prosthetic culture, arguing that we are now in a period of self-refashioning (prosthetic culture) in which two central processes – indifferentiation (the disappearance of the distance between cause and effect) and outcontextualization (where contexts are multiplied and rendered a matter of choice) – enable the thought of reflexivity to become objectified in itself. Together, the processes of outcontextualization and indifferentiation, Lury argues, have encouraged an experimental individualism, in which the subject is increasingly able to lay claim to features of the context or environment as if they were the outcome of the testing of his or her personal capacities. The source of authority is the self. Extension, attachment and detachment become a matter of scale and perspective, the way in which the self sees itself as entitled to experiment in the world. The disaggregated parts of individualism come to provide the resources for reconstituting the middle-class self, out of context, as if an experimental form of play (of enhancing the potential for dramatic performance and responsibility) lies in the choices made for this self rather than in relation to others as part of this middle-class re-formation. Franklin *et al.* (2000) identify a global trend, whereby nature becomes both culturalized and incorporated into the new self project through propriety branding, and used as a resource for self-making by those who have access to the knowledge to make use of resources,[6] whereby global nature becomes culture.

But what are the social relations and constituents of power and entitlement that allow the middle-classes to participate in the forms of exchange that enable them to resource themselves? We need to question what, who and how parts/objects/figures become available as a resource. We also need to think about the different economies of exchange, which, as Edward Said (1978) pointed out some time ago, are always uneven in the trading of culture. Papastergiadis (1999) describes these forms of exchange as a multidirectional circuit board, where connections and short-circuiting may occur. For instance, in the space of colonial encounters, Pratt (1992) shows how forms of uneven exchange bristle with conflicts and contradictions. The making of the new middle-class self is located and shaped by power and struggle, in which middle-class selves attempt to retain legitimacy and authority for the choices they make and the resources they use. But this authority is fragile and has to be continually asserted – through perspective. Turning nature into culture and using it as a resource produces new forms of legitimating, through culture. These legitimating strategies depend on making cultural difference more obvious and knowable. This process of making difference relies on a standard from which difference can be drawn and manifested in spatial organization (as the race theorists in the first section of this chapter ('Aestheticization of the self') demonstrate).

'New' middle-class lifestyles and omnivorousness

The concept of lifestyle is another way to theorize the emergence of the new middle-class. Lifestyle, Featherstone (1991) proposes, can best be understood in relation to the habitus of the new petite bourgeoisie, which, as an expanding class fraction centrally concerned with the production and dissemination of consumer culture imagery and information, is concerned to expand and legitimate its own particular dispositions and lifestyle. Central to most theories of lifestyle lies Bourdieu's topology of social space, as described in the introduction.

Bourdieu (1986) documents the rise, in France, of what he terms a new petite bourgeoisie, identifiable through lifestyles and tastes. However, as Lamont (1991; 1992) shows, there are significant differences between nations. The strong emphasis historically on high culture in France gives a different inflection to the evaluation of culture within different European traditions. A brief review of this research will reveal how these 'new' lifestyles are being formulated and spatialized, a 'new' middle-class in formation.

In *Distinction* Bourdieu (1986) demonstrated how the aesthetic disposition was inseparable from a specific cultural competence. Cultural competence could be known by the tastes held by people, especially their relationship to, and knowledge of, objects and practices. Central to the development of 'high' culture was the Kantian aesthetic based on the judgement of pure taste, which distinguished that which pleases from that which gratifies, 'to distinguish disinterestedness, the sole guarantor of the specific aesthetic quality of contemplation, from the interest of reason' [7] (Bourdieu 1986:5). The purifying, refining and sublimating of primary needs and impulses defined taste, and taste was always moral. The different ways of *relating* to objects and practices marked out the systems of dispositions and, as Bourdieu's classic comment notes: 'Taste classifies, and it classifies the classifier' (1986:6): 'In matters of taste, more than anywhere else, any determination is negation; and tastes are no doubt first and foremost distastes, disgust provoked by horror or visceral intolerance ("sick-making") of the taste of others' (Bourdieu 1986:56).

Cultural practice takes its social meaning and its ability to signify social difference and distance, not from some intrinsic property, but from the location of cultural practice in a system of objects and practices (Waquant 2000). Crucial to Bourdieu's analysis is his emphasis on knowledge, and the way it enables particular relations to objects/practices. It is not just a matter of obtaining objects and knowing how to use, play, experiment with them; rather, how they are conceptualized (objectified) by relations to others is what matters.

Bourdieu explores judgements made on the basis of taste, arguing judgement is always a moral judgement, a value of the person. All tastes, he argues, distinguish between practices and objects that do or do not function within the remit of moral personhood. So, if we relate his arguments back to those of the aesthetic/prosthetic self, what Bourdieu adds is a preliminary mapping of what counts as *worth*, knowing or having in the constitution of the self, and how this is always spatialized. This demonstrates even more vividly that *this is not just a self but a class formation*, premised on structural inequality and access to knowledge fought out in culture, and reliant on not being recognized as such: what Bourdieu calls mis-recognition. What is also significant is how certain tastes become institutionalized, protected by symbolic boundaries and forms of exclusion, so that the categories used by groups to make, recognize and 'cultivate differences' become legitimated over time (DiMaggio 1986).

Bourdieu argues that women are the predominant markers of taste. It is women's role to convert economic capital into symbolic capital for their families through the display of tastes. As Lovell (2000) points out, for Bourdieu women's status is as *capital-bearing objects*, whose value accrues to the primary groups to which they belong, rather than as capital-accumulating subjects in social space, whose strategic circulation plays a key role in the enhancement of the symbolic capital held by men. Women, for Bourdieu, rarely have capital-accumulating strategies of their own; they are repositories. This is most clearly shown in the diagram in *Distinctions* on 'the space of social positions', in which to include women would be to include them twice. Lovell argues that Bourdieu's attempts to understand gender in *Masculine Domination* are premised upon women as objects, in a similar way to how Levi-Strauss described women – as the basis of exchange.

In contrast, feminist analysis has revealed that women can be subjects with capital-accumulating strategies (e.g. Adkins 2000a; Lawler 2000b; Moi 1991; Munt 1995; Reay 1998; Skeggs 1997; Walkerdine 1989). Also, that gender struggles over the boundaries of taste and design have been significant to understandings of what actually counts as contemporary taste (e.g. Sparke 1995). Whilst Bourdieu shows that bodies are central to the embodiment of capital and taste, he describes a stable body in contrast to feminist views of leaky bodies (e.g. Gatens 1996). The body, for Bourdieu, is, as Probyn (2000a) points out, overdetermined. For Bourdieu (1986) the body is 'sign-bearing, sign-wearing', the 'producer of signs which physically mark the relationship to the body' (p.192). For Probyn, this figures a body that is strangely inert, a body that eats and is, in the end, eaten by the overdeterminations of culture. Bourdieu reads the lack of care of the body and appearance as a sign of moral laxity, whereas too much concern for the body and appearance is also read as a sign of feminine excess, and thereby morally dubious, repeating a long moral equation of appearance with femininity (Lury 1993; Nead 1988).

Bourdieu's work has been developed through national studies and challenged in a variety of ways. Savage *et al.* (1992) empirically demonstrate how the lifestyles of the middle-class are dependent upon very specific pursuits; their research distinguishes between three different types of middle-class lifestyle: the *ascetic* (public sector welfare professional); the *postmodern* (private sector professionals) and the *undistinctive* (managers and government bureaucrats). The postmodern lifestyle most closely relates to the arguments in this chapter, as those who live it are the ones who re-fashion themselves through specific cultural resources. Particularly noticeable from Savage *et al.*'s research is the link between high levels of educational attainment and engagement in new forms of body culture associated with keeping fit; this, they argue, is representative of the promotion of the self in which investment is made in the *storing* of cultural assets. But, they explain, this is also contradictory, as this group also indulge in some very non-healthy practices, mainly drinking, which makes them the calculating hedonists with strategic de-control, identified by Featherstone (1991), or the utilitarian pleasure seekers identified by Brooks (2001), who use their leisure pursuits to increase their productivity and market value.

Savage *et al.*'s research also shows how the management sector of the middle-classes are less likely to invest in their bodies and more likely to rely on organization assets.[8] The materialist world (rejected by the intellectual section of the middle-classes described by Bourdieu 1986) is now fully accessed for lifestyle resources. However, the centrality of Savage *et al.*'s argument rests on the fact that culture is *not the only asset* that is used in the formation of the middle-classes, as suggested by earlier aesthetic arguments. Rather, it is the combination of economic, property and organizational assets that enables a wide resource base. Their research also demonstrates that there is substantive evidence to suggest that the 'new' middle-classes are being formed through the professional private sector employees, those that Lash (1990) defines as the group who work on symbols rather than things, and thereby 'produce symbols which help to realize the value of other symbols' (p.251). These professionals legitimate themselves through their own production, comprising established, as well as more recent, professions; what Lash calls the 'post-industrial middle-class', a group whose lifestyle marks it out from other sectors of the middle-classes and who define themselves through cultural markers.

In a study of Australian taste cultures, Bennett *et al.* (1999) provide another national inflection, arguing, in a similar manner to Bonnie Erickson's work on Canadian taste formation, that Australians place emphasis on social rather than cultural capital for transmitting and maintaining distinctions. Bennett *et al.* found that the scales of value used by their research participants were, unlike Bourdieu's claims, not homologous. In Australia 'culturedness' was not particularly salient in the self-definition of the economically dominant social groups, with the exception of certain activities, such as going to the theatre, the ballet and the opera, which are at once prestigious and expensive. The Australian model of taste distinction is more in line with that of the US than France and the UK, leading Bennett *et al.* to argue that the primary mode of status distinction within Australia is conspicuous consumption, rather than the display of 'good taste'. Different systems, circuits of exchange and value attribution can therefore be seen as nationally specific, as they have to cohere with other modes of governance.

There is, however, growing evidence, especially in Canada and the US, first associated with the research of Erickson (1991; 1996); Peterson (1993); Peterson and Kern (1996), of 'cultural omnivores', a middle-class self-formation; a mobile and flexible body that can access, know, participate and feel confident about using a wide variety of cultures (from low to high). Peterson for instance, in a study of musical taste in the US, argues:

> Elite taste is no longer defined as an expressed appreciation of the high art forms (and a moral disdain or bemused tolerance for all other aesthetic expressions). Now it is being redefined as an appreciation of every distinctive form along with an appreciation of the high arts. Because status is gained by knowing about and participating in (that is to say, by consuming) all forms, the term omnivore seems appropriate.
>
> (Peterson 1993:169)

Peterson cites the rise of country music to aesthetic status in elite music magazines as a sign that US taste is being re-formulated. Yet, in a detailed empirical analysis of omnivorousness in the UK, Warde *et al.* (2000) urge caution. They identify at least three different interpretations of the significance of omnivorousness: tolerant pluralism, cultural symbolism and reinforcement of class distinctions. Unpacking the debates on omnivorousness and using the 1985–92 British Health and Lifestyle Survey, they find no evidence for omnivorous expansion. Instead, they show how there is a consolidation of the highbrow by those with access to, and high volumes of, types of capital. Warde *et al.* also draw attention to the work of Michelle Lamont (1992; 2000) to show how different moral values exist that challenge traditional distinctions of cultural tastes.

Erickson (1996) develops the themes of omnivorousness, in a study of private sector workers in Canada, demonstrating that understanding of taste and class cultures should not just be restricted to cultural objects. The most useful cultural resource, she maintains, is in fact social networks. Also, she notes, omnivores are alike 'only in the large number of tastes and practices that they have, not in having the same tastes and practices' (p.247); they have many social circles, a greater network and cultural variety, but do not share any one profile. This, she argues, is in opposition to Bourdieu's structural homologies that map taste and disposition onto position. Yet Warde *et al.* (2000) and Bryson (1996; 1997) disagree, contending that omnivorousness is a confirmation of class distinction, rather than a challenge to it; because all forms of capital become embodied in the middle-classes who can access and consolidate their interests.[9] Moreover, they maintain, the socially privileged do not give up highbrow activities; in fact they pursue leisure activities more assiduously and extend their range, demonstrating evidence of both omnivorousness and persistent distinction amongst the British middle-classes. So time, knowledge, information, bodily investment, mobility across cultural boundaries and social networking, all constitute resources for the formation of the new middle-class omnivorous self. The cultural omnivore, therefore, enables the middle-classes to re-fashion and re-tool themselves.

Whereas prosthetic and some aesthetic theories deconstruct the self into parts, omnivore theories assume the existence of an accumulative self. Also, the omnivore is counter-posed to the univore: that is, those with limited taste. Sarah Green[10] views this as evidence of the middle-classes appropriating what were previously upper-class dispositions of omnivorousness (such as expanding the self through the Grand Tour, the Left Bank and Greek classical knowledge). But what is significant is the transfer of sampling by the middle-classes to aspects of working-class (rather than 'foreign') cultures.

The use of categories uni/omnivore assumes that there is a particular type, even personality, generated through resources. This produces another contemporary version of the possessive individual. It is certainly an exchange-value, accumulative view of the self, enabling class formation through access to the requisite resources. Omnivorousness is a privilege restricted to the middle-classes and does not work in reverse because of the money, time and knowledge required to know what to access and how to use what has been accessed. The middle-classes are segmented also by the resources that are mobilized, as Savage *et al.* (1992) noted earlier.

Bourdieu's (1992) model of interest and investment underpins these different national systems of exchange upon which new middle-class formations are predicated. That interest and investment can be made is both presupposed and produced by the functioning of what he defines as historically delimiting fields. Each field calls forth and gives life to a specific form of interest, a tacit recognition of the value of the stakes of the game and of the practical mastery of its rules. He explains this through his concept of investment, which he defines as:

> The propensity to act that is born of the relation between a field and a system of dispositions adjusted to the game it proposes, a sense of the game and of its stakes that implies at once an inclination and an ability to play the game, both of which are socially and historically constituted rather than universally given.
>
> (Bourdieu 1992:118)

Instead of a model of the self, Bourdieu proposes the habitus, an internal organizing mechanism which learns, as a result of social positioning, how to play the game; dispositions arise from the fields to which one has access, knowledge and experience. But, asks Lovell (2000), how is it that women manage to develop a 'feel for the game' from which they are excluded by virtue of their sex? We might also ask how is it that the middle-classes become omnivores, if they have been excluded from other cultures? How do they gain access? How do they know what to plunder in order to make attachment and/or accrual of cultural resources? Is this why they can never get it right and become an object of ridicule in the symbolic critique of pretensions? And how is it that they can sample other cultures (for instance, ethnic food – see Warde *et al.* 2000) – whilst maintaining social distance from those that enable this cultural sampling? Is this just another form of commodity fetishism – cultural fetishism perhaps – which not only hides the production of culture, but the cultural inscription of the producers that enables the attribution of value?

Bourdieu actually argues against the Satrean idea of a self as a project to be worked upon. He is highly critical of any sense of a coherent whole and, in particular, exposes the illusion of biography, which works to generate specific forms of homogeneous totalizing personhood.[11] He shows how biography is shaped by assumptions about ascendancy in careers (a particular middle-class version of exchange and accumulation). He also dismisses personal style, explaining that it is always a deviation in relation to the style of a period or class. He focuses on habit in an attempt to decentralize the self, making it opposite to conscious action and will-power, preferring instead a model of disciplined bodies. Yet if we examine the many definitions of habitus offered by Bourdieu (1977; 1980/1990; 2000b) and Bourdieu and Waquant (1992) we can see that, whilst arguing against the concept of a coherent self, against biography, against conscious accumulation, the habitus is still premised on exchange-value and the ability to accumulate value through capital composition and volume: 'The habitus is a model of accumulation, based on knowledge of the game and how to play it' (Bourdieu 2000b:184).[12] Even if the body achieves this accumulation through its unconscious habitual actions:

> the habitus is the product of the work of inculcation and appropriation necessary in order for those products of collective history, the objective structures (e.g. of language, economy, etc.) to succeed in reproducing themselves more or less completely, in the form of durable dispositions.
>
> (Bourdieu 1977:85)

Even when exposing the arbitrary nature of value, the concept of investment is used to suggest that exchange-value:

> This value is such as to induce investments and over-investments (in both the economic and psychoanalytic sense) which tend, through the ensuing competition and rarity, to reinforce the well-grounded illusion that the value of symbolic goods is inscribed in the nature of things.
>
> (Bourdieu 1977:183)

This illusion of value generates relations to objects and things that is about investment. Investment, I'd argue, must be about a projection into the future of a self/space/body with value. We only make investments in order to accrue value when we can conceive of a future in which that value can have a use. So even if the habitus is not a conscious, rational, experimenting, playful self, it still works with an accumulative sense, premised on exchange-value. It is also driven by strategy (see *Pascalian Meditiations*, Bourdieu 2000b, in particular). When Bourdieu argues that the objective homogenizing of group or class habitus resulting from 'the homogeneity of the conditions of existence, is what enables practices to be objectively harmonised without any intentional calculation or conscious reference to a norm' (1977:80), he makes the subject the project of an unconscious desire to accumulate. Even when Bourdieu tries to challenge accusations of rational action in *Invitation to Reflexive Sociology* (Bourdieu and Waquant 1992), his metaphors collapse him back into exchange models.

Andrew Sayer (2001) and Peter McMylor (2001) draw attention to the ways in which Bourdieu's metaphors of capital are *always* forms of exchange-value. As Sayer notes, Bourdieu's analysis operates through economic categories (I'd argue metaphors). These inevitably have the effect of treating all matters, which are at least partly to do with recognition and how it is granted or withheld, as if they were to do with distribution – of capital and of symbolic profits. Moreover, Bourdieu not only uses economic categories of distribution where there is still place for categories of recognition, but categories which conflate rather than distinguish use-value from exchange-value. The struggles of the social field are precisely about the difference between these. Hence, they are *both* recognition and distribution struggles, both ethical and economic valuation. And politically, these struggles mis-recognize in two senses: hiding the workings of the powerful (in the traditional Bourdieuan sense), and also hiding the value of the working-class. Recognition struggles are not only about the relative rates of exchange of different forms of capital, but also the relative worth (use-value) of different kinds of goods/categories of people (Sayer 2001).

If all these different models of the middle-class self rely on the accumulation of value, we need to know how this value is attributed, known, accessed, used and accrued. It is to these matters that this chapter now turns.

Establishing value

The double capacity of the commodity to be exchange-value and ersatz use-value, to be the same and different, Baudrillard (1983) argues, distinguishes contemporary culture from the past. The movement towards the mass production of commodities and the obliteration of the original 'natural' use-value of goods by the dominance of exchange-value under capitalism, has resulted in the commodity becoming a sign. Consumption, then, must not be understood as the consumption of use-values, a material utility, but primarily as the consumption of signs (exchange-value). Cultural properties, bodies and bits of non/bodies (prosthesis) all have an exchange-value. Featherstone (1991) maintains that it is this dominance of the commodity as sign which has led some neo-Marxists to emphasize the crucial role of culture in the reproduction of contemporary capitalism. For Baudrillard (1983) this means that 'we live everywhere already in an "aesthetic" hallucination of reality' (p.148). The 'death of the social, the loss of the real, leads to a nostalgia for the real: a fascination with and desperate search for real people, real values, real sex' (Kroker 1985:5).

The difference between the aesthetic/prosthetic (AP), the reflexive self, and the omnivorous lifestyle can be seen in the way accrual works. The AP self moves from figure to figure, reliant upon knowledge about what figure to appropriate, what to attach, what choices to make. It is an entitled self that can cross boundaries, be flexible and mobile, that is concerned to (and can) authorize its own perspective and partiality. The theories of the omnivore (or habitus) are less about playfulness and experimentation and more about a stable self, one that accrues interest through investment over time. Peterson and Kern (1996) show how 'highbrows' are more omnivorous than others and that they become increasingly omnivorous over time. Whilst the AP self cannot lose knowledge easily, it is less based upon volume and more on surface; it is about the composition of the surface. The omnivore is dependent upon knowing the value of certain practices, of understanding the symbolic economy and being able to access it, whereas the AP self is about creating new values, a process of re-evaluation: it fine-tunes differences, making the knowledge more difficult to obtain (possibly why irony is so favoured, as it is an exclusive attribute). The AP self is more interested in boundary plundering than in boundary maintenance. There are two issues raised here. First, what is considered to be a resource needs addressing and, second, we need to keep in mind that it is not just cultural resources, but also social networks and relationships that are important in these new class formations.

Featherstone (1991) contends that it is cultural specialists and intermediaries who play a key role in establishing and translating value, because they have the capacity to ransack various traditions and cultures in order to produce new symbolic goods, and provide the necessary interpretations on their use. He shows how these new cultural intermediaries seek not to promote a single lifestyle, but to break new markets to cater for and expand the range of styles and lifestyles available to audiences and consumers. Bourdieu (1986) demonstrates how these cultural intermediaries adopt a learning-mode towards life, fascinated by identity, appearance and lifestyle to such an extent that they consciously invent an art of living, in which their body, home, car, etc., are all regarded as an extension of their persona which must be stylized to express their individuality. What is significant is that these intermediaries *can* access different fields. Where intermediaries used to be arbiters of highbrow taste (boundary maintenance), their role is now the *translation and evaluation* of other cultures. A corresponding shift occurs in middle-class formation reliant on achieving elite status through hiding and restricting knowledge and practices, to one in which status is achieved through the display of this knowledge and practice: exclusivity to transparency.

Knowledge about other cultures and the display of one's access to the culture and resources of others are central in this process. Black working-class culture, for instance, has long been plundered for its cultural attributes, such as music and fashion, that can be re-packaged to sell elements of it to a white audience that would not otherwise have access. In the selling of black culture it is not just objects that are sold, rather the exchange-value is based on attributing to the object particular properties of black culture more generally, affects such as credibility and 'cool'. Elements of black culture are extracted and made available for attachment and detachment on the white market. But, as Diawara (1998) points out, this is a one-way process. For instance, the abstraction of cool from dangerous only works when applied to white bodies; the long history of racism semiotically sticks cool and dangerous together when applied to black bodies. The value depends on to which body the affect is attached.

Hauser (1982) illustrates, similarly, how the white working-classes have long served to function as an attached affect of resistance for middle-class artists. He notes how artists live cheek by jowl with the working-classes in the low-rent areas of large cities, cultivating similar manners, valuing spontaneity and anti-systematic values; values which challenged the controls and conventions of the respectable middle-classes. The UK pop band Pulp epitomized a similar phenomenon in their immortal lyric for the track *Common People*: 'I want to live like common people, I want to do whatever common people do, I want to sleep with common people like you', and the riposte: 'You'll never live like common people, you'll never do what common people do, you'll never fail like common people, you'll never watch your life slide out of view, and dance and drink and screw 'cos there's nothing else to do' (written by Cocker/Senior/Mackay/Banks/Doyle, *Common People*, 1995, Island Records).

The riposte makes explicit the two different knowledge systems in play: the bourgeois desire to be 'common' will always be exposed because it has not been acquired through the right experiences. There are limits to appropriating affect. However, there is a considerable debate about the terms of cultural appropriation. Appropriation has been defined as the taking from a culture that is not one's own: of intellectual property, cultural expressions or artefacts, history and ways of knowledge. From Ziff and Rao's (1997) analysis of appropriation three general points emerge: first, appropriation concerns relationships among people; second, it occurs through a wide range of modes and, third, it is widely practiced. They argue that if we conceive of the numerous acts of appropriation that happen all around us in a vast number of creative domains, cultural influences blend, merge, and synthesize.

James Clifford (1992) makes a similar point. Reflecting on the discontinuity of cultures and traditions, and the fracturing of images of cultural purity in the modern world, he suggests that 'cultural' difference is no longer a stable, exotic otherness; rather, self-other relations are matters of power and rhetoric rather than essence. However, difference, even if produced by rhetoric (or cultural rather than biological essentialism, as above), is still coded and valued as difference, and some differences are valued more than others. Moreover, as Featherstone (1991) notes, in order to open up new markets consumer culture needs to differentiate and encourage the play of difference, but these differences must be socially recognized and legitimated: total otherness, like total individuality, is likely to be unrecognizable and hence without value. Thus different systems of exchange and the fields that shape them determine the value that can be attributed. Following Annette Weiner (1992), use-value can also be established from that which cannot be exchanged, that which can instead be retained.

In a study of UK club culture Sarah Thornton (1997) uses Bourdieu's analysis to show how different forms of capital (cultural – such as haircuts, style, being gendered, knowledge of particular music and social activities – and who you know, the groups you associate with) are forged to make a form of 'sub-cultural capital' which has a currency outside of the 'legitimate' circuits of capital. So knowing about white label pre-release dance records does not have much value outside of the field of the sub-culture and is unlikely to improve chances of social movement (unless you are lucky enough to work for a specialist music company). But knowledge has an intermediary exchange-value when it can be converted into economic capital. Although Thornton argues that sub-cultural capital is not as class-bound as cultural capital, her research tends to suggest otherwise. For instance, she shows how the distinctions between different sorts of music and their use have strong class, sexuality and gender signs: Handbag House, Sharon and Tracey Music, Cheesy House do not have a convertible value; rather, they are signals of the 'mass', an inscription that marks the unknowing, uncritical, tasteless group, from which the sub-culture draws its distinction. What Thornton identifies as sub-cultural capital could be seen as a form of mis-recognition of a version of middle-class plundering, appropriation and distinction-making. Just as with most popular music, the working-classes (usually male) function as a resource that can be used for the career-making of middle-class music industry intermediaries. I am not suggesting that there is not a mixed-class dance culture, rather that those who can make their knowledge of the culture work for them are far more likely to be middle-class because it is about access to resources. In the conversion from cultural to economic capital the middle-classes are likely to be the ones who have access to the social networks in the industry that can enable the conversion to be made. They will have had access to, and learnt how to convert themselves into subjects with exchange-value. There is a difference, and I'd argue it's a class difference, between those who just enjoy the dance music culture for pleasure and those who can put it to work for them to increase their exchange-value (their capital composition and volume).

Mis-recognition, in this sense, works like Marx's theory of commodity fetishism: the theory of the magical power of the commodity which, stripped of its basis in historical social relations of unequal power, appears merely as the consequence of a contractual exchange between equivalents (Marx 1967:163–77). The power necessary to make a conversion is not recognized. Fetishes, then, emerge from cultural accumulation when utilized as capital. But some groups are even beyond fetishizing. For instance, as discussed in Chapter 5, Haylett (2001) revealed how the white working-classes have not just been plundered for culture, but have also been used as symbols of a generalized 'backwardness', a constitutive limit, necessary to figure the middle-classes as positioned at the 'vanguard of the modern' and in a moral category referring to liberal, cosmopolitan, work and consumption-based lifestyles and values.

So, whilst some aspects of the working-classes can be usefully opened up and commodified as cultural properties, exchange-values, attachments or prosthesis, other parts of working-class culture are beyond appropriation. But this may be because they are trying to defend their culture, to block exchange, for nothing is given in return.

In their research Bennett *et al.* (1999) discuss the proclamations issued between 1559 and 1597, seeking to regulate sumptuary practice in England and Wales. These proclamations contained explicit instructions about what was proper or improper, decorous or indecorous, in the use of valued goods by the different degrees of social rank,[13] *codifying and imposing values upon a set of material objects and their proper use* within the framework of a status system. The proclamations legislated the 'proper use' within a set of relations between cultural goods and a system of social power. The taxonomic regimes that govern cultural practice in modern social formations are considerably less inflexible than those governed by strict custom or by the authority of church and state, but, they argue, we can still identify similar systems of codification, what they call 'regimes of value'.

They also challenge Bourdieu's restricted definition of field-delimited high cultural (capital) taste, on the basis of the singular logic of the homology between the hierarchical ordering of cultural domains and the stratified order of social class (Bourdieu 1986). Their definition allows space for Clifford's (1988) 'art-culture system', a system which classifies objects and accords them value relative to one another; it also establishes the context in which they properly belong, and between which they circulate (Lury 1997a).

Appadurai (1986) argues that the movement of goods within and across societies is shaped by the distribution of a combination of technical, social and aesthetic knowledge in the pathways through which they flow. The knowledge available on these pathways is unevenly distributed and attributed with unequal values. Knowledge is also a contested domain in which challenges to the value and meaning of 'things' is in constant flux. Even if a particular object or practice is attributed value in circuits of exchange and flows, this may not be the way it is received and converted for use.[14] For instance, Willis *et al.* (1990) show how a process of 'grounded aesthetics' may take place which converts commodities into local use-value through modification which makes them appropriate to cultures for which they were not intended. Also, research shows how the middle-class are not valued or authorized by the working-class, nor are middle-class self-dispositions desired. In fact, the middle-class are regularly viewed as having moral flaws in terms of snobbery, elitism and competitiveness or pretentiousness (Skeggs 1997), rather than attachment to family, sincere personal relations, loyalty and honour (Lamont 2000).

However, a whole raft of institutional apparatus exists to institutionalize entitlements. Margaret Davies (1998), for instance, details how the law converts entitlements into property defining an 'exclusive territory of rights and responsibilities attaching to each owned thing' (p.155). Drawing on Derrida's (1974) 'metaphysics of the proper' she charts how the proper[15] designates the connection of a name to a thing, e.g. the right thing. Yet, as she shows, the thing drops out of the property relation: 'It is the relation which constitutes the property: the thing does not motivate ownership. I could compare this to the way in which the thing or the referent drops out of the structure of signification' (Davies 1998:159).

Exclusion from the relationship to the proper entitlement structures significance. So it is not just the value generated from a system of exchange but the way relationship to exchange is institutionalized. There is a right way to appropriate, one has to be *marked as entitled* in the first place:

> The proper entitles in the sense of giving identity and boundaries to an object, and in the sense of giving authority to a person or term which defines the existence of the object. The proper is right, in the sense of appropriate, but it also points to certain inherent rights.
>
> (Davies 1998:165)

The decision to propertize or not constructs the object.[16] The purpose of property law is to create scarcity and value in objects (in intellectual property law this is by prohibiting uncontrolled imitation).[17] These legal entitlements are made available to those who fit their proper position. So appropriation of others can be established as an entitlement to others that constructs them as object or part object. Those who have access to law and inhabit the proper positions can make use of this. But it is not only authorization of entitlements by law; Bourdieu also sees taste as a process which classifies through the use of authorization as well as ridicule. Radin (1993) details how a history of property entitlements generates the terms of person-hood (exemplified in possessive individualism). This means that the more closely connected to personhood, the stronger the sense of entitlement and the more likely entitlements are institutionalized in law. If you aim to like something or judge something without the appropriate entitlement, you will be the subject of ridicule[18] (Cook 2000:102). Herzfeld (1999) argues that the rhetoric of identity makes property relations integral to governance by categorizations. So those who occupy proper categorizations can authorize their relationships within the appropriate regime of values.

This has led to many contestations over appropriation. Weiner (1992), for instance, shows how inalienable possessions, that is those possessions felt to represent the identities of the transactors themselves, become a site of legal and cultural struggle. Identity, she argues, depends on maintaining an exclusive association with a distinctive set of symbolic practices; this is culture as property. Even when identity symbols do not figure as goods in any system of exchange, and indeed are not even economic assets in any obvious sense, Harrison (1999) notes that they are, however, capable of being copied.

The different types of personhood produce different entitlements and authoriza-tions. How these are institutionalized is central to how different systems of exchange and use-value can operate.

Conclusion

Theories of the self assert an assumed and often unrecognized class position, reproducing a form of entitlement to others, their cultures, bodies and practices. This entitlement operates as a form of mis-recognition (in the sense identified by Bourdieu), in which it is understood as a technological effect, an aesthetic composition, a form of de-differentiation, experimentation, a lifestyle. The disposition of entitlement is one of the most obvious ways that class is written on the body, as it can be read as rights, privilege, access to resources, cultural capital, self-authorization and propriety.

Just as personhood was once only available to the upper-classes, we now see that certain formations of personality are extended and made available to the middle-classes. Personhood and selfhood are both a product of, and produce, class inequality. Claiming selfhood can be seen as performative of class, as selfhood brings into effect entitlements not only denied to others, but reliant on others being made available both as a resource and a constitutive limit. Thus, we can identify a new form of possessive individualism based on experimentation, 'doing' and affect, in which processes of out-contextualization and in-differentiation, as identified in the formation of the prosthetic self in prosthetic culture by Lury (1998), are class-specific formations. These entitled selves and class formations are nation specific and also indicative of the use and access to different resources by different factions of the middle-classes.

To have entitlement is to be part of a system of exchange in which difference is materialized by culture, through authorization by cultural intermediaries and their institutionalized practices. Entitlement is also about the ability to authorize and institutionalize one's perspective in order to literalize and legitimate the practices of oneself. This self-authorizing of perspective makes possible a variety of different types of appropriation – from fetishism to mediation – and enables the conversion of cultural capital into symbolic capital. Yet working-class culture is not point zero of culture; rather, it has a different value system, one not recognized by the dominant symbolic economy. The forms of exchange in which the working-classes can engage are different, for they are not seen to possess any of the entitled selves (and subsequent entitlements, projections and legitimations) identified in this chapter. The working-classes do not use, accrue and develop culture in the same way; the working-classes' relationship to culture is different.

Culture, as an exchange-value in self-formation, becomes a resource, a form of property and, therefore, propertizable. Propertizing personhood entails a shift in perspective, from exchange as objects and/or labour, to exchange as a focus on the *relationships of entitlement* to others. For Marx, the transformations of objects into possessions is through labour; now, I'd argue, it is also through culture, whereby particular forms of culture are made into objects to be possessed. A focus on culture transfers our attention to the form the transactions take and the power that informs these transactions and to how different forms of exchange create different relations. One of the great mis-recognitions of Western modern society, Strathern (1999) argues, is to view the market itself as a coherent and overarching 'system' that accords exchange-value in a homogeneous way. Rather, such transactions generate the impression of a system.

This is not to deny the importance of economic organization, labour, work, etc., but to suggest that culture is an exchange-value too, that can also be made subject to appropriation, exploitation, legalization, etc., but also resistance. Culture also involves labour; it is produced. This is not a model about cultural incorporation (c.f. Williams 1973) in which the base incorporates and nullifies working-class culture, or even leaves the radical potential of some of it behind (e.g. Grossberg 1988); instead, it is a model which sees class struggle partially fought out through entitlement to the cultures, experiences and affects of others, whereby not just working-class labour but also culture becomes a resource, plundered for elements made useful to others. This could be seen as a peculiarly British take on class relations, but I'd argue it has much wider applicability, as evidenced in global marketing and the deployment of similar strategies across race, gender and sexuality (Franklin *et al.* 2000).

But the working-class do not just figure as a culture to be plundered for opening out of new markets and useful attachments, as dramatic and performative. Rather, the progressiveness of the new middle-class self is predicated on holding in place that which must signify stagnation and immobility. The working-class is fragmented as a resource that functions in a variety of ways to sustain the modernity of factions of the middle-class. The working-class is both fixed in place so that others can move, but also available as a resource that can be used. So the political rhetoric described in Chapter 5 fixes, whilst the representations outlined in Chapter 6 enable exchange-value to be identified, and used by those who utilize the 'selves' described in this chapter. These are the conditions of possibility that shape class relations.

Yet the working-class, both within and outside the circuits of symbolic distribution, resist appropriation, continually threatening to expose and ridicule the pretensions and inaccuracy of new middle-class formations. Therefore, the fragility and vulnerability of the new middle-class self has to be continually authorized and asserted, continually struggling to be taken seriously, and seen as worthy of moral authority. Entitlements have to be institutionalized, perspectives authorized, and property legitimated. This is where class struggle is being fought. The next chapter shows how this takes place spatially and through particular gendered and sexed configurations, by which members of the new middle-class try to constitute themselves as subjects with value.

9 Beyond appropriation

Proximate strangers, fixing femininity, enabling cosmopolitans

This chapter develops the themes of the last, focusing on 'new' aesthetic and prosthetic middle-class selves by drawing attention to the types of *relationships* between different classes. It illustrates how different dispositions – 'the cosmopolitan' and 'the excessive' – are read and constituted as classed positions. To explore these classed relationships I rely on an account of context, of how some physical spaces bring together groups into proximity that would otherwise remain separate. These encounters force a reading of proximate bodies and, in some cases, generate a need for boundary maintenance.[1] It is not just the encounter but the relationships generated from the encounter between bodies that rely on prior systems of inscription – rhetoric, representation, discourse – identified in previous chapters, that provide methods for reading others. This chapter shows how the reliance on systems of inscription, and their accordant value, positions some groups as the ground of fixity, otherness, strangerness and danger. This sets limits on how they can be used and appropriated, and exposes the limits to exchange-value accumulative selves.

The chapter begins with a frame that charts how some bodies are made readable, analyzing the significance of visible classifications. It then explores how visibility and readability inform new theories of cosmopolitanism to analyse how cosmopolitan dispositions are figured. Moving on, it details how too much visibility sets limits on the exchange-value that is attributed to particular bodies, exposing the constitutive limits of the cosmopolitan. This chapter is, therefore, not just about who can appropriate for their self-constitution but about who and what is appropriable; not only who is entitled, but *who can be propertized*. As before, moral attribution underpins the forms of exchange. The chapter draws on some empirical research findings to illuminate the points being made.

Aesthetics, Eagleton (1989) argues, is the space that mediates between property and propriety through which structures of power become structures of feeling. He describes how manners operate as the crucial hinge between ethics and aesthetics. The meticulous disciplining of the body enables the conversion of morality to style, aestheticizing virtue. This is especially the case on women's bodies, as the latter section of this chapter will demonstrate.

Some people, however, have no choice about visibility. Black women and men, for instance, are always read through highly visible systems of colour coding. Ahmed

(1998b) notes that for most black women and men, skin is seen as a stained physical 'reality' that cannot be transformed or contained. It is the physicality. Gunew (2000) outlines how, in academic theory, the visible body is used to explain differences, evoking the incommensurability of post-colonial theory (the untranslatabilities of cultural difference) and the 'lifestyle incompatibilities' of 'culturalism', cultural racism or prosthetic legitimation (see Chapter 8). This reliance on visibility is at the core of what Balibar (1991) calls 'academic racism', which mimics scientific discursivity by emphasizing 'visible evidence', a 'violent desire for immediate knowledge of social relations' (p.19).

The emphasis on visible evidence also operates legally to circumscribe who is made public and who can have access to the private. Berlant and Warner (1998), for instance, chart how gay men have legally been deprived of the 'private' in US law, and Moran (1997) provides legal evidence to illustrate how the state intervenes in gay male lives in the UK, denying them the 'private' privileges accorded to heterosexuals. As Weeks (1981) argues, in relation to gay men, they are read as *the* sign of sex; some people are made visible and public, whilst others are allowed to occupy and have access to the private.

It is interesting that radical politics have relied on this method of visible public classifications to make political claims. Fraser (1999) suggests that we explore the constitutive limits that enable the articulation of any form of classification. She observes how the forms of politics that literally can be made visible have an advantage. This visibility is produced through a process of materialization that constitutes the 'matter' of bodies. Matter does not exist in and of itself, outside of discourse; rather it is repeatedly produced through performativity. Performativity is that which 'brings it into being or enacts that which it names' (Butler 1993:134). For queer politics, the desire to make visible, to bring the queer body into view, is the way in which matter is converted into politics; the queer body is brought into being. This relies on becoming visible, but, as Fraser points out, it also relies on a particular aestheticization of the body. This aestheticization, Hennessy (1995) argues, obscures the social relations that make it possible. For example, only some bodies can be visibly outed; for instance, black bodies are read always as black in the Western world; gay men are read as the sign of sex. Theories of performativity, therefore, assume a body that can be read and known that the performativity can be recognized and people want to actively take up forms of identification via visible classification (e.g. queer). As my earlier *Formations of Class and Gender* (Skeggs 1997) ethnography demonstrated, however, white working-class women may not want to be recognizable, to identify or to performatively aestheticize their body in a way circumscribed by prior systems of visible recognition which, as the rest of the book has demonstrated, work to constantly devalue them. For black women, too, who are constantly made visible in conditions not of their own choosing, Ahmed (2000) notes that performativity of categorizations may not be an option. The re-appropriation of signifiers by radical politics at the level of the symbolic may, therefore, only work for some. Challenging signifiers may also have no impact at all (for instance, ironic masculinity may only serve to reinforce power and not destabilize at all: see Cronin 2000a).

The prior debates about the aesthetic/prosthetic, or omnivorous middle-class self in Chapter 8, rely on this process of making visible, for only already visually evaluated body parts, practices or culture can be used as a resource in the process of self-making. And it is the job of cultural intermediaries to make visible what was previously hidden, thereby attributing new value to new visibilities. I now want to explore how this works through theories of cosmopolitanism.

Discrepant cosmopolitans

Becoming user-friendly

We can identify two major strands of cosmopolitanism:[2] incorporation and universalism. The former is represented by Zizek (1997), who argues that cosmopolitanism can only ever be incorporating as it is a product of the cultural logic of global capitalism. Zizek makes his arguments through examples of US multiculturalism:[3]

> Multiculturalism involves patronising Eurocentrist distance and/or respect for local cultures without roots in one's own particular culture. In other words, multiculturalism is a disavowed, inverted, self-referential form of racism, a racism with a distance – it respects the Other's identity, conceiving the Other as a self-enclosed 'authentic' community towards which he [sic], the multiculturalist, maintains a distance rendered possible by his privileged universal position. Multiculturalism is a racism which empties its own position of all positive content (the multiculturalist is not a direct racist, he doesn't oppose to the Other the particular values of his own culture), but nonetheless retains this position as the privileged empty point of universality from which one is able to appreciate (and depreciate) properly other particular cultures – the multicultural respect for the Other's specificity is the very form of asserting one's own superiority.
>
> (Zizek 1997:44)

A cosmopolitan citizenship is, therefore, based on one's ability and resources to participate in the global capitalist economy. For Zizek the only two contemporary alternatives for citizenship are a cosmopolitan global capitalism or totalitarianism, nationalism and fascism. This is similar to Brennan (1997), who maintains that cosmopolitanism inevitably makes one complicit with global formations of capital. The second contrasting perspective is presented by Cheah (1998) and Beck (2000). Cheah argues that cosmopolitanism has the potential to 'better express or embody genuine universalism',[4] and Beck (2000) suggests that cosmopolitanism is the way in which we can learn 'how to imagine, define and analyse post-national, transnational and political communities' as a way of understanding the second stage of modernism (p.90).

Work on cosmopolitanism tends to emphasize that cosmopolitans are at the privileged, empowered end of what Massey (1994) terms the power-geometry of time-space compression (see Chapter 3 on mobility). Cosmopolitans are seen as elite professionals in high-status occupations, members of what Leslie Sklair (2001) calls the transnational capitalist class, or what Robbins (2001) terms 'the liberal managerial class'. However, Pnina Werbner (1999) argues that 'even working-class labour migrants may become cosmopolitans, if willing to engage with the Other' (p.18).

The majority of debates about cosmopolitanism are made through three different discourses: cosmopolitan as anti-national, as a form of consumption, and as a form of subjectivity. In this section of the chapter the emphasis is on the latter two and how they intervene in the polarized positions represented by Zizek and Brennan in opposition to Cheah and Beck. Beck's desire for learning how to have solidarity with strangers can also be seen as Zizek's fantasy of incorporation. However, Beck (2000) does note that: cosmopolitan society means cosmopolitan society and its enemies. Just as there are, to borrow Lash's (1994) terms, reflexivity winners and losers, for Beck there are similarly cosmopolitan winners and losers. Central to these different positions is the understanding that culture is a property that can be owned in particular ways by certain groups. The *relationship of ownership and entitlement* for culture is central to understanding class differences.

The most frequently used definitions of cosmopolitanism assume that to be cosmopolitan one has to be able to appropriate, distinguish and claim to know the other in order to generate authority and disposition from this knowing. Ulf Hannerz (1996) maintains that:

> A more genuine cosmopolitanism is first of all of an orientation, a willingness to engage with the Other. It entails an intellectual and aesthetic openness toward divergent cultural experiences, a search for contrasts rather than uniformity. To become acquainted with more cultures is to turn into an aficionado, to view them as artworks. At the same time, however, cosmopolitanism can be a matter of competence, and competence of both a generalised and a more specialised kind. There is the aspect of a state of readiness, a persona; ability to make one's way into other cultures, through listening, looking, intuiting, and reflecting.
>
> (Hannerz 1996:103)

A more detailed articulation of Bourdieu's (1986) analysis of how class is formed through knowledge and disposition would be hard to find; as would a greater sense of entitlement. To turn the intellectual gaze into a form of knowledge and competence for one's own enhancement is precisely how cosmopolitanism as a disposition is generated. This must involve access to the cultures of others, turning them into objects of distanced contemplation for oneself. The intellectual cosmopolitans learn to know themselves through travelling through the cultures of others. This then is the aesthetic/prosthetic self, shopping, sizing-up the value of what is available, participating in the art-culture system of otherness, where others become a resource – in the propertizing of the self. The property of this possessive individual is premised on access to valued cultural resources; on accruing cultural value through drawing to oneself the culture of others.

Cosmopolitanism, therefore, as an *embodied entitled subjectivity* relies on the requisite cultural resources (time, access, knowledge) for generating the requisite dispositions. Beck (2000) suggests that we have entered the second stage of modernity, in which not only have relations between and beyond national states altered, but so has the inner quality of the social and political. This, he argues, makes cosmopolitanism an institutionalized learning process; learning to know how to make cultural judgements about what is worth appropriating to produce ourselves as cosmopolitan. Also, as Skeggs (2001; 2002) and Zizek (1997) note, global capitalism is devoted to exploiting difference and marketing it as multicultural and/or cosmopolitan. In order to know who, how and why to engage with others we also need to know their value; is their culture worth knowing, experimenting with? And value is established through different symbolic economies (such as those outlined in the previous chapter: taste, art-culture system, lifestyle), in different fields.

To make this point more clearly, I will now digress into a brief analysis of a local gay space that prides itself on having value by being both sub-cultural and cosmopolitan. A great deal has already been written about this area.[5] The area is the 'gay Village' in Manchester, a north west city in the UK, the heart of the industrial revolution from where Engels famously worked and funded Marx (see Wheen 1999). The area developed from the de-industrialized space of warehouses and canals, its modern reincarnation produced by the independent initiative of two local gay entrepreneurs. The space now includes over 50 bars and restaurants and is principally a space for leisure consumption. Some key members of the area have been recruited by the City Council to a team to generate international investment for Manchester.[6] For instance, Joanna, from *Marketing Manchester*, notes:

> It is obviously a unique selling point that Manchester has. It has taken time to get it accepted by some of the board in our organization; however, the fact that the council are seen to be gay friendly, the minister of tourism is, or it comes under his department, and the BTA (British Tourism Authority) have now decided to actively and openly promote the UK, it has gained credence and I've been able to suggest that this could be an official policy now and it is one of our target markets.
>
> (Key Informant Interview, 1998)

The development of the concept 'global gay' signals both those who consume and sites of consumption (Altman 1996; 1997; 2001). In a gay take on the multiculturalism of the Zizek–Beck debate, similar issues are raised. The 'global gay' is most likely to be represented as a model global consumer, contributing disproportionately to transnational flows of capital through participation in, for example, global gay tourism (Evans 1993; Altman 1996; 1997; 2001). In terms of cosmopolitanism this represents particular issues, similar to those expressed in the multicultural debate (and multicultures are about sexuality as well as race). On the one hand the rise of the 'global gay' has been celebrated as a form of queer politics – 'We're here, we're queer' and other events are organized around this global association, such as corporate and institutionalized *Mardi Gras* in Sydney and Manchester. Moreover, the global gay is incited to consume (places and bodies) through a range of travel guides and adverts in international pink papers and magazines (*Spartacus* is an international bestseller and most tourist guides list lesbian and gay spaces). The Internet has enabled further global communication (although usually restricted to Anglo/Spanish speakers). However, on the other hand, the cosmopolitan losers' side, the argument is that global gay discourse represents Western gay men as a cipher for hyper-mobile, affluent and privileged consumers. Peter Jackson (1999) berates those who deploy the term 'global gay' to describe the internationalization of Western gay identity. He argues it is a term plagued by ethnocentrism, which reduces indigenous cultures and discourses to specific commercial spaces.

Yet, within the local space itself, campaigning group Healthy Gay Manchester spatialize and mark their presence in the village through symbolic adornment with banners and flags, and describe the Gay Village as the pride of Europe:

> Manchester's stature as a European gay Mecca continues to thrive as visitors flock from all over to sample its unique spirit. At the heart of this fast-growing, post-industrial city sits the eclectic café society of the Lesbian and Gay Village – a cosmopolitan showcase bursting with pride, and one of the queerest pieces of real estate Europe has to offer.
>
> (*Healthy Gay Manchester's Guide to Lesbian and Gay Greater Manchester*,
> Healthy Gay Manchester, 1998)

Interestingly, this HIV campaigning group draws attention to the real estate value of the area. The tourist board, local and national listing magazines (reliant usually on PR or press releases), TV programmes on loft living and estate agents' publicity similarly reproduce the Village as cosmopolitan, diverse, tolerant and European (even global). Those who own businesses in the Village market it as an integrating, mixed space which has one essential feature, '*gayness*': 'Obviously the village is grown on the back of the fact that this is a lesbian and gay space. The reason that people come here is for the gayness of it, even if they are not gay' (John, Marketing Director, Metz Bar).

Tellingly, one of the major clubs in the area is called 'Essential'. Lury (1997b:82) describes as 'discrepant cosmopolitanism' the ways in which

> the designated objects of cosmopolitanism become marked with particular qualities, such as friendly, fun and fashionable; the *user-friendliness* of objects, a user-friendliness as the quality in objects that reciprocates the open-mindedness of people.

In this case the marketing of 'gayness', of gay people, becomes a way of both essentializing and trading on a particular lifestyle, turning that lifestyle into a commodifiable object. The essentializing of gayness is a requirement for marketing the area, as our focus groups have consistently shown. The 'gayness' of the area makes it unique, gives it its sub-cultural and cosmopolitan character, and 'gayness' is used to draw people of other sexualities into the village. For instance, Julie, a straight woman from our focus group, notes: 'Gay people just have this liberated – you can do whatever you like type attitude' (SW Manchester Focus Group 2). Gayness, therefore, can be easily branded – it has a quality that can be read back onto the space. It fulfils the requirements identified by Zizek for a multicultural global market. It has a warm and user-friendly quality, perfect for discrepant cosmopolitans, perfect for the entitled-discerning, mobile cosmopolitan.

But to work as a marker of cosmopolitanism the space also has to be safe. Propriety is central to the ways in which consumers and users of the village are able to make investments in it (Moran and Skeggs 2001a; 2001b). In terms of queer politics this has paradoxical effects, producing in the gay male body both the sign of propriety and the 'essence' of sex. Gay men are culturally essentialized – branded – through sexuality in a way that can now be seen as a cultural property with marketable value.[7] Zizek would argue that they have been incorporated into the capitalist nexus, whereas Beck (2000) would read the incorporation differently, as 'strangeness is replaced by the amazement at similarities' (p.88).

Mica Nava (1996), however, argues against the simple equations of cosmopolitanism with the imperatives of global capital or liberal humanism, and suggests other alternatives. Because, she contends, gender is usually overlooked as emphasis is placed on men, gay and straight, in cosmopolitan debates other readings have been ignored. In an historical examination of Selfridges department store in London, she shows how the marketing relied on 'cosmopolitan campaigns', focusing on the Russian dancer Nijinsky:

> It is interesting to note that gay-male creations of male sexuality and the eroticised male body – in this instance Diaghilev's shaping of Nijinsky – seem to have opened up for women spectators during this period more active and desiring libidinous fantasies.
>
> (Nava 1998:177)

And, we could argue, public space. Whilst exotic gay male sexuality was used (and branded) by Selfridges as a marketing strategy to generate new shoppers, the side-effect of this was to enable a reshaping of gendered fantasies and heterosexual possibility. Here we see cosmopolitanism offering gains for some groups at the expense of others, all understood through distinctions made on the basis of class: remember only middle-class women were positioned as respectable in public (e.g. Walkowitz 1989; Nead 1988), as potential shoppers. In our contemporary research we find striking parallels with Nava's research on the gender aspect, in which white working-class heterosexual women are using gay space to:

- reject traditional hetero-masculinity;
- assert their claim on public space not of their own making (the use of the village for all women parties);
- facilitate a transitional space for moving through sexualities;
- enjoy the voyeuristic pleasure of looking.

However, their presence in the space creates particular problems for lesbians who then feel displaced from the space for which they campaigned politically, but from which they have also been marginalized as consumers (see Skeggs 2001).

Differences *and* connections are drawn in the gay space, but these have very particular effects. For instance, in a response to the 'Integrate don't Discriminate' campaign of Metz bar, we hear a call for a return from café culture to sub-culture. Making the space cosmopolitan appears to have entailed significant losses:

> In hindsight it seems that as a group we were more strongly defined from outside, through marginalisation, and now that marginalisation has been diluted. Instead of pariahs we have become little more than a bit of cosmopolitan flavour among the students and parties of office workers on a Friday night out.
>
> (Scott Smith, 1999, Healthy Gay Manchester Newsletter)

Claiming that the space offered a sense of community ten years ago (1989), Scott Smith argues that it was not the homophobia that killed the space but the power of cash. He equates cosmopolitanism with consumption, himself a necessary commodity in this process, and the loss of marginalization as necessary to the gay community. So, whilst some respectable gay men and straight women can enjoy the space, others feel displaced and objectified. Those drawn into the area must be of a particular type.[8] There are, however, some who destroy the cosmopolitan flavour entirely. They stop making it user-friendly, block branding, interrupt incorporation, disturb the fascination with others, disrupt propriety, and generate fear and danger. And guess who they are?

The cosmopolitan limit

Those who represent the limit to the use of space and experience are *always* read though classification systems based on visibility, on their clothing, their body (shapes, sizes, walks) and their aurality (language and noise level). Consider the following, for instance:

> Yes, I know the lad that stands on the door of Velvet with the bouncers. He works in the bar, he's a little sweetheart and I remember once I was stood on the door with him, it was on a Saturday. So I stood on the door and it was such an eye-opener, it was such an experience because stood there for that very short half hour, at the end of it I went 'How do you do this job?' because the amount of gangs of lads with the checked polo shirts – they call them Opal Fruits. They must ring each other up and say are you wearing the green one tonight? You know what I mean they've all got different colours on ... And they just wouldn't leave it alone and the same thing with gangs of girls that came up to the door you know with the little fluffy bras and he just said no.
>
> (Louise, Manchester Straight Women, Focus Group 4, 2000)

The Opal Fruit shirt is the key signifier of belonging to the working-class and works like the little fluffy bra to signify tastelessness. Noted for their tenacity, the really distinguishing feature is that the working-class appear in 'gangs'. (Note that in prosthetic theories of the self you cannot attach a gang.) Lads and scallies are rarely represented historically in the singular. Such men are also in the space for the wrong reasons:

> It's one of those bars you do go there to cop off it's really horrible … I went in once for a drink and all it is everyone is staring at one another seeing who they can chat up next, it's just like a dating agency and – *Salford* started going in there, *gangs of Salford* and *Cheetham Hill* they all started going in there and it got to the stage the police were patrolling the outside of Mash and Air. They had cameras, they had a big van outside and cameras were running on it.
>
> (Louise, Manchester Straight Women, Focus Group 4, 2000)
> (emphasis added)

The danger signs are developed further through reading behaviour as a lack of appropriate education and knowing how to use the space correctly; importantly, their geographical tag is a signifier of class. They are identified as coming from the poorest areas and estates. They are gangs of Salford (note not people from) and Cheetham Hill (the myth of Gunchester as Manchester).[9] Geography is read as culture to locate their difference. These gangs have entered the village, a space of user-friendly propriety, from a position of geographical fixity, a mechanism by which they can be known, placed and contained, into a space of mobile users. And they entered it in the wrong way, to cop off. To authenticate the threat that they represent to the space, police with cameras enhance the narrative.

However, most bizzarely, the gangs from the marginalized areas do not represent the greatest threat, *but … hen parties*:

Ali: Then you'll see packs of girls …

Raj: Mm, hen parties

Ali: Hen parties. You'll see it all over the place where you'll walk past and they'll be scratching themselves and skitting themselves and all the rest of it but they will wait in the queue. You know, there'll be at least 15 girls or whatever.

> (Manchester Gay Men, Focus Group 3, 2000)

Not only can hen parties be easily identifiable (noise, appearance, use of space), they embody en masse nearly every negative class, sexual and gender association. They travel in 'packs' (at least 15!) and they are bodily repulsive through behaviour, such as scratching and skitting (skitting is the polite shorthand for 'taking the piss' which means that anything within the space becomes a potential object of humour). They are ubiquitous. They take over the hard-won space. They are definitely out of place, excessive in every way: alchohol, noise, femininity, bodily display, often excessive heterosexuality. This is all coded as the ultimate in tastelessness, as Pete notes:

Yeah, I mean like we talked about the Northern Quarter, a lot of my straight friends go out there 'cos that is the new up-and-coming area. The Village is seen as cheesy – 'cos we are getting hen parties, we are getting your ... do you know, the trendier people who are using it when Manto's first started, they are now moving on to *other areas, so you are getting your more you know, coach loads from Oldham and Rochdale* and that sort of place.

(Pete, Manchester Gay Men, Focus Group 2, 2000)

(emphasis addded)

Pete's comments show how the fickle nature of gay consumption is tied into cultural capital and the place-making of distinctions. The whole of the Village has become so infiltrated by hen parties from geographically named satellite towns that they no longer work to signify trendiness, and dilute the user-friendly gay essence necessary for discrepant cosmopolitanism. Such is the disgust and ubiquity of hen party invasion that two of our key informant interviewees went out of their way to distinguish themselves from hen parties. For instance:

Lucy: (bar manager Via Fossa) We don't get hen parties or anything like that, you know, we're not like mainstream Yates's-straight-women, we're not, you know.

Steph: (bar manager Manto) I see some terrible sights over the weekend, like hen parties dragging 'L-signs' and blow-up men, dolls sort of things like that ... I don't think it's the right space for them. That's what I think personally. But there are bars further up the street that do cater for straight women.

Paul: (researcher) What, Manto's not the right place for straight women?

Steph: Trendy women, yeah. Trendy, but not the normal everyday Sharon and Tracey I would say 'No'. I don't think that you would enjoy yourself in Manto. You're best going somewhere like Bar 38 where it's the complete opposite.

(Manchester Key Informant Interviewees, 1998)

Just as Sarah Thornton's trendy clubbers used direct references to working-class 'Sharon and Tracey' (see Chapter 8), 'Sharon and Tracey' is again a semiotic shorthand for the wrong sort of woman. From the above bar manager's comments we can see that, in order to sustain their commercial viability, bars promote themselves in a way that institutionalizes class representations. They define themselves in opposition to that which disturbs their forms of address to other potential customers. Yates Wine Lodge, the stereotype par excellence of a working-class locale, is held as the absolute other, exactly what Via Fossa and Manto are not, according to their managers. Hen parties disturb marketability; their bodies and presence disturb user-friendliness.

But why? Why are they such a threat? To disrupt propriety and entitled cosmo-politanism is one thing, to be marked out so clearly that such women become a performative, almost an unchallenged, citation, taken up and spoken to expel the other, is another. The ubiquity of the threatening hen, I'd argue, draws attention to how space figures in the making and maintenance of class distinction. The unusual thing about the Village is the range of different people who use it. Our census survey found almost every identity category possible, including those who could or would not identify themselves along a gender/sexuality/race/class axis. The proximity of all these different groups in one small space produces easy readings (or mis-recognition: Skeggs 2001) made through visible interpretations, informed by historical taste classifiers. The hen parties' proximity in space, their obviousness, their visibility, embodies and condenses on the body prior historical classification systems, enabling them to be easily read and attributed with no value. This leads to their becoming the most regularly cited target of disruption to the space. They come to stand in for all that threatens the space: heterosexuality, women in public and out of control and working-class. The 'scally' (working-class male) is put to the same use, but as the scally also has a double meaning as 'bit of rough' (potential rent boy or gay), it is less easy to condense its readability, to make the same distinction.

As Bhabha (1996) noted in Chapter 8, proximity – not distance – now figures and makes a difference. The dangerous other does not threaten; rather, the proximate stranger who is not easily identifiable presents anxieties. The inability to draw distance and distinguish dangerous others means that proximity continually poses a symbolic threat to the boundary maintanance of the self, for those who can have a self. This has led to what Ahmed (2000) identifies as 'stranger fetishism', which works simultaneously to expel the stranger as the origin of danger, but also (through multiculturalism) to welcome some strangers as the origin of difference, a potential object of consumption with possibilities to propertize. This process also takes place in gay male culture, especially around the figure of the skinhead. According to Nayak (1999), skinheads purposely generate a trademark in themselves through clothing and, in particular, the haircut. This produces a geometry of menace, and also a form of protection of their image as white, heterosexual working-class hard men. This was an image produced in opposition to the perceived effeminacy of the middle-class hippy. But, as Healy (1996) shows, this cannot always be guaranteed, as the take-up of the skinhead trademark has long been in place in gay culture. The working-class gay male is welcome as a marketable sign of cosmopolitanism, safe and user-friendly, whilst the working-class woman signals that which is not cosmopolitan.

Ahmed notes that stranger fetishism can be read not only as a displacement of social relations onto an object (in the traditional Marxist take on fetishism), but also through the transformation of objects into figures: 'stranger fetishism is a fetishism of figures; it invests the figure of the stranger with a life of its own insofar as it cuts "the stranger" off from histories of its own determination' (p.5). She shows how narratives that construct 'the strange culture' as their object (distance) are also contaminated by that very object (by proximity). They involve, simultaneously, social and spatial relations of distance *and* proximity. 'Others become strangers (the ones who are distant), and other cultures become strange cultures (the ones who are distant), only through coming too close to home, that is, through the proximity of the encounter or "facing itself"' (p.12). This may be what Beck (2000) means when he calls for embracing the stranger. But, as our research indicates, there are some strangers who are beyond embrace. Their differences cannot be made user-friendly. They only hinder the development of cosmopolitan dispositions.[10] They are *beyond appropriation*, because they do not offer any cultural value to the self that accumulates or plays with others.

Also, it is not just whole bodies or cultures that are fetishized in 'stranger danger'; rather, aspects of bodies and cultures are read as strange, dangerous or appropriable. So, whole bodies and cultures are not taken on in the construction of the aesthetic/ prosthetic self, but rather the aspects that can be fetishized, which are seen to add value to the self who has entitlement and access to, and is powerful enough to appropriate, others/strangers. Understanding of distance, proximity, danger, strangers and safety is informed by symbolic systems of exchange in which bodies are attributed value (moral value, commodity, sub-cultural, etc.). When bodies which have different symbolic values enter the same space, the readings are made through the relations of potential exchange. Ahmed argues:

> When we face others, we seek to recognise who they are, by reading the signs on their body, or by reading their body as a sign. As I will argue, such acts of reading constitute 'the subject' in relation to 'the stranger', who is recognised as 'out of place' in a given place. The surprising nature of encounters can be understood in relation to the structural possibility that we may not be able to read the bodies of others. However, each time we are faced by an other whom we cannot recognise, we seek to find other ways of achieving recognition, not only by re-reading the body of this other who is faced, but by telling the difference between this other, and other others. The encounters we might yet have with other others hence surprise the subject, but they also reopen the prior histories of encounter that violate and fix others in regimes of difference.
> (Ahmed 2000:8)

The bodies that circulate and encounter each other in gay space have already been pre-coded for reading, reliant on a visual system of encoding which enables appearance and behaviour to be read and recognized through already established interpretative systems. These symbolic systems have a long history in which bodies are allocated to positions and values in symbolic space.

Traditional understandings of boundary maintenance between groups that rely on the attribution of morality to some groups and not to others do not work in gay space, where historically most of the groups who occupy the space have been historically marginalized, made immoral and used to demarcate boundaries.[11] In a study of the historical epistemology of boundary maintenance, Sonya Rose (1999) shows that when communities become unsure of their identities, moral 'boundary crises' are produced, so they can retain and maintain knowledge of who they are and from whom they are under threat. She demonstrates how frequently moral fears about women's sexuality have been used to shore up the many legitimation crises in masculinity. But this 'gay' space offers a different challenge to boundary maintenance; taste rather than morals becomes significant, provoking the label stranger-danger.

Fixing femininity

The tastelessness of the hen display is, I'd argue, closely related to the distance that is drawn between the hen and respectable femininity. Historically, the categorization of working-class women who were coded as inherently healthy, hardy and robust – often masculinized (whilst also, paradoxically, a source of infection and disease) was made against the frailty of middle-class women. Working-class women were also involved in forms of labour that prevented femininity (appearance and characteristics) from ever being a possibility.[12] Thus, for working-class women, femininity was never a given. Both black and white working-class women were coded as the sexual and deviant other against which femininity was defined (Gilman 1992). Similarly, Hart (1994) charts how, when the category 'lesbian' entered discourse, it did so through an alignment with black, ethnic and white working-class women. Working-class women were not expected to inhabit femininity in the same way as middle- and upper-class white women. Femininity was always something that did not designate working-class women precisely: a sign under which they could not and did not belong. But their distance from it was a requirement for the comfortable occupation of femininity by others who had access to the necessary economic and cultural resources.

So the highly visible, scantily dressed women who make up the 'hen parties' are very much a product of this classificatory history. They are not the universal 'pan-feminine' identified by Stacey (2000), but the localized and particular, read as repositories of negative value, bad taste and culture (as bad-objects rather than subjects) – even though, in terms of the alternatives available, they are strategically investing in themselves and attempting to convert their cultural into economic capital (Lovell 2000; Skeggs 1997). The reading of some women's bodies as excess has long functioned to reproduce traditional distinctions based on class and sexuality.

In a similar way to the middle-class feminist readings of Dolly Parton (as documented by Tyler 1991), Patrick (2001), in a reading of Dusty Springfield shows how the fashioning of feminine excess as a way of 'authenticating' the performance of drag queens enabled feminist critics to also read her as a parody of femininity.[13] In fact she was drawing on the glamour associated with American film stars, which Wilmer (1989) notes was drawn from black female and male music culture, to generate what was read as her feminine excess. For black performers this was always read as not just feminine but also sexual excess (Davis 1995). *Feminine excess means women with visible sexuality*. It is marked on their bodies and coded as tasteless. Femininity without excess is the terrain of the middle-class (as Chapter 6 showed).[14]

Feminist queer theory has often reproduced this excess = tasteless formula. For instance, Biddy Martin (1996) notes how efforts to introduce desire into the definition of lesbianism, and distance it from imperatives to identify with and as feminine-women, have cast (feminine) gender as mere masquerade or as a constraint to be escaped, overridden, or left aside, as the more radical work of queering the world proceeds. Sexuality is cast as that which offers the potential of superseding gender, leaving femininity behind. It is, Martin argues, *the fixed space* from which all others can move (signified by Female-To-Male or Transsexuality: see Halberstam 1998).[15] Martin argues that we need to 'stop defining queerness as mobile and fluid in relation to what gets construed as stagnant and ensnaring' (Martin 1996:46).

Christine Holmund (1993) notes how the femme lesbian, along with the butch clone, and the passing black person, are signs of a refusal of the reduction of the body to a sign of truth. By disrupting the heterosexual matrix and reversing its connections, the femme lesbian blocks easy readability.[16] Yet what is often ignored in the recent feminist queer critiques is that this exchange mechanism is firmly anchored in class; a point well made by earlier lesbian analysis (e.g. Nestle 1987; Lapovsky Kennedy and Davis 1993). So when these encounters occurred in toilets during our research in the Village, the following readings were made:

C: … the only problems that I've ever had in places like Paradise [gay male club] or sort of now really at Manto [urban regeneration gay bar] is from straight women, there's always straight women at those places and they do look at you, like if you go to the toilet.

M: Yes. And when you're in a toilet queue and you've got all these women with like big platform shoes and little short skirts and loads of make-up, and you just, but you do really feel like you're in a minority in the toilet queue and you feel that you, you sort of … I immediately feel like really masculine, loads bigger than them, loads fatter than them, obviously I'm not fat at all, but you know they're all like anorexic, they probably take too many drugs or whatever. And you just feel really, you feel really invaded in your own space and they can't wait to get out again to be with the gay male friends who they think they're really safe with.

J: I was stood in the queue at Manto, I was watching one of those little micro-skirted girls and every lesbian that came out was like with their head down, oh you know … Wouldn't dream of looking. Sort of like, just felt like, you know, just trying to take up as little space as possible. This is a gay space and yet these women …

M: I know like putting hair in your face.

                                              (Manchester, Lesbian Seedcorn Focus Group, 1998)[17]

In these examples, it is not hen parties but excessively feminized singular bodies that are being read in close proximity. Whilst noting that the women who appear feminine are assumed to be heterosexual, and also that they are read through devalued class signifiers of excess (big hair, short skirts, lots of make-up), what is surprising here is the power that the normative feminine invokes, generating comparisons and self-judgement (of fat, masculinity, etc.) and provokes embodied feelings of shame (head held down). This is the language of evaluation, and those who appear feminine are authorized and granted the power (in this small space) to evaluate others. This is a surprising authorization for those who inhabit a category – femininity – that has so little wider symbolic exchange-value. Paradoxically, those who provide the authorization for femininity are also those who have chosen not to invest in it.

There are two types of recognition at play here. First, there is the Fraser (1995) and Taylor (1994) type of politics of recognition, in which certain bodies are read, through their appearance (and dispositions), as having no value. Second, mis-recognition in Bourdieu's sense occurs when symbolic capital has been acquired by a successful act of legitimation which itself veils the social processes and structures that are necessary to existence, so femininity is read as a natural or individualized personality disposition, a form of cultural essentialism. This mis-recognizes the structural and historical formation of femininity, in which working-class women are positioned as immoral and tasteless because of their concern with appearance, one of the only forms of cultural capital on which they can draw. The appearance of femininity in a gay male space simultaneously produces the first and second mis-recognitions. So, it is not a straightforward analysis of dangerous scallies and hen parties, but a way in which class is produced in the contemporary through the historical systems of reading visible bodies that is brought into play, making invisible once again the restricted access to different forms of capital imposed on certain groups of women, and making invisible the labour and social relations that underpin the imperatives and necessity for particular forms of femininity.

Working-class women doing femininity to excess are not read as parodic or ironic, but as authentic, the real from which tasteful distance must be drawn.[18] This is not authenticity with value (as documented in Chapter 6) but the wrong authenticity. But this is a *reading of the surface rather than a reading of the relationships that constitute the object* in the first place; a reading which displays the class-based invest-ments of the reader. These readings must represent a desire by the mobile to fix others and to mark boundaries and distinctions so as not to disrupt their fought-for and/or entitled cosmopolitan pleasures. This is not far from the readings that have been made of pornography, another form of sexual excess. And I now digress into this debate to make the point about making class distinctions from surface readings.

Critiques of pornography are often the product of one class's visceral intolerance of the sexual taste of another (Jancovich 2001). Or rather, I'd argue, it is the split projections of one class's tastes onto another, so that they – the classmaking, the judgement – cannot be held responsible for them but the other can. Mark Jancovich details how even alternative avantgarde feminist performance artists such as Annie Sprinkle, who supposedly challenges and deconstructs pornography, still requires a stable pornographic other against which to define their transgressiveness as an act. As Laura Kipnis (1999) has pointed out, the moral outrage at pornographic forms can often be seen as the desire to distance oneself from, and if possible banish from existence, the cause of one's distress – that is, the sexual expression of people unlike oneself; the excessively sexual stranger. Even 'alternative culture' therefore relies on the foundational ground of class which itself produces it in the very act of defining against it.

There are similarities here with the wider critique of disgust. Stallybrass and White (1986:191) maintain that the rise in the threshold of the disgust function, which Elias (1982) identifies, also bears the offprint of desire for the expelled other, and this becomes the source of fascination, longing and nostalgia. And Roberts (1999a) documents how both disappointment and disgust have framed many of the observations of the middle-class observers who have studied the working-class, who never live up to their expectations: they never have the right things, the right attitudes, the right bodies, the right taste. They are just not user-friendly.

So, whilst the working-class appear as symbolically undervalued, Stallybrass and White (1986) argue that we also need to think that what is socially peripheral is often symbolically central. This can be seen alongside Derrida's notion of the logic of supplementarity, whereby it is not always a fear of otherness but an obsession with otherness that enables obsession to be structured symptomatically. The 'hen-party' signifier condenses a whole range of anxieties and says more about the investment in propriety than about the women themselves.

The hen parties show how working-class women are fixed, categorized, classified, pathologized, projected onto, used as boundary markers. This is not just through the government rhetoric, institutionalized practices, popular and academic representations outlined in the book so far in which the working-class are made to stand in for backwardness and the threat to multicultural modernization; it is also in the space of the encounter, even in liberal cosmopolitan space, where the working-class woman again stands for all that is bad, disgusting, intolerable and disruptive. As a figure she is matter out of place, the repository of middle-class fears and fantasies.

Conclusion

Linklater (1998) argues that a cosmopolitan position would need to bring the 'other' into an extended dialogue. Or, as Nick Stevenson (2002) notes:

> A genuinely cosmopolitan dialogue would need to avoid the negative representations of 'alien' cultures, while deconstructing the assumption that 'national' or 'local' conversations have the right to override the interests of 'insiders' over those of 'outsiders'. In these terms cosmopolitan moral progress can be accounted for when 'they' become 'us'.
>
> (Stevenson 2002:11)

Stevenson (2002:11) asks, 'How do people begin the process of thinking and feeling like cosmopolitans?', how do *they* 'become' translated into '*us*'? We could answer by saying when they are hailed, interpellated, recognized as cosmopolitans. But in order for this to take place, systems of interpretation, reading and recognizing need to be established which do not hold some as the fixed and foundational ground from which others can become cosmopolitan. But, as the majority of this book has shown, it is necessary for some to maintain distinctions and boundaries. 'They' can never be 'us' because they are, by necessity, the prior ground for the constitution of 'us' in the first place. The institutionalized and propertized entitlements of 'us' require that 'they' stand and work as the projected distanced object. We should rephrase the question, 'How will the mobile cosmopolitan middle-class effect changes to their relationships with those they can only render without value?' If current academic theorizing is any measure, the failure to deal with issues of class suggests this is not currently happening and is unlikely to happen in the future. In fact, Stevenson argues that Beck (1992) presents the most sustained cosmopolitan vision through his thesis of 'reflexive modernization', but, as earlier critiques have shown (here and Adkins 2002a; Adkins and Lury 1999), reflexivity is a privileged disposition that reinforces entitlement rather than de-differentiates social divisions, and individualization is a position only available for some. When Stevenson (2002:11) argues that 'the version of cosmopolitanism I wish to defend has more to do with ethics and selfhood than explicit concerns with ideology', he forgets that ethics and selfhood are forged; that is, productive of, and known through, prior classification systems in which some forms of ethics and selfhood are not available to all. Cosmopolitanism is a disposition made in the way of all dispositions; that is, by way of distinction and differentiation (cf Bourdieu 1986; 1987; 1989). Cosmopolitanism, like propriety, individualization and reflexivity, makes class by its *constitutive exclusion*. But this is always based on reading bodies through established symbolic visible classifications.

Even desire, Zizek (1996) argues, is known through the visual. The original question of desire is not directly 'What do I want?' but 'What do others want from me?' 'What do they see in me?' 'What am I for others?' (p.117).[19] So we should not be surprised that working-class femininity is fetishized as strange. A physical space of such intense proximity like Manchester's gay Village represents a threat not only to moral order, but also to the political visibility generated by the marginalized. She (the hen) is the stranger who can be fetishized as dangerous precisely because she isn't. She represents a safe threat for (as feminine) she has little value in the symbolic exchange systems that really count. By threatening the production of gay space as normative and safe for consumption the hen is most definitely not the object or resource of 'distanced contemplation' or user-friendliness required by the cosmopolitan aesthete. She embodies the source of anxiety and fear on which the cosmopolitan depends to expel their distastes. Her expulsion enables multi-cultures to be made corporate through their 'essential' difference, their commodifiable value (Zizek 2002).

And, as Beck (2000) notes, cosmopolitan society also includes its enemies. As terms like cosmopolitanism come to replace those of distinction and difference, we should remember the political and economic impetus behind them. Cosmopolitanism has always been about making distinctions – that is its premise. Cosmopolitanism is a particular variant of the formation of the new middle-class self; it is aesthetic, prosthetic and omnivorous, making judgements about discerning taste wherever it goes. Here, in a physical space enabled by the blatant relationships of consumption, we can see how this works by dividing groups by class in order to make them amenable to commodification. Even political claims-making becomes measured through propriety. Class divisions interrupt both participation in one's own consumption, the consumption of others and in being consumed. This suggests that political struggles have moved far beyond identity and recognition – even if the aesthetic and visual are used to produce knowledge – to where the emphasis needs to return to capitalism's power to produce, constitute and utilize 'difference' as a marketable commodity in a hierarchy of moral tastes. Just as Haylett (2001) describes (in Chapter 5) how the white working-class were represented in political rhetoric as the blockage to the development of multicultural modernism, here white working-class women are being represented as the blockage to respectable consumption and respectable-marginalized gay identity politics, not only out of place, but also disruptive. That such a powerless group has figured for so long as the threat to the moral order should not surprise us, as they are par-excellence the visual representation of the constitutive limit for middle-class self-production; they are there by necessity.

10 Conclusion

Changing perspectives

Class struggle is alive and well, highly apparent in the circuits of symbolic distribution, as this book has shown. In fact class is so ubiquitous, one wonders why all the energy, anxiety and aggressive denial is put into proving that the working-class either does not exist or, if it does, is worthless. Why is so much time and effort put into discrediting those whose access to power is so highly restricted? Why do academics, politicians and media producers continually euphemize the working-class, whilst simultaneously reproducing middle-class experience as universal, through their own perspectives? Class struggle is not just about collective action, for when are we aware of physically encountering a class? But it is also about the positioning, judgements and relations that are entered into on a daily and personal basis. Living class, which I'd argue is different from class-consciousness,[1] is very much part of how class is made.

The book has shown in some detail how perspectives are made from classed positions. This conclusion aims, therefore, to argue for a change in focus,[2] to draw attention to the *value* of culture, but also to expose the interests inherent in the theories that we already have. Rather than viewing the world from a position of privilege, which assumes the possibility of self, individualization, reflexivity, choice, mobility and entitlement, this book asks what interests lie behind these ideas and concepts? What motivates and breathes life into their existence? For some time now middle-class social theorists (following the capitalist metaphor mode) have studied themselves: their investments, their interests, their mobility, their accumulations of capital, their social networks, even their intimacy. I think it is time we asked about the limits to these partial experiences. Let's stop theorizing the conditions of possibility of the middle-classes, and think instead of those who cannot make the same investments, who are not flexible or mobile. Of course, this may not be so interesting to those who find themselves endlessly fascinating, but it may produce better social theory.

Overall, this book has been about four processes: first, how categorizations of class (both working and middle) are made in the contemporary, and how this symbolic struggle has very real effects on value, national belonging, interpretation of experiences and the propertizing of culture. Second, how culture as a resource is not equally available to all. Culture can be used by the middle-classes as a resource to increase their exchange-value, establishing relations of entitlement, but that same culture cannot be converted for the working-classes. Third, how, in the processes of categorization and exchange, there is always an underlying assumption about who can have a self. Fourth, how specific perspectives, theories and methods are promoted as morally good, generating a self only for those with privilege. When all these processes are brought together it is possible to see how symbolic exchange enables culture to be used as a form of property, something that can be accumulated to modern possessive individuals (in their variant range), increasing their value and ability to move across social space.

An analysis of these processes demonstrates how some cultures are differently valued depending on who can *deploy them as a resource*. This opens up ways of thinking about exploitation and exclusion as matters within, alongside, but also beyond production and into more generalized exchange. If, as has been suggested by numerous theorists, we are in a period of capitalist organization in which affect, experience and hyper-commodification can be put to work to produce value for 'flexible capitalism', then we need to think about how these values are generated, and for and from whom. Hopefully, this book has established how this value-generating process is very much about class struggle, and the shifting emphasis on culture as a source of economic value means that we need to pay close attention to how culture is being deployed. But the fact that 'culture' as a term has always been slippery means we must define it not just as symbolic, but also as a resource in the practices and relationships in which we daily engage.

Using culture as a resource is one of the ways morality is coded into social relations and institutionalized through property relations, most obviously institutionalized through law. Morality is always present in the 'social contract', through the ways we know and relate to others in civil society. This conclusion, therefore, draws all these different threads together, and considers the consequences of the processes of class formation that have been identified throughout the book. This chapter is organized into three sections. The first explores the consequences of propertizing culture, the second examines the gap between the politics of recognition and contemporary class formations, and the third analyzes the political significance of the use, transfer and conversion of ethics and affect as cultural resources.

Propertizing, entitlement and resourcing the self

Property is a metaphor for an array of concepts centred on hierarchy, purity and limitedness. It is defined through exclusivity, sovereignty, self-identity, law, territory, boundaries, title and unity. Davies (1998) details how property-thought, or thought of the proper, regulates not only the distribution of resources in society, but also our conceptions of self, knowledge, group identity, sexual identity, law and language. Property is no longer a thing, a relationship between a person and a thing, or a network of relationships between persons with respect to things, or even a bundle of rights.[3] Instead, property is determined as a *set of entitlements*, which are exclusive to an owner, or to the holder of the proprietary *interest*. Property defines an exclusive territory of rights and responsibilities attaching to each owned thing. All concepts of personhood and personality are structured through concepts of property, which rely on systems of knowledge (Davies identifies the law) to turn elements of persons into objects of knowledge. The principle feature of converting persons into property is based on a 'right' to *exclude others*, so the 'right' of property sets up 'rights' of exclusion (Davies 1994; 1998). But, I'd argue, it is not just a right to exclusion, but also a simultaneous right of access, of entitlement. Exclusion from, and access to, objects, people and practices to propertize are central to both the formation of the possessive individual (in its various new configurations: aesthetic, prosthetic, reflexive, rational, enterprising, omnivorousness), and the exclusion of others from self-formation.

A focus on property is helpful because it draws attention to how property and propriety have long been central to the formation of the middle-class self, how ownership, exchange and morality are always intimately connected. This has been theorized for some time via Kant, Nietzsche, Hegel, Marx and Macpherson, to name a few, who have linked property and exchange relations to formations of selves, subjects, individuals and forms of personhood. The self has always been conceived as something premised and reliant on owning and knowing. In Hegel (1821/1967), for instance, only in the process of appropriation is personality realized. Yet these perspectives are always focused on the lives, access and entitlements of the middle-class. As Steedman, Poovey and Bennett make absolutely clear, the working-class self was not formed through the possibilities for appropriation and propertizing; instead, its formation was the constitutive limit to those very actions.

The social contract was devised on *relationships* between those who were not considered to be propertizable to each other. Pateman (1988), for instance, demonstrated how middle-class men related to each other precisely because they were *not* potential property for each other. Moreover, they were given public recognition on the basis of being a property holder; and subjectivity was not possible for those who did not own property. Therefore, the *relationships* between things, people and practices structure class relations, not always as direct exploitation, but as the *use of others as resources*, who are excluded from the same process. The relation constitutes the property – not the thing, person or practice that is being exchanged – although it helps if the resource is user-friendly and not too different to be attached to the self without ridicule. This process is similar to the way in which the referent drops out of the structure of signification, as in Saussure's theory; exclusion structures significance. So the initial referent 'working-class culture' disappears when this culture is used in the formation of the middle-class self.

The decision to propertize or not constructs the object as property. In conventional property analysis, Davies (1998) shows, the object is regarded as 'proper'[4] or not 'proper' and, therefore, subject or not subject to the imposition of a property regime. However, the law of intellectual property amply demonstrates that it is the law that creates property, and confers certain characteristics on physical and abstract objects, rather than simply recognizing them as already proper. The improper can be used if those who have the symbolic power (such as the law and media) decide that certain characteristics have value and can be made proper;

hence, the expansion of new markets for the media by inclusion of the improper and immoral previously excluded; the translation of improper to proper depends, of course, on who makes the evaluation, and this is a class relation.

Whilst the middle-classes are busily propertizing their accumulative, exchange-value selves through the use of, attachment to, detachment from and experiment-ation with cultures not of their own making (and I am being purposely polemic), the working-classes make culture that is defined as deficit, their selves as abject, and their value use-less. In the contemporary the impossibility of a working-class self is not articulated widely (although still present in political rhetoric); instead, a universalistic self is presented as if it is available for all, when in fact the access to the resources to make the self is not equally available. The risk-taking, enterprising, mobile, reflexive, individualistic self, or the 'subject of value', deemed necessary by global economic rhetoric, requires access to the right resources to produce itself. As Bennett (2003) shows, the historical assumptions about the one-dimensional self (as opposed to the dual morality or the depth required for reflexivity), are being reproduced in the contemporary, through what he calls a 'modern cultural fact', generated through theories and perspectives on 'everyday life'. In discussing the literatures on everyday life, he notes:

> This literature does exhibit similar properties in the distinction it draws between two different modes of relation to the everyday life which depend on similarly differentiated architectures of the self. On the one hand, there are those who are said to live spontaneously at the level of everyday life, reproducing its habitual routines through forms of consciousness and behaviour that remain resolutely single-levelled.
>
> (Bennet 2003:3)

Moreover, modern forms of cultural governance are split in their logic according to the historical depth or the shallowness of the selves with which they have to deal. If there is a perceived layered self, liberal forms of indirect governance are possible; if the self is either denied an interior space or denied completely, more direct forms of rule are perceived to be necessary, and other foci, such as culture or the mass, replace the self. Using culture as a resource not only generates proprietal investment in some selves, it also institutionalizes rights to protection, enabling self-governance. This leads to different forms of control and new forms of exploitation.

The ability to propertize one's self and one's culture (as an exchange-value) generates new forms of exploitation based on immateriality (alongside the existence of traditional exploitation from production). Any theory of exploitation, Sorenson (2000a) argues, defines a process by which the holder of an economic property right obtains an advantage at the expense of persons without these rights. So when culture can convert into a property right at the expense of the person who cannot hold these rights to culture, then exploitation can occur. Moreover, an accumulative model of self, premised on accruing value for the future, contributes further to generating inequality; for the ability to perceive future returns on wealth reflects the different life conditions, as those poorer can see less chance of future gain. The distinction between *temporary* and *enduring* exchange-value is central to the analysis of class formation as process, or what Bourdieu identifies as the volume and composition of capitals over time. We can also observe an extension of ownership, from economic goods, to the ownership of oneself thorough one's labour power, and finally to the ownership of one's self through access to cultural properties. However, certain dispositions cannot be rented, appropriated and exchanged. This is because dispositions can be defended, or are the constitutive limit that puts them beyond exchange-value. Other dispositions are non-exchangeable because they are culturally essentialized, and thus assumed to already exist as part of, say, gendered or raced personhood.

If class is made from evaluations we need to think about the basic ontological conception of value as a virtual dimension, in which forms of appearance dissimulate its real nature and content (Smith 1994b). Whereas money was always seen to be the appearance of the measure of value, immanent in commodities, I'd argue that now exchangeable culture also generates value, by attributing social features to people, relations and artefacts that enhance their value beyond the monetary. Marx (1967) describes how value does not have its description branded on its forehead, rather value transforms every product of labour into a social hieroglyphic. In other words, value is inherently misrepresentative of its social content, hence the mis-recognition of the working-class when it is represented as having no value. In the present, culture becomes a hieroglyphic when transferred from those who generate it.

The attribution of exchange-value to culture is a reversal of the historical process, as seen in Chapter 1, when I discussed Stallybrass's (1998) analysis of the development of European personhood, in which 'the primitive' imputed affect via history and memory to objects and people, in opposition to the European colonialist who was only interested in exchange-value. Now, however, the use of culture enables the dissimulation of affect, which can be propertized onto selves, people and practices; but, for those who can mobilize and convert culture, their exchange possibilities – hence value – are consolidated even further. So, using authenticity, for instance, generates added value beyond the monetary, but ultimately, the middle-classes can enhance their overall value capitals, extending their resources in volume, composition and across time.

The ability to propertize culture in the making of a self, therefore, becomes central to how class is made in the contemporary. The entitlement and access to the resources for making a self with value are central to how the middle-class is formed; they have access to others' culture as a resource in their own self-making. In the relationship of entitlement class is lived and experienced. But this is also about exclusion from the ability to propertize cultural resources; from access to the very resources for making the 'subject with value'. *The relationships of entitlement and exclusion establish the basis for cultural exchange, in which new forms of exploitation are shaped.* But value is mis-recognized in this process (only ever recognized as exchange-value), because those who are excluded from propertizing their culture are also excluded from the circuits of symbolic control and distribution. I now want to explore the political consequences of using and mis-recognizing culture.

Political consequences

The conceptualization of subjectivity did not seem politically important until the demise of the sovereign mode of government; for only when individuals were allowed to govern themselves did it seem necessary to understand how they did so (Poovey 1998). Because the working poor were seen to be incapable of self-formation and governing themselves, they were subject to external controls. This, I'd argue, is reproduced in contemporary political rhetoric, which suggests (and literally repeats through the iteration of discourses of the moral underclass), that the working-classes need controlling, whilst the middle-classes are producing new forms of personhood, in which self-governance is assumed.

We see the disparity in the way different forms of governance are enacted in the debates on the politics of recognition; a politics which, Fraser (1995) argues, shapes the landscape of political representation in the West. To make a recognition claim one must first have a recognizable identity, and this identity must be 'proper': that is, it must have recognizable public value. This immediately presents a problem for those who are not considered to have 'proper' identities and are continually mis-recognized; it also presents a problem for those who are forced to inhabit an identity category not of their own making (see Chapter 3), as well as those who are forced to be visible in order to be seen to have a recognizable identity.[5] The debates surrounding recognition politics are well rehearsed (see for instance, Adkins 2002c; Fraser 1999); here, however, I want to focus on one angle – that of entitlement, exclusion and interest.

Brown (2001) reveals how liberal discourse converts political identity into essentialized private interest; disciplinary power converts interest into normativized social identity manageable by regulatory regimes. Thus 'disciplinary power politically neutralises entitlement claims generated by liberal individuation, while liberalism politically neutralises rights claims generated by disciplinary identities' (pp.205–6). As a consequence, identity claims re-legitimate capitalism through a formulation of justice, which re-inscribes a bourgeois ideal as its measure. American identity politics, she claims, has been achieved through a renaturalizing of capitalism:

> Identity politics may be partly configured by a peculiarly shaped and peculiarly disguised form of class resentment, a resentment which is displaced onto discourses of injustice other than class but a resentment, like all resentments, which retains the real or imagined holdings of its reviled subjects as objects of desire.
>
> (Brown 2001:206)

Brown explores how other identities depend on class, whereby the enunciation of politicized identities through race, gender and sexuality require – rather than incidentally produce – a limited identification through class, and 'may specifically abjure a critique of class power and class norms insofar as these identities are established *vis-à-vis* a bourgeois norm of social acceptance, legal protection and relative material comfort' (p.207). Just as propertizing culture is essential to middle-class self-formation, so is the desire for the protection of the law and for the entitlements of civil society. Propertizing and protection rely on a notion of a possessive individual who can receive legitimate recognition from the state. Yet for those who are positioned as abject, underclass, beyond the nation and without the right cultural capital, this legitimate recognition is not offered. In fact, the excluded are the foundation of the state's exclusion.

This means that forms of recognition are in place that draw upon and reproduce the exchange-value view of personhood, which again protects and propertizes the values of the middle-class by excluding the working-class. For instance, O'Neill (1999)[6] shows how Adam Smith in *A Theory of Moral Sentiments* proposed that the concern with appearance (with recognition) was about the corruption of moral character. Notwithstanding the way in which femininity comes to be a sign of this immorality, O'Neill notes how Smith draws a distinction between the appearance of worth and the real worth of character. Central to Smith's moral theory is the Aristotelian distinction between 'the love of praiseworthiness' and 'the love of praise', which he compares to the contemporary politics of recognition. To desire to be praiseworthy is to desire those characteristics for which praise is owed, whereas the desire for praise itself is properly parasitic on the desire for praiseworthiness: the former deserves it, the latter is just appearances. Vanity is defined as the love of praise for its own sake, divorced from the relationship to the characteristics that are praiseworthy. O'Neill argues that this distinction between praise and praiseworthiness can be connected to two contemporary debates: the first is the proposition that appearance is all, or everything is sign-value, or abuse-value, or symbolic exchange. The second is that the desire for recognition appears to be like the love of praise (not praiseworthiness), for it is based simply on categorical position, not labour or character, but symbolic positioning rather than objective worth or use-value.

Hegel (1821/1967), too, distinguishes between the possessive self-seeking self and those people who desire recognition for the competencies and skills they have within a community of skills. It could be argued that the contemporary use of identity as cultural capital to claim recognition has effaced its use-value, and instead used cultural capital as exchange, for a positional good. This is why the distinction between use- and exchange-value is in danger of collapse. O'Neill draws attention to the arguments of public intellectuals like Fukuyama (1992) in which the love of praise and the love of praiseworthiness have become identical. For Fukuyama the love of praise alone moves the individual, in which there is no distinction between looking good and being good, where worth lies in appearance and appearance is something that is vied over by competitors in a market, in which the idea of independent worth disappears. O'Neill reveals how this definition of what counts as worth is used in recent understandings in the sociology of science, often by the 'reflexive theorists' (of Chapter 7), who reduce everything to exchange-value:

> Scientists are investors in credibility. The result is a creation of a *market*. Information now has value because ... it allows other investigators to produce information which facilitates the return of invested capital. There is a *demand*

from investors for information which may increase the power of their own inscription devices, and there is a *supply* of information from the other investors. The forces of supply and demand create the *value* of the commodity.

(Woolgar and Latour 1979:206) (emphasis in original)

What counts as value is the market in credibility (appearances). Any scientific worth outside of these standards of appearance is not recognized. Science is thus described in the image of a commercial society, where the market establishes the rules, logic and value; the scientist is the self-interested accruing individual, this time interested in accruing credibility rather than money directly, in which all communication is reduced to strategic action. This repetition of the exchange-value self as the valuable recognizable self has been shown throughout the book to be produced across a range of symbolic sites. Yet for some groups recognition is just not possible or accessible, because they are positioned as the constitutive limit for recognition (as we saw in Chapters 8 and 9).

Likewise, Zizek (2002) points out how for some groups, self, recognition and humanity are never a political possibility. He draws on the category of *homo sacer* from Giorgio Agamben (1998) to describe those groups who are now designated in the West as having no worth whatsoever.[7] Whilst Zizek explores the *homo sacer* in the context of the reshaping of global politics, in which some groups are made to disappear from humanity, his analysis offers us some clues as to how this process takes place within the nation. For instance, the spatial apartheid, the cultural funda-mentalism and the abject agency, attributed to the working-class in the UK, Europe and US, enable the identification of the 'enemy within'.[8] As Zizek points out:

> The division friend/enemy is never just a recognition of factual difference. The enemy is by definition always (up to a point) *invisible*: it cannot be directly recognized because it looks like one of us, which is why the big problem and task of the political struggle is to provide/construct a recognizable *image* of the enemy[9] ... In short, 'enemy recognition' is always a performative procedure which brings to light/constructs the enemy's 'true face'.
>
> (Zizek 2002:5) (emphasis in original)

Zizek further draws on the Kantian category of *Einbildungskraft* – the transcendental power of imagination – to show how, in order to recognize the enemy, one has to 'schematize' the logical figure of the enemy, providing it with concrete features that will make it into an appropriate target of scorn, hatred and struggle. I hope the book has documented how a similar process occurs with the working-classes, in which a great deal of energy goes into inscribing, depicting, categorizing and degrading the working-classes as enemy. Also, in the performative procedures that bring recognition, this recognition only works for those who can be projected onto, rather than positioned by, these procedures.

We need to shift perspective, therefore, from recognition and think instead about who is being made invisible and who is emphatically denied in the process of recognition. And why does this continue to occur, especially when we have known for such a long time that what appears as symbolically undervalued and socially peripheral is usually symbolically central (Stallybrass and White 1986)? This may be one of the explanations for the prolific ubiquity of class representations. Following Derrida's notion of the logic of supplementarity, the obsession with otherness enables obsession to be structured symptomatically, insofar as represent-ations of the working-classes condense a whole range of anxieties, enabling anxiety to be expressed, known and become governable.

The representations we have of the working-classes have, for a long time, enabled them to be fixed, categorized, classified, pathologized, projected onto and used as boundary markers. This is achieved across a powerful conglomeration of symbolic systems: government rhetoric, institutionalized practices, popular and academic representations. The working-classes are recognized, but not in the terms of liberal individualism; rather they are mis-recognized as a symptom of an anxiety, without humanity – mis-recognized in order to be denied recognition. Moreover, political change is not likely to be achieved by challenging the rhetoric, discourse and representation of recognition. As Smith (1994a) notes in relation to Thatcherite homophobic discourse:

> 'Positive images' offer an interpretation of homophobic discourse, and con-struct a counter-discourse, but they do not interrupt the entire process whereby the coherence of a political project is established through the construction of demon figures. The *investment* in the process remains unchallenged.
>
> (Smith 1994:191)(my emphasis)

This is why we need to understand the interests and investments made in the relationships that enable difference to be mis-recognized but also used as a resource.

In Nietzsche's (1969) account, the strategies of evaluation, interpretation and containment operate through the deployment of metaphysical fictions, and these are central to the challenge made through ressentiment. Self-consciousness, for Neitzsche, can only be produced through the evaluation structure of the other; the judgement of the 'other' becomes the very structure for the apparently autono-mous 'self' formation of the self. Yet I want to show how the effect of judgement impacts upon ressentiment and is employed as a resource by different groups differently.

But, politically, as shown in Chapter 6, these positions, mis-recognitions and supplementary evaluations are rarely inhabited and accepted by the working-class. In this lack of fit between position and disposition, recognition and mis-recognition, we can see contemporary class struggle. We see also challenges made by the critiques of pretensions that deny the power of judgement and authorization to those who are in a relationship of power to the working-class. And we see struggle more force-fully in the expression of ressentiment and resentment to which I will now turn.

Ressentiment, affect and ethic

What Nietzsche calls slave morality produces identity in reaction to power; any identity rooted in this reaction achieves its moral superiority by reproaching and defining power and action as evil. Therefore, identity structured by this ethos of slave morality becomes deeply invested in its own impotence, even while it seeks to assuage the pain of its powerlessness through its vengeful moralizing and its reproach of power. Brown argues that:

> Politicised identity, premised on exclusion and fuelled by the humiliation and suffering imposed by its historically structured impotence in the context of a discourse of sovereign individuals, is as likely to seek generalised political paralysis, to feast on generalised political impotence, as it is to seek its own or collective liberation through empowerment.
>
> (Brown 1995:217)

For Nietzsche, ressentiment and vengefulness represent the desire to deaden pain by means of affects. Ressentiment is a triple achievement, for it produces an affect (rage, righteousness) which overwhelms the hurt; a culprit responsible for the hurt; and a site of revenge to displace the hurt (a place to inflict hurt as the sufferer has been hurt). These operations ameliorate and externalize what is unendurable. Slaves become good by depicting the master as bad and themselves as morally superior. Revenge, Nietzsche maintains, is a reaction, a substitute for the capacity to act, producing identity as both bound to the history that produced it, and as a reproach to the present, which embodies that history. In this schema, ressentiment is the moral strategy of the powerless (but also those who have access to identity), who challenge the judgements of the powerful; an attempt at de-authorization by denying the powerful the right to the moral high ground.

What is interesting in modern studies of ressentiment is how it is deployed by those who are *not* powerless. Brown (1995), for instance, maintains that due to global contingency and de-sacrilization, 'the late modern subject quite literally seethes with ressentiment' (p.215). She considers recent moralizing politics – that is, those based on a foundational claim to truth and injury – to mark a crisis in political teleology. Moralism has appeared because, in the Nietzschean sense, it is a reaction to and recrimination by those who feel they are losing the power that they once had (or would have had as a result of their positioning). So they mobilize their own felt exclusion. Powerful groups, who feel they do not have enough power, attempt to shape the political landscape by enunciating, dramatizing and inscribing their loss through the claim to pain and by mobilizing resentment.[10] Here I distinguish between ressentiment (an expression of powerlessness) and resentment (an expression of the powerful). This enables us to see why it is corporate businessmen who freely use the language of class to legitimate their actions, as described by Frank (2001). Or, how and why the language of corporate multiculturalism can make use of injury claims which de-legitimate the everyday suffering of others (see Chapter 5 and Rouse 1995).

This, however, is very different to those who have no access to shaping the political landscape and cannot make known their exclusion, injury and pain. This difference is made most explicit in Rouse's (1991) examples of how migrants are forced to take on political identities not of their own making, in order to have access to state resources. This forced recognition is almost identical to the process whereby the working-class were offered subjectivity though legal interlocutors, but only if working-class experience could be narrated and interpreted through state definitions.

Cameron McCarthy (2000) extensively documents how the suburban middle-class in the US use the discourse of resentment to claim and legitimate moral authority. He reveals how, in the early 1990s, *Time* magazine published two articles documenting the rise of the suburban middle-class. These articles fetishized crime and violence, transmuted in the language of the coming invasion of the abstract racialized working-class other.[11] In opposition to Jameson's (1981) proposal that postmodernism, or the logic of late capitalism, sets a new 'emotional ground tone' about the waning of affect or the loss of feeling, McCarthy argues instead that, in the US, through the manipulation of difference, a powerful *concentration of affect and a strategic use of emotions produce a moral re-evaluation*. A critical feature of discourses of resentment is dependence on processes of simulation, that is, the middle-class comes to 'know' its inner-city other through an imposed system of infinitely repeatable substitutions and proxies: census tracts, crime statistics, tabloid newspapers and television programmes (p.285). Or, as Berlant (2002) demonstrates, such knowledge is attained by the mimesis of the affect of pain and suffering. Resentment, therefore, is an affect distinguished first of all by its concern and involvement with the powerful winning power. McCarthy contends:

> A new moral universe now rides the underbelly of the beast – late capital's global permutations, displacements, relocations and reaccumulations. The effect has meant a material displacement of minority and other dispossessed groups from the landscape of contemporary political and cultural life. That is to say, increasingly the underclass (sic) or working-class subject is contemporaneously being placed on the outside of the arena of the public sphere as *the middle-class subject-object of history moves into occupy and to appropriate the identity of the oppressed, the racial space of difference*. The centre becomes the margin.
>   (McCarthy 2000:285) (emphasis added)

Yet Brown (2001) argues that, when the middle-class use moralism via resentment, moralism becomes the reinstatement of a hegemonic form, marking analytic impotence and political aimlessness. Investment in pain closes down the possibility of a painless future. This means that the problematic of pain is installed at the heart of the demand for political recognition, the pain of the powerful, which can be co-opted into the production of national sentimentality – the rhetoric of a promise that a nation can build across fields of social difference through channels of affective identification and empathy (Berlant 1997). The nation imagined in this reactive rhetoric is dedicated not to the survival or emancipation of traumatized marginal subjects, but to the freedom of the innocent, the moral, and the good.[12] The citizen becomes a trauma-affect and effect, requiring protection and political reparation; the general scene of public citizenship is suffused with a practice of making pain count politically. In this political model of identity, framed by recognition, shaped by liberalism, articulated by resentment, trauma stands as truth, and is intensely individuating. The harm, injury and damage wreaked on those made non-human are not recognized, and everyday suffering goes unnoticed. The powerless simply become an affect, a resource to be plundered to gain the political and moral ground that has been lost by the powerful.

According to Toby Miller's (1993) analysis of late-capitalism, such ethical resource deployment is entirely fitting for capitalist systems that are, by definition, contradictory. Capitalism in its various manifestations requires workers who are 'subjects of value'; it also requires selfish utilitarian consumers. Yet these requirements are in opposition to the selfless communitarian citizens capable of self-governance. This contradiction produces what he defines as a state of 'ethical incompleteness', which is partially managed by the state in its attempts to encourage loyalty, but is also potentially assuaged through consumption. However, Miller's description of the state of ethical incompleteness also provides the space for the political claims for ethical completeness in which identities bounded with the moral authority arising from their status as victims of injury or harm, claim recognition not only for power, rewards and protection, but also for completeness, for being seen to have moral value. Claims for recognition are claims to be seen as capable of self-governance, but also a call upon the law for protection; the modern version of vengeance is 'both an intense emotion and a cool, calculating strategy' (Solomon 1999:127) based on an economy of return; a re-venge[13] (see Moran and Skeggs 2003). In a similar move to the one documented above by Poovey (1998), recognition based on the affects of ressentiment, pain and injury, also requires a form of subjectivity that is denied to the working-class.

And, in a similar move to the Aristotelian desire for praise, just being middle-class is seen to be enough to make a political claim and to demand protection from the State. This reduces morality to an exchange-value, and means that groups compete and trash the moral claims of their competitors in their desire for moral completeness. Not only are the affects, or even metaphysics, of working-class injury used and converted into political value by the middle-class, but also, as Gary Tedman (1999) demonstrates, working-class affects are packaged and marketed at the aesthetic level to sell products. Alienation has been used by the music industry for a long time to sell its products (think Nirvana, rap music and Eminem in particular).[14] Working-class antagonisms create commonly felt estranged emotions, forms of sensuous alienation, which the entire culture industry attempts not only to sublimate onto safe pathways, but also to brand products through affect.

This means that the working-class, defined as unworthy of national belonging, or as *homo sacers*, cannot establish any rights from the nation through the politics of recognition; this can only be done through mis-recognition, which simultaneously makes use-value invisible whilst obsessively defining their potential for exchange. Even working-class alienation can be used as a resource, an exchange-value to enhance products, politics and identities of others.

This is what I think is significant about the contemporary: the extension of the dual process of defining the enemy as not just enemy, but also as useful, as a cultural resource. The broadening out of this process into material and marketable aspects, by the use of affect, marks how class is presently in formation; in particular, the extension of attributions of authenticity and the genuine to aspects of working-class lifestyles. This extension involves not just the masculine criminally glamorous, but also the attempt to incorporate the anti-pretentious critique into the mainstream as well as its hedonism, de-control, loyalty, grit, fun, non-seriousness, even alienation.[15] These affects mark 'the real'. Seabrook (2000) demonstrates that these affects are the most profitable associations to be added to practices and objects.

But what does it mean to divorce affects from the site of their production and re-attribute them to others? And what does it mean to produce forms of positive affectivity, in which a particular sort of personhood is generated because it is worth exploiting? How do those with few alternatives manage to resist becoming the sort of person that is seen to be marketable and valuable to middle-class culture – but not to themselves, rather to those who see their lifestyle as worth copying without the consequences?[16] And what does it feel like to watch the powerful parade pain for political gain?

Whilst recognition politics becomes the ground for the middle-classes to regroup their interests and investments, attempting to gain the moral and national high ground, other groups shape their ethics differently. For those unable to participate in recognition politics, the ethical struggles often occur around use rather than exchange-values. Kathleen Stewart (1996), for instance, describes how a whole community forms itself through 'just-talk', talk of fairness and kindness that glues people together and is based on values of care rather than exchange. The significance of loyalty and honour has also been well documented in studies of working-class life (Duneier 1992; Lamont 2000; Willis 1977; Mac an Ghaill 1994). Respectability, arguably a value imposed through middle-class evangelical moralism, has also been given a different shape and value when translated into working-class lives (see Skeggs 1997). But the emphasis on moral authority, produced from recognition politics, means that many of these values cannot be recognized by the middle-class commentators, those who can only see from their own position and are unable to extend their perspectives beyond an exchange-value, an entitled, accumulative, demanding way of being in the world.

This is why, I'd argue, morality needs attention. We need to move beyond exchange-value now that we know how it works. McMylor (2001) argues that we have become so entrenched within the neo-liberal value economy of capitalism that we have even come to evaluate morality on the basis of interests. Yet, after years of markets and individualism, he also points to the revival of an ethical discourse, citing Habermas's 'the genesis of values', to Robert Young's radical science, to the political theory of Norman Geras, as the means by which issues of ethical justice are returning to the political agenda. McMylor identifies this shift, promoted by a form of Marxism, as based on concepts of justice, rather than reliant on Hegelian notions of history. This shift is a critique of Kantian rule-based morality (of the 'thou shalt' type) and promotion of an Aristotelian-based virtue ethics. McMylor suggests that looking beyond modernism to the classics gives us perspectives not focused on the economy and rule-based systems. He turns to Alistair McIntyre, who proposes that, instead of thinking about morality in inherently rational terms such as gains, losses and interests, we should focus on the use-value of goods or practices, which have a worth intrinsic to themselves, or a community, rather than a value that can be exchanged.

But we also need to be aware of how this worth can be mobilized, not just to market goods, but to produce business practice. An 'ethical turn' has recently been identified in the US; following the scandals of Enron and WorldCom, the business world had to clean up its act. To do so it used ethical discourse to demonstrate integrity, namely 'enlightened self-interest'.[17] This is precisely not the sort of ethics to which I refer. I reference that which cannot be used, that which has real integrity; something quite rare in an exchange-value Western world. And it is the rarity of integrity that makes it in such demand, for it is one of the cultural practices that is difficult for the accumulative self to access, the prosthetic self to play with, or the omnivore to taste. Authenticity and integrity are ethical qualities that cannot be easily exchanged; they may be one aspect of cultural capital that cannot be harnessed by those intent on increasing their value at the expense of others. Yet, interestingly, it was the display of production of the self as an ethical imperative that propelled possessive individualism into existence (and then law). So we can see two different ethics in operation; one that fits the exchange-value model – the 'enlightened but self-interested' middle-class self – but also one beyond this ethical imperative, a subjectivity with worth, with use-value. The ethical imperative of global economic rhetoric, condensed into the 'subject of value', is a very different motivation to that which is produced for its own sake.

This is why I suggest that we turn our perspective to use-value, to that which is praiseworthy for its own sake, to that which is not exchangeable and cannot be put to use to enhance the middle-class self. As Spivak (1990) suggests, use-value is precisely what disrupts the chain of value connections, because it is beyond value, understood in traditional economistic terms. Moreover, use-values can only be known when they are put to use, so they force a focus on the uses of culture, relations and practice. This means we can explore how something has different values in different contexts, enabling us to break through the dominant symbolic understandings premised on exchange. Spivak argues that value is a *catachresis*: contra to Marx, it has no literal origin or referent, because use-value will always exceed that which it claims to represent.

Conclusion to conclusion

We need to reinvigorate class analysis and deal with the contemporary shifts in neo-liberal governance and transnational flexible capitalism. We require an understanding that goes beyond the 'economic' and exchange to understand the consequences of cultural struggle and how this is part of new marketization, new attributions of value, new forms of appropriation, exploitation and governance, and new selves. We must rethink contemporary class struggle and focus on the relationships of entitlement to the cultures and affects of others. This perspective enables us to see where, how and why working-class culture becomes fixed, but plundered: elements for others to use and morally authorize themselves. When the middle-classes appropriate parts of working-class culture as a resource, they only take the bits that are useful, such as the criminal associations, the sexuality, the immoral bits; essentializing qualities with the working-classes. That is, the plundered attributes have to remain associated with the 'originary' group in order to guarantee the attribution of 'the real' and authentic. The relationship of entitlement and extraction simultaneously fixes the cultural feature in the group from which it was extracted, whilst making it a mobile resource for the one who can use it. This proposed change in perspective requires that we also understand how the middle-class is also being re-constituted, in which its progression and progressiveness are predicated on holding in place – fixing – that which must signify stagnation and immobility.

I'm aware that I may have fallen into the trap that Bourdieu is accused of making, whereby economic metaphors are used to illuminate social and cultural processes, so that terms like investment and interest reproduce an accumulative, capitalist-based model. But, I shout loudly, the purpose has been to show how some people do actually fit and benefit from shaping themselves through these capitalist metaphors of profit and loss, depreciation and inheritance, interest and investment. If culture is made into a property that can be exchanged for value across a range of sites, then it is important not to lose sight of the broader framework that enables, indeed compels, some selves to operate in this way. Moreover, when more and more aspects of culture are opened out and exploited by capitalism, or used as resources in nation-building and governance, it is useful to know what is appropriable and what is not, and what are the consequences of this. If our understandings of class are shaped by these processes, in which the symbolic is central, then mis-recognitions of use-value will occur, whereby the referent (the working-class) disappears. We should know if people are being classified, positioned, known and mis-recognized as *homo sacers*, without any value whatsoever or without agency and only addiction, or with only the capability of making bad choices from bad culture. This is why we need to change perspectives to ones that bring these processes to light rather than keeping them in the dark.

It is also important to identify sites of resistance. The working-class, both within and outside the circuits of symbolic distribution, resist appropriation, and continually threaten to expose and ridicule the use of their culture. The pretensions and inaccuracy of the new middle-class formations are being constantly undermined.[18] This exposes the fragility and vulnerability of the middle-class self, which has to assert itself in order to assuage anxieties of power-loss, to be taken seriously and be seen as worthy of moral authority. That entitlements have to be institutionalized, perspectives authorized and property legitimated, means that, ultimately, they can be challenged. And they are. This is class struggle made through culture in which value is continually contested.

Notes

1 Making class: inscription, exchange, value and perspective

1 However, this has a long and difficult history and it could be argued that the 'Blues', as a form of music appropriated by white musicians, was the site where 'cool' as an attribute was formed. That it sticks to black bodies in a way that it does not to white bodies is about the repetition of association between dispositions and bodies over a long period of time, in which it is not just about the power of those who can influence the dominant cultural symbolic economy, but also about those who have shaped the symbolic through oppositional struggle. Thanks to Lisa Adkins for bringing the work of Diawara to my attention.

2 When playing blackness becomes ironic, as in the *Shrek* donkey, or Will Smith in *Men in Black*, we know that the use of blackness as 'cool' has been well established as a cultural resource when it can be destabilized by those who have the closest attachment to it.

3 As Evans (1993) shows, contemporary identity politics movements of sexual campaigning were forged through a particular variety of 1960s bourgeois individualism.

4 Strathern names the 'logic of commodity perspective' as the bourgeois perspective.

5 This is not dissimilar to Foucault's subjectification of the body by discourse.

6 As Bogard notes this is very close to Foucault's position: discourses do more than signs to designate things. It is the practical deployment of forces on bodies, in ways that harness their energies, hierarchize them and make them functional.

7 As Deleuze and Guattari (1987) point out, the power of Marx's analysis was his ability to understand how capitalism could work its own contradictions (although ultimately predicting that this would be its downfall).

8 To make this point I am focusing on femininity as appearance. It also has a value as a form of nurturing and care (see Skeggs 1997).

9 This is a very different definition of social capital to that made by Putnam (1995), who sees social capital as a source of trust in community formation.

10 This is made more even more explicit in Bourdieu (1999), where the original French title *La Misère du Monde* suggests economic poverty alongside moral poverty. Impoverishment and suffering are seen to be moral practices.

11 See Butler (1999).

12 Porter also charts how the self-centredness, formerly considered to be a sin by the Church, was transformed into the *raison d'être* of the modern psyche.

13 See Stedman Jones (1971).

14 Sarah Green (2003) argues that this also produces people who were neither self nor other, but fundamentally *uninteresting*. Also see Auge (1995).

15 See Gittins (2002).

16 This is made most explicit in black female Rap music (see Skeggs 1994b).

2 Thinking class: the historical production of concepts of class

1 They are also implicated in responses to art. As Guillory (1993) observes, 'the problem of aesthetic judgment was as essential to the formation of political economy as the problem of political economy was to the formation of aesthetics' (p.303).

2 The word 'commodity' only accrued its contemporary meaning of an 'exchangeable good' in the eighteenth century. Before that it simply meant a useful good: that is, it was defined by use-value rather than exchange-value (see Rowling 1987).

3 This approach has also been developed in another direction via 'governance' in which market interests, come to order aspects of life often believed to be private, are investigated (see Rose, N. 1989; 1992).

4 Yeo (1993) shows how middle-class women used working-class women to clean the dirty bits, enabling the middle-class to appear as hygienic.

5 Game theory, revised by John Forbes Nash in the 1950s, who subsequently won the Nobel prize for it, is based on a group of mathematical propositions that attempt to predict the outcome of competitive situations in which different parties may make different decisions when their interests conflict.

6 Trautmann (1997) argues that there is a problem with the term orientalism because it collapses two quite different phenomena: the earliest sense of 'indo-mania' and then the later orientalism of the nineteenth-century British evangelical liberals who are 'indophobes'. Indomania was part of a more generalized search for the source of universal spirituality.

7 There is some debate over how the term culture is used. Initially, as Slater (1997) points out, the word itself came into existence in response to the emergence of market society.

8 See Walkerdine and Lucey (1989) for an almost exact replication of this statement in the contemporary discourse of working-class women.

9 Although they were initially devised some 30 years ago.

10 For a very thorough and comprehensive coverage of these debates, see Savage (2000).

3 Mobility, individualism and identity: producing the contemporary bourgeois self

1 In the UK the RAE has occurred every four years in social science departments and every six years in humanities departments, to assess the productivity of academics. It is a powerful audit device tied into research funding. The difference between the grades (1–5*) has been estimated to be £100,000 per department. It reproduces and institutionalizes inequalities between universities.

2 Urry is also, significantly, UK Chair of the 2001 Sociology RAE panel.

3 See Stanko (1988); Stanko and Curry (1997).

4 The project on 'Violence, Sexuality and Space' was funded by the ESRC (grant no. L133251031) from May 1998 to May 2001. The research data was produced by Bev Skeggs, Les Moran, Paul Tyrer, Karen Corteen and Lewis Turner. See http://les1.man.ac.uk/sociology/vssrp for an outline of the project and list of publications. A book of the research: *Sexuality and the Politics of Violence* is published by Routledge.

5 To re-gender mobility would also involve replacing the term 'flaneur' which has become resolutely identified as *the* (male) figure of modernity (even after heroic attempts have been made to appropriate it for lesbians, see Munt (1995).

6 This develops a previous position in which market regulations produce individualism, by which an individual's biography becomes defined by the state (Beck and Beck-Gernsheim 1995).

7 Frank (1997) shows how advertising has to appear to be more 'radical' than market speak.

8 Abercrombie, Hill and Turner (1986) identify a number of different definitions of individualism, individuality and individuation:

Individualism, was in origin mainly a political and subsidiarily an economic doctrine relating to the rights and obligations of persons that was associated with political theory of the seventeenth century, which later heavily influenced British and American culture. Individuality is concerned with the education of inner feeling and subjectivity. By contrast, individuation is a bureaucratic procedure that uniquely identifies individuals for the purpose of social administration and control.

(Abercrombie, Hill and Turner 1986:2)

4   The subject of value and the use-less subject

1   Readership is 91 per cent male, and its circulation in 2001 was 780,000 readers; although based in the UK, over half of its circulation is in the US.

2   The proportion of households in the UK without any assets whatsoever doubled between 1979 and 1996. Some 50 per cent of adults have less than £500 of disposable financial wealth and between 47 per cent and 64 per cent of families earning under £20,000 per annum have no savings at all (Regan 2001).

3   In *Formations of Class and Gender* (Skeggs 1997) I documented how the women used caring as an asset not to accrue value but to put a floor on their circumstances.

4   This is made most clearly explicit in Rational Action Theories that bring the self-interested accruing individual to the forefront of social theory.

5   The political rhetorics of class

1   David Selbourne (1994) a New Labour guru, maintains that the performance of duty is the morally superior, as well as the historically prior, constituent of human association.

2   This administering to the poor is not at all unlike at the turn of the century (Hall 1979), where middle-class women carved out space from domestic responsibilities by attempting to morally reform the poor, or gentlemanly social reforms focused on bringing 'rough lads' to civilized manhood (Haylett 2001).

3   Although this is going to be increasingly more difficult after the collapse of Enron and other major corporates, and the exposure of Anderson's corrupt accounting practices.

6   Representing the working-class

1   See political theorist Seymour Martin Lipset's (1959) essay, 'Working-class authoritarianism', which equated fascism with authoritarianism as a working-class personality trait.

2   This is not to argue that there is anything like a perfect representation. Representations by definition are partial. They are re-presentations, thereby offering the potential to include *and* exclude.

3   Although Campbell (1987) argues that during an earlier period the upper-class romantic poets provided the conditions for modern hedonism, in which pleasure was separated from physical satisfaction, pursued in the art of daydreaming.

4   Smith (1999) has shown how early photographs in the US were used in a similar way as representations of working-class women's appearance, as 'vehicles of gendered and racialised interior essences' (p.4).

5   Unlike Anglo/US debates on transexuality and transgender, Kulick shows how Brazilian travesti do *not* define themselves as women.

6   See Jones (1994) and Mercer (1987) for a description of how different values have been attached to and contested over black hair.

7   This becomes more complicated, as the re-valuing occurred through a 'black is beautiful' campaign that urged the growing of hair into a 'natural' style, which became known as an 'Afro'.

8 This is somewhat paradoxical if we think of the history of primitivism and the association of the working-class with nature, where they were assumed to *be* natural.

9 Yellow brassy blonde on an upper-class body would not be read as working-class but would be offset by other signifiers such as height, skin tone and body size (Bourdieu 1986).

10 We are aware of the irony of the attempts to make a gay space pure, but see Moran and Skeggs (2001a; 2001b).

11 However, Probyn (2000a) notes a problem with Bourdieu's analysis: 'This is a body that is strangely inert. The body that eats is in the end eaten by the overdeterminations of culture' (p.29).

12 It could be argued that this process is well developed in drug use: the branding of ecstasy names the experience – e.g. lamborghini, mitsubishi, doves, jungle fever, most wanted, disco biscuits, etc.

13 The name itself – Bouquet – immediately confronts the possibility for pretension. It is variously named 'bucket', or the emphasis is put on French pronunciation (often viewed as a British middle-class affectation).

14 The upper-class, Sarah Green (personal communication) notes, would consider drawing attention to class to be very vulgar indeed.

15 Gittins (2002e) describes the proliferation and fascination with criminality, arguing that the 'lauding of violent crimes and gangsters as contemporary cultural icons has clearly been one of the most pernicious media trends of the last decade' (p.12).

16 Class resentment, hatred and antagonism were clearly apparent in my earlier ethnography (Skeggs 1997).

17 Thanks to Karen Corteen for drawing my attention to this (and many more!).

18 Thanks to Josie Dolan for providing me with this newspaper article.

19 This process of deflecting judgment by denigrating the potential judges is particularly well visualized in rap music where black females are subject to a wide range of abuse which undermines their potential to judge men (see Skeggs 1994). It could be argued that the systematic denigration of women is a mechanism to reduce their power to make judgements about men.

20 For a sophisticated and subtle reading of how class informs the interpretation of TV see Seiter (1999).

7 The methods that make classed selves

1 Here I distinguish between the concept of the self as a coherent unity, a category which has been developed in Western societies through the methods outlined in this chapter and through the 'psy' sciences (see Rose 1989), and the concept of subjectivity which is not coherent and which we all live with in ways we do not often know (see Skeggs 1997).

2 This may present particular problems for the use of Bourdieu's concept of habitus, that in its formation is the 'internalization of externality'. This is how he holds together the objective social structure with the subjective world in which social relations become embedded social practices.

3 See Smith (1988) for a detailed analysis of how textual mediation works to produce femininity.

4 Walkerdine and Lucey (1989) show how this morality is reproduced in contemporary child development discourses.

5 Although, as Gilman (1990) shows, the undeserving poor, from which the recuperable were drawn, were made up of a variety of ethnicities.

6 Probably one of the most famous of these is the story of Hannah Cullwick who kept diaries for her employer Arthur Munby, who had a fascination and fetish with the dark, dirty, strong bodies of working-class women (see McClintock 1995).

7 Vincent (1981) shows how many were written as challenges to the assumption that immorality increased with poverty.

8 Berlant (2001) argues that contemporary expressions of self-expressivity and self-reflexive personhood link norms of expressive denegation to genres that conventionalize and make *false equivalents* among diverse traumatic consequences. She shows how the appropriation of legal rhetoric in tales of testimony aims to claim the authority of self-evidence (as opposed to authority bequeathed by institutions).

9 Rap music and white British film have reproduced this narrative of the emasculating woman who interferes in the real business of friendship between men.

10 Just as standpoint was something the researcher used to take on behalf of others, which then became a means of asserting individual and self-authority (seeProbyn (1993b; Skeggs 1995).

11 Although, as Boyne (2002) notes, this is exactly what he doesn't do in *The Weight of the World*. See also McRobbie at hhtp://www.les1.man.ac.uk/sociology/bourdieu conference.

12 Thanks to Andrew Sayer for clarifying this and for a development of this argument (see Skeggs 1994).

8 Resourcing the entitled middle-class self

1 Featherstone (1991) shows how there are three senses in which we can speak of the aestheticization of everyday life. First, we can refer to those artistic subcultures which produced Dada, the historical avant-garde, surrealist movements in World War One and the 1920s, which sought in their work, writings, and in some cases lives, to efface the boundary between art and everyday life. Second, the aestheticization of everyday life can refer to the project of turning life into a work of art. The third sense of the aestheticization of everyday life refers to the rapid flow of signs and images that saturate the fabric of everyday life in contemporary society. Theorization of this process has drawn much from Marx's theory of the fetishism of commodities which has been developed in various ways by Lukacs, the Frankfurt School, Benjamin, Haug, Lefebvre, Baudrillard and Jameson.

2 Personal communication.

3 Following Adam Smith, Marx distinguished use-value from exchange-value: usefulness, which cannot be quantified, from the ability to exchange with other commodities, which can be quantified. Every commodity has a use-value, but not every use-value is a commodity, for use-values, which are either freely available or are not exchanged, have no exchange-value (Fine 1975). The question Marx wanted to answer is what the determinant is of the relationship of exchange of commodities. What causes them to be equivalents in exchange? This, he argued, was the product of human labour. A use-value is not a commodity unless it embodies a labour cost (and is exchanged). Thus, the property that all commodities have in common, that creates the relations of exchange, is that they are the product of labour.

4 See Debbie Fallon (2000) for how this is worked through in state rhetoric on teenage pregnancy. Unpublished paper presented to University of Manchester postgraduate forum.

5 Strathern does not use the concept of the self, which assumes a Western model of coherence.

6 See Castree (2003) for an account of 'prospecting' whereby global companies work at converting nature into a resource.

7 Cook (2000) argues that Bourdieu's critique of taste is itself marked by its own aesthetic moments. The 'anti-Kantian' aesthetic is not simply presented as one further datum in an enterprise of the social critique of taste. Bourdieu prefers it to what he presents as the emotionally cold formalisms of high bourgeois taste. He invites his readers to give new value to a mode of judgement, which is presented as socially despised. He therefore, Cook argues, makes a judgement of taste between judgements of taste.

8 They also note significant age and regional differences between different factions of the middle-classes.

9 Their research suggests that education, income, age, social network connections and gender are all highly significant in determining levels of participation in leisure and cultural pursuits.

10 Personal communication.

11 See Bridget Fowler's (2002) paper on obituaries.

12 This also presupposes a particular model of acquisition, through the body: 'We learn bodily, the body is a memory pad' (Bourdieu 2000b:141).

13 In fact – as is evidenced by their continual repetition – these laws, with their petulant denunciation of 'excess', were widely flouted, but, they argue, this is not the point (Bennett, Emmison and Frow 1999).

14 Coombe (1993), however, points out that the most powerful are able to utilize this system of value to consolidate their own interests legally. So the 'value' of a product, in other words, lies in the exchange-value of its brand name, advertising image, or status connotations – the distinction it has in the market. Monopoly of the trademark or 'commodity sign' is crucial to corporate capital, often the most valuable of corporate assets and the most important site of capital growth and investment. In practice, this means that the more powerful the corporation, the more success-fully it can immunize itself against oppositional cultural strategies.

15 'Proper ... adj. 1.1. Belonging to oneself for itself; (one's or its) own; owned as property; that is the, or a, property or quality of the thing itself, intrinsic, inherent'. *Oxford English Dictionary* (Davies 1998:163).

16 Thus it is the relationships that enable exchange that produce what appears to be a system of exchange and the product of that exchange.

17 Davies (ibid.) shows how in the US self-ownership is legally recognized to the extent that a person may sue if another appropriates their identity for a commercial purpose.

18 Bourdieu (1986) defines the practices perceived as pretensions as a result of the manifest discrepancy between ambition and possibility. It is the un-hinging of practice from position that makes the pretentious so obvious: practice out of place.

9 Beyond appropriation: proximate strangers, fixing femininity, enabling cosmopolitans

1 See Ahmed (2000); Frank (2001); Spivak (2000).

2 I'd like to thank Jon Binnie for drawing my attention to this area, and being so generous with time and ideas.

3 Zizek could be criticized on the basis that he focuses his attention on corporate multiculturalism, rather than that which has not been in/corporated.

4 Recently Judith Butler (2001) has argued that genuine universalism is a racialized myth. She notes how culture itself is defined through cultural properties which are dependent upon the symbolic order of race (whilst also constitutive of this symbolic order). Thus any claim to univer-sality must be a fetishized desire which eludes the propertizing of cultural processes of exchange.

5 The project on Violence, Sexuality and Space was funded by the Economic and Social ResearchCouncil (ESRC) (grant no. L133251031), see http://www.les1.man.ac.uk/sociology/vssrp.

6 See Mellor (1997) for an account of how and why Manchester chose a policy of 'cultural' regeneration, rather than one of economic regeneration, that could have attended to inequalities in the city.

7 There is only one lesbian bar in the area. Our space census found that within the 13 venues selected to sample, 19.8 per cent of the users were lesbians compared to 35.9 per cent gay men, 19.5 per cent straight women and 13.6 per cent straight men; bi-women and men comprised 6.7 per cent and 1 per cent were transgender. See *Citizen's Inquiry Report* on website: http://www.les1.man. ac.uk/sociology/vssvp. for full details.

8 There is obviously a paradox built into this too, for if too many straight people enter the Village its gayness will be diluted. Yet the Village could not be economically sustained without a broader population.

9 During the 1980s Manchester was represented in the local and national media as a dangerous place, because two local gangs (from Moss Side and Cheetham Hill), whose activities were premised on drug dealing, were fighting each other in a 'turf war'. This representation was milked in the marketing of pop groups from the area to generate a sense of danger and authenticity (e.g. Stone Roses, Happy Mondays, Oasis, etc.).

10 Many of the debates about tourism follow similar lines; certain forms of 'aboriginal' or 'native' groups do not display user-friendly behaviour, thereby limiting their potential for appropriation; or they are not 'authentic' enough for Western consumers (see Blundell 1994).

11 Rose (1999).

12 See 'Discussion of Formations of Class and Gender' (Skeggs 1997) in Chapter 7 for an extended account of the development of textually mediated classed femininity.

13 No doubt this was why she was used in the Pet Shop Boy's video.

14 Or femininity can be excessive as play and parody if there is enough cultural capital elsewhere embodied that can offset the reading of the morally unworthy on the excessive body.

15 In the Female-To-Male project, femininity is always fixed, but fixed centrally in heterosexuality. Sexuality is often the mechanism by which the crossing occurs and masculine positions become the emblem of mobility. Tyler (1991) draws attention to theories that distinguish between simulation and representation. Those who can draw distance from the representation are seen as capable of simulation, those who cannot are fixed by the representation. However, I'd argue that working-class women can and do resist fixing through processes of dis-simulation and dis-identification (see Skeggs 1997).

16 This is why the femme has always been a problem in lesbian bars, as documented by Nestle (1987) who shows how femmes are usually read with suspicion (as Butler suggested earlier) and through heterosexuality; a potential collusion with the enemy.

17 Because these quotes are from the pilot research, we have anonymized the participants. In the focus groups of the main research project participants were asked to choose their own pseudonyms that are used in the earlier examples. Thanks to Lucie Scott and Carole Truman for running this group.

18 Bhabha (1986), describes a similar necessary distancing at work in the colonial imaginary.

19 Zizek (1989) makes the distinction between imaginary and symbolic identification: imaginary identification is identification with the image in which we appear likeable to ourselves, with the image representing 'what we would like to be'; symbolic identification is identification with the place from where we are being observed, from where we look at ourselves so that we appear to ourselves likeable, worthy of love (p.105).

10 Conclusion: changing perspectives

1 Theories of class-consciousness assume that the working-class person will develop an awareness of their positioning and therefore come to operate through class interests (Marx's 'class for itself'). I'd argue, following my previous research, that it is much more complex. People may have an awareness of how they are positioned, they may hate the middle-classes, they may also resist the positioning and find alternative ways of presenting their own interests, which may have specific class consequences (see Skeggs 1997).

2 Castree (1996/7) suggests that this is an essential epistemological move because it reaffirms vision as central to theoretical understandings, at a time when great efforts are going into making the workings of capitalisms invisible. Yet, Gunew (2000) draws attention to the problems of paying too much attention to the visual, at the expense of the cultural. To rephrase Gayatri Spivak, even if the subaltern could speak, would we hear her?

3 This, Davies (1998) argues, illustrates the adaptability of the concept of property to increasingly complex capitalist configurations.

4 The 'metaphysics of the proper' and the corresponding characteristics of self-possession, Derrida notes, mean that the proper is properly untranslatable: a proper name designates the connection of a name to a thing, without any conceptual element which would mediate the connection, meaning that it has the appearance of being 'outside' the ordinary circulation of signifiers and signifieds which constitute language (Davies 1998:18).

5 Butler (1990) assumes that anyone can participate in exposing the fiction of sexual identity. Yet for many lesbians and gays, who have not had the social resources or mobility to insulate themselves from heteronormativity's insistence that sex equals gender, drag has not been so much playful subversion as a painful yearning for authenticity, occasionally with brutally violent results (see Hennessy 2000).

6   O'Neill (1999) illustrates how the supposed move to a sign-based economy, in which all use-value is effaced by exchange, is in fact not a modern idea but an old one, a concern about morality.

7   In ancient Roman law *homo sacer* referred to somebody who could be killed with impunity and whose death had no sacrificial value.

8   This was made completely explicit in Margaret Thatcher's 'war' on the miners in the 1980s; she identified the miners as the 'enemy within', the threat to the stability of the good of the nation.

9   Zizek (2002) argues that Jews are the best example of the enemy par excellence

> not because they conceal their true image or contours but because there is ultimately nothing behind their deceiving appearances. Jews lack the 'inner form' that pertains to any proper national identity; they are a non-nation among nations, their national substance resides precisely in a lack of substance, in a formless infinite plasticity.
>
> (Zizek 2002:5)

10 Reed (1995) argues that the majority of Americans feel fear, shame and helplessness because of the continuing degradation of socio-economic life and the continual anxiety associated with fear. The US has become a dangerous domicile. He makes the comparison to domestic abuse (to conflate the specific abuse of women with generalized suffering again).

11 He shows how these articles offer a dystopic chronology in two instalments: in the first phase, indigenous criminal elements take over the small-town rural suburbs. In the second phase, nameless third-world infidels housed in the UN make a final conquering manoeuvre to rush the whole nation, making their first point of attack a leafy Michigan suburb. In the articles murder and mayhem are everywhere.

12 Berlant (1997) describes the adult without sin to be most effectively represented by foetal person-hood:

> The foetus was an American to identify with, to aspire to make a world for: it organized a kind of beautiful citizenship politics of good intention and virtuous fantasy that could not be said to be dirty, or whose dirt was attributed to the sexually or politically immoral.
>
> (Berlant 1997:201)

13 One context in which the rationality of vengeance is made is through the link between retribution and vengeance. Through this link the credit/debt metaphor of retribution is connected to the idea of vengeance. The 're' of re-venge draws attention to the fact that vengeance is a response to, and the return of, a prior act: a re-payment. This re-turn places vengeance in the frame of a potentially civilizing economy of violence: just desserts. In turn, just desserts connotes equality, balance, harmony and stability (Moran and Skeggs 2003).

14 It is also interesting how these ciphers of alienation eventually become incorporated, through attribution with middle-class cultural capital; designated as poets or artists.

15 Perfectly encapsulated by Eminem's video *Without You*.

16 Wallace (1993) has shown how this process has had devastating consequences for the reproduction of black masculinity, whereby the sexually powerful, glamorous image of the male 'gangsta' has led to high mortality rates. The combination of lack of alternatives and some value from within local communities and symbolic legitimation generates a form of affectivity.

17 See popular discussion by Garfield (2002) and Bell (2002).

18 Or the derision aimed at the new legions of social workers brought in to modify the behaviour of the unruly working-class (Skeggs 1997).

Bibliography

Abercrombie, N., Hill, S. and Turner B. (1986) *Sovereign Individuals of Capitalism*, London: Allen and Unwin.

Adkins, L. (1995) *Gendered Work: Sexuality, Family and the Labour Market*, Buckingham: Open University Press.

—— (2000a) 'Mobile desire: aesthetics, sexuality and the "lesbian" at work', *Sexualities*, 3(2): 201–18.

—— (2000b) 'Objects of innovation: post-occupational reflexivity and re-traditionalisation of gender', in Ahmed, S., Kilby, J., Lury, C., McNeil, M. and Skeggs, B. (eds) *Transformations: Thinking Through Feminism*, London: Routledge.

—— (2001) 'Cultural feminisation: "money, sex and power" for women', *Signs*, 26(3): 669–97.

—— (2002a) 'Reflexivity and the politics of qualitative research: who speaks for whom, why, how and when?', in May, T. (ed.) *Companion to Qualitative Research*, London: Sage.

—— (2002b) *Revisions: Gender and Sexuality in Late Modernity*, Buckingham: Open University Press.

—— (2002c) 'Sexuality and economy: historicisation vs deconstruction', *Australian Feminist Studies*, 17(37): 31–41.

Adkins, L. and Lury, C. (1999) 'The labour of identity: performing identities, performing economies'. *Economy and Society*, 28(4) November: 598–614.

Agamben, G. (1998) *Homo Sacer: Sovereign Power and Bare Life*, Stanford, CA: Stanford University Press.

Aglietta, M. (1987) *A Theory of Capitalist Regulation: The US Experience*, London: Verso.

Aherne, C. and Cash, C. (2000) *The Royle Family: The Scripts Series 2*, London: Granada.

Ahmed, S. (1998a) *Differences that Matter: Feminist Theory and Postmodernism*, Cambridge: Cambridge University Press.

—— (1998b) 'Tanning the body: skin, colour and gender', *New Formations*, 34: 27–43.

—— (2000) *Strange Encounters: Embodied Others in PostColoniality*, London: Routledge.

Ahmed, S. and Stacey, J. (2001) 'Testimonial cultures: an introduction', *Cultural Values*, 5(1): 1–6.

Ahmed, S., Kilby, J., Lury, C., McNeil, M. and Skeggs, B. (eds) (2000) *Transformations: Thinking Through Feminism*, London: Routledge.

Altman, D. (1996) 'Rupture or continuity? The internationalisation of Gay Identities', *Social Text*, 48: 77–94.

—— (1997) 'Global gaze/global gays', *GLQ: A Journal of Lesbian and Gay Studies*, 3:417–36.

—— (2001) *Global Sex*, Chicago: Chicago University Press.

Amariglio, J. and Callari, A. (1989) 'Marxian value theory and the problem of the subject', *Rethinking Marxism*, 2(3): 1–30.

Appadurai, A. (ed.) (1986) *The Social Life of Things*, Cambridge: Cambridge University Press.

Arditi, J. (1999) 'Etiquette books, discourse and the deployment of an order of things', *Theory, Culture and Society*, 16(4): 25–48.

Arrighi, A. (1994) *The Long Twentieth Century*, London: Verso.

Atkinson, P. (1990) *The Ethnographic Imagination*, London: Routledge.

Auge, M. (1995) *Non-Places: An Introduction to an Anthropology of Super Modernity*, London: Verso.

Back, L. and Quaade, V. (1993) 'Dream utopias, nightmare realities; imagining race and culture within the world of Benetton advertising', *Third Text*, 22: 65–80.

Bailey, P. (1998) *Popular Culture and Performance in the Victorian City*, Cambridge: Cambridge University Press.

Bakhtin, M. (1981) 'Discourse in the Novel', in Holquist, M. (ed.) *The Dialogical Imagination*, Austin, Texas: University of Texas Press.

—— (1984) *Rabelais and His World*, Bloomington: Indiana University Press.

Balibar, E. (1991) 'Is there a "neo-racism"?', in Balibar, E. and Wallerstein, I. (eds) *Race, Nation, Class: Ambiguous Identities*, London: Verso.

—— (1999) 'Class racism', in Torres, R.D., Miron, L.F. and Inda, J.X. (eds) *Race, Identity and Citizenship: A Reader*, Oxford: Blackwell.

Bar On, B.-A. (1993) 'Marginality and epistemic privilege', in Alcoff, L. and Potter, E. (eds) *Feminist Epistemologies*, London: Routledge.

Barret-Ducrocq, F. (1992) *Love in the Time of Victoria: Sexuality and Desire among Working-Class Men and Women in Nineteenth-Century London*, London: Penguin.

Barzel, Y. (1997) *Economic Analysis of Property Rights*, Cambridge: Cambridge University Press.

Baudrillard, J. (1983) *Simulations*, New York: Semiotext(e).

Bauman, M. (1998) *Work, Consumerism and the New Poor*, Buckingham: Open University Press.

Beck, U. (1992) *Risk Society: Towards a New Modernity*, London: Sage.

—— (2000) 'The cosmopolitan perspective: sociology of the second age of modernity', *British Journal of Sociology*, 51: 79–105.

Beck, U. and Beck-Gernsheim, E. (1995) *The Normal Chaos of Love*, Cambridge: Polity Press.

Beck, U., Giddens, A. and Lash, S. (1994) *Reflexive Modernisation: Politics, Tradition and Aesthetics in the Modern Social Order*, Cambridge: Polity Press.

Becker, G. (1996) *Accounting for Tastes*, Cambridge, MA: Harvard University Press.

Bell, D. (1993) *Daughters of the Dreaming*, second edition, St Leonards, NSW, Australia: Allen and Unwin.

—— (2002) *Ethical Ambition*, London: Bloomsbury.

Bell, D. and Nelson, T. (1989) 'Speaking about rape is everybody's business', *Women's Studies International Forum*, 12(4): 403–47.

Bennett, T. (1998) *Culture: A Reformer's Science*, London: Sage.

—— (2003) 'The invention of the modern cultural fact: toward a critique of the critique of everyday life', in Silva, E.B. and Bennet, T. (eds) *Contemporary Culture and Everyday Life*, Durham: Sociology Press.

Bennett, T., Emmison, M. and Frow, J. (1999) *Accounting for Tastes: Australian Everyday Cultures*, Cambridge: Cambridge University Press.

Berlant, L. (1997) *The Queen of America Goes to Washington City: Essays on Sex and Citizenship*, London: Duke University Press.

—— (2000) 'The subject of true feeling: pain, privacy, politics', in Ahmed, S., Kilby, J., Lury, C., McNeil, M. and Skeggs, B. (eds) *Transformations: Thinking Through Feminism*, London: Routledge.

—— (2001) 'Trauma and ineloquence', *Cultural Values*, 5(1): 41–58.

—— (2002) 'Forgetting love, remembering everything: now voyager'. Paper presented to University of Manchester.

Berlant, L. and Freeman, E. (1993) 'Queer nationality', in Warner, M. (ed.) *Fear of a Queer Planet: Queer Politics and Social Theory*, Minneapolis: University of Minnesota Press.

Berlant, L. and Warner, M. (1998) 'Sex in public', *Critical Inquiry*, 24(Winter): 547–66.

Bernstein, B. (1971) *Class, Codes and Control*, London: Routledge and Kegan Paul.

Beynon, H. (1999) 'A classless society?', in Beynon, H. and Glavanis, P. (eds) *Patterns of Social Inequality*, Harlow: Pearson Education Ltd.

Bhabha, H. (1986) 'The other question: difference, discrimination and the discourse of colonialism', in Barker, F. (ed.) *Literature, Politics, and Theory: Papers from the Essex Conference, 1976–84*, London: Methuen.

—— (1994) *The Location of Culture*, London: Routledge.

—— (1996) 'Rethinking Authority: interview with Homi Bhabha', *Angelaki*, 2(2): 59–65.

Billig, M. (1987) *Arguing and Thinking: A Rhetorical Approach to Social Psychology*, Cambridge: Cambridge University Press.

Blundell, V. (1994) '"Take home Canada": representations of Aboriginal peoples as tourist souvenirs', in Riggins, S.H. (ed.) *The Socialness of Things*, Berlin: Mouton de Gruyter.

Bogard, W. (1998) 'Sense and segmentarity: some markers of a Deleuzian–Guattarian sociology', *Sociological Theory*, 16(1): 52–74.

Boltanski, L. (1979) 'Taxonomies sociales et lutte de classes. La mobilisation de la "classe moyenne" et l'invention des "cadres"', *Actes de la Recherche en Sciences Sociales*, 29: 75–105.

Bondi, L. (1998) 'Gender, class and urban spaces: public and private space in contemporary urban landscapes', *Urban Geography*, 19(2): 160–85.

Bonnett, A. (1998) 'How the British working-class become white: the symbolic (re)formation of racialised capitalism', *Journal of Historical Sociology*, 11: 316–40.

Bourdieu, P. (1977) *Outline of a Theory of Practice*, Cambridge: Cambridge University Press.

—— (1979) 'Symbolic power', *Critique of Anthropology*, 4: 77–85.

—— (1980/1990) *The Logic of Practice*, Oxford: Oxford University Press.

—— (1985) 'The social space and the genesis of groups', *Theory and Society*, 14: 723–44.

—— (1986) *Distinction: A Social Critique of the Judgement of Taste*, London: Routledge.

—— (1987) 'What makes a social class? On the theoretical and practical existence of groups', *Berkeley Journal of Sociology*: 1–17.

—— (1988) *Homo Academicus*, Cambridge: Polity Press.

—— (1989) 'Social space and symbolic power', *Sociological Theory*, 7: 14–25.

—— (1992) *Language and Symbolic Power*, Cambridge: Polity Press.

—— (1993) *Sociology in Question*, London: Sage.

—— (2000a) *Les Structures Sociales de L'économie*, Paris: Sevil.

—— (2000b) *Pascalian Meditations*, Cambridge: Polity Press.

Bourdieu, P. and Waquant, L. (1992) *An Invitation to Reflexive Sociology*, Chicago: University of Chicago Press.

—— (2001) 'NewLiberalSpeak: notes on the planetary vulagate', *Radical Philosophy*, 105: 1–6.

Bourdieu, P., Accardo, A., Balazs, G., Beaud, S., Bonvin, F., Bourdieu, E., Bourgois, P., Broccolichi, S., Champagne, P., Christin, R., Faguer, J.P., Garcia, S., Lenior, R., Oeuvard, F., Pialoux, M., Pinto, L., Podalydes, D., Sayad, A., Soulie, C. and Waquant, L.J.D. (1999) *The Weight of the World: Social Suffering in Contemporary Society*, Cambridge: Polity Press.

Bower, L. (1997) 'Queer problems/straight solutions: the limit of the politics of "official" recognition', in Phelan, S. (ed.) *Playing with Fire: Queer Politics, Queer Theories*, New York: Routledge.

Boyne, R. (2002) 'Bourdieu: from class to culture', *Theory, Culture and Society*, 19(3): 117–28.

Brainerd, L. (1991) 'International Monetary Programme', Brussels, IMP.

Brennan, T. (1997) 'At home in the world: cosmopolitanism now', Cambridge, MA: Harvard University Press.

Brenner, J. (2001) *Women and The Politics of Class*, New York: Monthly Review Press.

Bromley, R. (2000) 'The theme that dare not speak its name: class and recent British film', in Munt, S. (ed.) *Cultural Studies and the Working-Class: Subject to Change*, London: Cassell.

Brooks, D. (2001) *Bobos in Paradise: The New Upper Class and How They Got There*, New York: Simon and Shuster.

Brown, W. (1995) 'Wounded attachments: late modern oppositional political formations', in Rajchman, J. (ed.) *The Identity in Question*, London: Routledge.

—— (2001) *Politics out of History*, Princeton, NJ: Princeton University Press.

Brunsdon, C. (1997) *Screen Tastes: Soap Opera to Satellite Dishes*, London: Routledge.

Brydon, A. (1998) 'Sensible shoes', in Brydon, A. and Niesson, S.A. (eds) *Consuming Fashion: Adorning the Transnational Body*, Oxford: Berg.

Bryson, B. (1996) 'Anything but heavy metal: symbolic exclusion and musical dislikes', *American Sociological Review*, 61: 844–99.

—— (1997) 'What about the univores? Musical dislikes and group-based identity among Americans with low levels of education', *Poetics*, 25: 141–56.

Burke, K. (1962) *A Rhetoric of Motives*, New York: George Brazillier.

Butler, J. (1990) *Gender Trouble: Feminism and the Subversion of Identity*, London: Routledge.

—— (1993) *Bodies That Matter: On the Discursive Limits of 'Sex'*, London: Routledge.

—— (1997a) *Excitable Speech: The Politics of the Performative*, New York: Routledge.

—— (1997b) 'Merely cultural', *Social Text 52/53*, 15(3 & 4): 264–77.

—— (1999) 'Performativity's social magic', in Shusterman, R. (ed.) *Bourdieu: A Critical Reader*, Oxford: Blackwell.

—— (2001) 'Is kinship always heterosexual?'. Opening Keynote for CATH (Centre for Art, Theory and Humanities) at the University of Leeds, Leeds.

Butsch, R. (2001) 'American movie audiences of the 1930s', *International Labor and Working-Class History*, 59(Spring):106–20.

Byrne, B. (2003) 'Reciting the self: narrative representations of the self in qualitative interviews', *Feminist Theory*, 4(1): 29–49.

Callinicos, A. (2001) *Against the Third Way*, Cambridge: Polity Press.

Callon, M. (1998) *The Laws of the Market*, Oxford: Blackwell.

Campbell, C. (1987) *The Romantic Ethic and the Spirit of Modern Consumerism*, Oxford: Blackwell.

Cannadine, D. (1998) *Class in Britain*, New Haven: Yale University Press.

Carling, A. (1990) *Social Division*, London: Verso.

Carrier, J.G. (ed.) (1997) *Meanings of the Market: The Free Market in Western Culture*, Oxford: Berg.

Carter, E. (1990) 'Design, class and lifestyle: a West Berlin perspective', *Magazine of Cultural Studies*, 2(8–11 October).

Castree, N. (1996/7) 'Invisible leviathan: speculations on Marx, Spivak, and the question of value', *Rethinking Marxism*, 9(2):748–78.

—— (2003) 'Bioprospecting: from theory to practice (and back again)', *Transactions of the Institute of British Geographers*, 28(1): 35–55.

Chanfrault-Duchet, M.-F. (2000) 'Textualisation of the self and gender identity in the life story', in Cosslett, T., Lury, C. and Summerfield, P. (eds) *Feminism and Autobiography*, London: Routledge.

Charlesworth, S. (2000) *A Phenomenology of Working-Class Experience*, Cambridge: Cambridge University Press.

Cheah, P. (1998) 'Introduction part II: the cosmopolitical – today', in Robbins, B. and Cheah, P. (eds) *Cosmopolitics: Thinking and Feeling Beyond the Nation*, Minneapolis: University of Minnesota Press.

Clifford, J. (1988) *The Predicament of Culture*, Cambridge, MA: Harvard University Press.

—— (1992) 'Travelling cultures', in Grossberg, L., Nelson, C. and Treichler, P. (eds) *Cultural Studies*, London: Routledge.

Code, L. (1995) *Rhetorical Spaces: Essays on Gendered Locations*, London: Routledge.

Cohen, G. A. (1988) *History, Labour and Freedom: Themes from Marx*, Oxford: Clarendon.

—— (1995) *Self-Ownership, Freedom and Equality*, Cambridge: Cambridge University Press.

Connor, S. (1993) 'The necessity of value', in Squires, J. (ed.) *Principled Positions: Postmodernism and the Rediscovery of Value*, London: Lawrence and Wishart.

Cook, J. (2000) 'Culture, class and taste', in Munt, S. (ed.) *Cultural Studies and the Working-Class: Subject to Change*, London: Cassell.

Coombe, R. (1993) 'Publicity rights and political aspiration: mass culture, gender identity and democracy', *New England Law Review*, 26: 1,211–80.

Cornell, D. (1993) *Transformations: Recollective Imagination and Sexual Difference*, London: Routledge.

Cosslett, T., Lury, C. and Summerfield, P. (eds) (2000) *Feminism and Autobiography: Texts, Theories, Methods*, London: Routledge.

Cowie, E. (1978) 'Woman as sign', *m/f*, 1: 49–64.

Crompton, R. (1993) *Class and Stratification: An Introduction to Current Debates*, Cambridge: Polity Press.

Crompton, R., Devine, F., Savage, M. and Scott, J. (eds) (2000) *Renewing Class Analysis*, Oxford: Blackwell.

Cronin, A.M. (2000a) *Advertising and Consumer Citizenship: Gender, Images and Rights*, London: Routledge.

—— (2000b) 'Consumerism and "compulsory individuality": women, will and potential', in Ahmed, S., Kilby, J., Lury, C., McNeil, M. and Skeggs, B. (eds) *Transformations: Thinking Through Feminism*, London: Routledge.

Crossick, G. (1991) 'From gentlemen to the residuum: languages of social description in Victorian Britain', in Corfield, P.J. (ed.) *Langauge, History and Class*, Oxford: Blackwell.

Curran, M.M. (1999) 'Not working in the inner city: unemployment from the 1970s to the 1990s', in Beynon, H. and Glavanis, P. (eds) *Patterns of Social Inequality*, Harlow: Pearson.

Daley, J. (1994) 'The Janet Daley column', *The Times*, London: 16.

David, M. (1980) *The State, the Family and Education*, London: Routledge and Kegan Paul.

Davidoff, L. and Hall, C. (1987) *Family Fortunes*, London: Hutchinson.

Davies, M. (1994) 'Feminist appropriations: law, property and personality', *Social and Legal Studies*, 3: 365–91.

—— (1998) 'The proper: discourses of purity', *Law and Critique*, IX: 147–73.

—— (1999) 'Queer property, queer persons: self-ownership and beyond', *Social and Legal Studies*, 8(3): 327–52.

Davis, A.Y. (1995) 'I used to be your sweet mama: ideology, sexuality and domesticity in the blues of Gertrude "Ma" Rainey and Bessie Smith', in Grosz, E. and Probyn, E. (eds) *Sexy Bodies: The Strange Carnalities of Feminism*, London: Routledge.

Davis, M. (1990) *City of Quartz*, London: Verso.

Day, G. (2001) *Class*, London: Routledge.

de Certeau, M. (1988) *The Practice of Everyday Life*, London: University of California Press.

de Certeau, M. and Giard, L. (1998) *Culture in the Plural*, Minneapolis: University of Minnesota.

de Groot, J. (1989) '"Sex" and "race" the construction of language and image in the nineteenth century', in Mendus, S. and Rendall, J. (eds) *Sexuality and Subordination*, London: Routledge.

de Lauretis, T. (1984) *Alice Doesn't: Feminism, Semiotics, Cinema*, London: Routledge.

Deleuze, G. and Guattari, F. (1977) *Anti-Oedipus: Capitalism and Schizophrenia*, New York: The Viking Press.

—— (1987) *A Thousand Plateaus: Capitalism and Schizophrenia*, Vol. 2, Minneapolis: University of Minnesota Press.

Derrida, J. (1974) *Of Grammatology*, Baltimore: Johns Hopkins University.

Devine, F. (1997) *Social Class in America and Britain*, Edinburgh: Edinburgh University Press.

—— (1998) 'Class analysis and the stability of class relations', *Sociology*, 32(1): 23–42.

Diawara, M. (1998) 'Homeboy cosmopolitan: Manthia Diawara interviewed by Silvia Kolbowski', *October*, 83(Winter): 51–70.

DiMaggio, P. (1986) 'Cultural entrepreneurship in nineteenth-century Boston: the creation of an organisational base for high culture in America', in Collins, R., Curran, J., Garnham, P., Scannell, P., Schlesinger, P. and Sparks, C. (eds) *Media, Culture and Society: A Critical Reader*, London: Sage.

Diprose, R. (1994) *The Bodies of Women: Ethics, Embodiment and Sexual Difference*, London: Routledge.

Dodd, N. (1994) *The Sociology of Money: Economics, Reason and Contemporary Society*, Cambridge: Polity Press.

Donzelot, J. (1979) *The Policing of Families: Welfare versus the State*, London: Hutchinson.

Douglas, M. and Isherwood, B. (1980) *The World of Goods*, Harmondsworth: Penguin.

Douglas, S.J. (1994) *Where the Girls Are: Growing up Female with the Mass Media*, London: Penguin.

Dowling, R. (1999) 'Classing the body', *Environment and Planning D: Society and Space*, 17: 511–14.

du Gay, P. (1996) *Consumption and Identity at Work*, London: Sage.

Duneier, M. (1992) *Slim's Table: Race, Respectability and Masculinity*, Chicago: University of Chicago Press.

Durham, M. (1991) *Sex and Politics: The Family and Morality in the Thatcher Years*, Basingstoke: Macmillan.

Eagleton, T. (1989) 'The ideology of the aesthetic', in Hernadi, P. (ed.) *The Rhetoric of Interpretation and the Interpretation of Rhetoric*, Durham, NC: Duke University Press.

Ehrenreich, B. (1990) *Fear of Falling: The Inner Life of the Middle-Class*, New York: Pantheon.

—— (2001) *Nickel and Dimed: On Not Getting By in America*, New York: Henry Holt.

Elias, N. (1982) *Power and Civility: The Civilising Process*, Vol. 2, New York: Pantheon Books.

Elster, J. (1985) *Making Sense of Marx*, Cambridge: Cambridge University Press.

Enevold, J. (2000) 'Men and women on the move: dramas of the road', *European Journal of Cultural Studies*, 3(3): 403–21.

Engels, F. (1844/1958) *The Condition of the Working-Class in England*, St Albans, Herts: Panther.

Erickson B. (1991) 'What is good taste for?', *Canadian Review of Sociology and Anthropology*, 28: 255–78.

—— (1996) 'Culture, class and connections', *American Journal of Sociology*, 102: 217–51.

Evans, D. (1993) *Sexual Citizenship: The Material Construction of Sexualities*, London: Routledge.

Evans, M. (1999) *Missing Persons: The Impossibility of Autobiography*, London: Routledge.

Fairclough, N. (1991) 'What might we mean by "enterprise discourse?"', in Keat, R. and Abercrombie, N. (eds) *Enterprise Culture*, London: Routledge.

—— (2000) *New Labour, New Language?*, London: Routledge.

Fallon, D. (2000) *State Rhetoric on Teenage Pregnancy*, Postgraduate Student Forum, University of Manchester.

Fanon, F. (1986) *Black Skin, White Masks*, London: Pluto Press.

Featherstone, M. (1982) 'The body in consumer culture', *Theory, Culture and Society*, 1(2): 18–33.

—— (1991) *Consumer Culture and Postmodernism*, London: Sage.

Featherstone, M., Hepworth, M. and Turner, B.S. (1991) *The Body: Social Process and Cultural Theory*, London: Sage.

Felski, R. (1995) *The Gender of Modernity*, Cambridge, MA: Harvard University Press.

—— (2000) 'Being reasonable, telling stories', *Feminist Theory*, 1(2): 225–30.

Field, N. (1995) *Over the Rainbow: Money, Class and Homophobia*, London: Pluto.

Finch, L. (1993) *The Classing Gaze: Sexuality, Class and Surveillance*, New South Wales, Australia: Allen and Unwin.

Fine, B. (1975) *Marx's Capital*, London: Macmillan.

—— (1999) 'A question of economics: is it colonising the social sciences?', *Economy and Society*, 28(3): 403–25.

—— (2001) *Social Capital versus Social Theory: Political Economy and Social Science at the Turn of the Millennium*, London: Routledge.

Fine, B. and Lapavistas, C. (2000) 'Markets and money in social theory: what role for economics?', *Economy and Society*, 29(3): 357–82.

Fligstein, N. (2001) *The Architecture of Markets: an Economic Sociology of Twenty First Century*, Princeton, NJ: Princeton University Press.

Florida, R. (2002) *The Rise of the Creative Class: and How it's Transforming Work, Leisure, Community and Everyday Life*, New York: Basic Books.

Forde-Jones, C. (1998) 'Mapping social boundaries: gender, race and poor relief in Barbadian plantation society', *Journal of Women's History*, 10(3): 9–31.

Foucault, M. (1966) *The Order of Things*, London: Tavistock.

—— (1974) *The Archaeology of Knowledge*, London: Tavistock.

—— (1979) *The History of Sexuality: Volume One, an Introduction*, London: Penguin.

—— (1988) 'The ethic of care for the self as a practice of freedom', in Berauer, J. and Ramussen, D. (eds) *The Final Foucault*, Cambridge, MA: MIT Press.

Fowler, B. (2002) 'Bourdieu's obituaries'. Paper presented to the 'Feminists Evaluate Bourdieu' Conference, University of Manchester, 2002. See http://www.les1.man.ac.uk/sociology/bourdieu conference.

Frank, T. (1997) *The Conquest of Cool: Business Culture, Counterculture and the Rise of Hip Consumerism*, Chicago: University of Chicago Press.

—— (2001) *One Market Under God: Extreme Capitalism, Market Populism, and the End of Economic Development*, New York: Doubleday.

Franklin, S., Lury, C. and Stacey, J. (2000) *Global Nature, Global Culture*, London: Sage.

Fraser, M. (1999) 'Classing queer: politics in competition', *Theory, Culture and Society*, 16(2): 107–31.

Fraser, N. (1989) *Unruly Practices: Power, Discourse and Gender in Contemporary Social Theory*, Cambridge: Polity Press.

—— (1995) 'From redistribution to recognition? Dilemmas of justice in "post-socialist" age', *New Left Review*, 212: 68–94.

—— (1997) 'Heterosexism, misrecognition and capitalism: a response to Judith Butler', *Social Text 52/53*, 15(3 & 4): 279–89.

Fronsman, B.C. (1992) *Common Whites: Class, Culture in Ante-Bellum North Carolina*, Lexington: University of Kentucky Press.

Frow, J. (1995a) *Cultural Studies and Cultural Value*, Oxford: Oxford University Press.

—— (1995b) 'Elvis's fame; the commodity form and the form of the person', *Cardoza Studies in Law and Literature*, 7: 131–71.

Fukuyama, F. (1992) *The End of History and the Last Man*, London: Hamish Hamilton.

Garfield, S. (2002) 'Is the age of integrity dawning?', *Observer*, 10 November, London.

Gatens, M. (1996) *Imaginary Bodies: Ethics, Power and Corporeality*, London: Routledge.

Genovese, E.D. (1975) *Roll, Jordan, Roll: The World the Slaves Made*, New York: Pantheon Books.

Giddens, A. (1991) *Modernity and Self-identity: Self and Society in the Late Modern Age*, Cambridge: Polity Press.

—— (1998) *The Third Way*, Cambridge: Polity Press.

—— (2000) *The Third Way and Its Critics*, Cambridge: Polity Press.

Gilman, S.L. (1990) '"I'm down on whores": race and gender in Victorian London', in Goldberg, D.T. (ed.) *Anatomy of Racism*, Minneapolis: University of Minnesota Press.

—— (1992) 'Black bodies, white bodies: towards an iconography of female sexuality in late nineteenth-century art, medicine and literature', in Donald, J. and Rattansi, A. (eds) *'Race', Culture and Difference*, London: Sage.

Gilroy, P. (1987) *There Ain't no Black in the Union Jack*, London: Hutchinson.

—— (1990) 'One nation under a groove: the cultural politics of "race" and racism in Britain', in Goldberg, D.T. (ed.) *Anatomy of Racism*, Minneapolis: University of Minnesota Press.

Gittins, I. (2002) 'Crim Watch', *The Guardian*, 20 July, London.

Goldthorpe, J. (1996) 'Class analysis and the re-orientation of class theory: the case of persisting differentials in educational attainment', *British Journal of Sociology*, 45: 211–33.

—— (2000) 'Rent, class conflict, and class structure: a commentary on Sorenson', *American Journal of Sociology*, 105(6): 1,572–82.

Goody, J. (1983) *The Development of Family and Marriage in Europe*, Cambridge: Cambridge University Press.

Graham, S. and Marvin, S. (1998) *Net Effects*, London: Comedia/Demos.

Gramsci, A. (1971) *Selections from Prison Notebooks of Antonio Gramsci*, London: Lawrence and Wishart.

Granovetter, M. (1981) 'Towards a sociological theory of income differences', in Berg, I. (ed.) *Sociological Perspectives on Labour Markets*, New York: Academic Press.

—— (1995) *Getting a Job: A Study of Contacts and Careers*, Chicago: Chicago University Press.

Granovetter, M. and Swedberg, R. (eds) (1992) *The Sociology of Economic Life*, Boulder, CO: Westview Press.

Green, S. (2003) *Boundaries at the Margins: The Greek-Albanian Border*, Chicago: Chicago University Press.

Greer, G. (2001) 'Long live the Essex girl', *The Guardian*, 10 March, G2: 8.

Gregory, C.A. (1997) *Savage Money: The Anthropology and Politics of Commodity Exchange*, Amsterdam: Harwood Academic Publishers.

Griffin, C. (1992) 'Fear of a black (and working-class) planet: young women and the racialisation of reproductive politics', *Feminism and Psychology*, 2(3): 491–4.

Griffin, P. (1999) 'Architectural notes', *City Life*.

Griller, R. (1996) 'The return of the subject? The methodology of Pierre Bourdieu', *Critical Sociology*, 22(1): 3–28.

Grossberg, L. (1988) *It's a Sin: Essays on Postmodernism, Politics and Culture*, New York: Power Publications.

Guillory, J. (1993) *Cultural Capital: The Problems of Literary Canon Formation*, Chicago: Chicago University Press.

Gunew, S. (2000) 'Operatic karaoke and the pitfalls of identity politics', in Ahmed, S., Kilby, J., Lury, C., McNeil, M. and Skeggs, B. (eds) *Transformations: Thinking Through Feminism*, London: Routledge.

Gupta, A. and Ferguson, J. (1997) 'Discipline and practice: "The field" as site, method and location in anthropology', in Gupta, A. and Ferguson, J. (eds) *Anthropological Locations: Boundaries and Grounds of a Field Science*, Berkeley, CA: University of California.

Hage, G. (1998) *White Nation*, Melbourne and London: Pluto Press.

Halberstam, J. (1998) *Female Masculinity*, Durham, NC: Duke University Press.

Hall, C. (1979) 'The early formation of Victorian domestic ideology', in Burman, S. (ed.) *Fit Work for Women*, London: Croom Helm.

Hall, S. (1981/1990) 'The whites of their eyes: racist ideology and the media', in Alvarado, M. and Thompson, J.O. (eds) *The Media Reader*, London: British Film Institute.

—— (1990) 'Cultural identity and diaspora', in Rutherford, J. (ed.) *Identity, Community, Difference*, London: Lawrence and Wishart.

Hannerz, U. (1996) *Transnational Connections: Culture, People, Places*, London: Routledge.

Haraway, D. (1990) 'A manifesto for cyborgs: science, technology and socialist feminism in the 1980s', in Nicholson, L. (ed.) *Feminism/Postmodernism*, London: Routledge.

—— (1991) *Simians, Cyborgs, and Women: The Reinvention of Nature*, London: Free Association Books.

Hardt, M. and Negri, A. (2000) *Empire*, Cambridge, MA: Harvard University Press.

Harrison, S. (1999) 'Identity as a scarce resource', *Social Anthropology*, 7(3): 239–51.

Hart, L. (1994) *Fatal Women: Lesbian Sexuality and the Mark of Aggression*, London: Routledge.

Hartigan Jr, J. (1992) 'Reading trash: deliverance and the poetics of "White Trash"', *Visual Anthropology Review*, 8(2), Fall.

Hartmann, P. and Husband, C. (1974) *Racism and the Mass Media*, London: Davis Poynter.

Harvey, D. (1993) 'Class relations, social justice and the politics of difference', in Keith, M. and Pile, S. (eds) *Place and the Politics of Identity*, London: Routledge.

Hauser, A. (1982) *The Sociology of Art*, London: Routledge and Kegan Paul.

Haylett, C. (2000) '"This is about us, this is our film!" Personal and popular discourses of "underclass"', in Munt, S. (ed.) *Cultural Studies and the Working-Class: Subject to Change*, London: Routledge.

—— (2001) 'Illegitimate subjects? Abject whites, neoliberal modernisation and middle class multiculturalism', *Environment and Planning D: Society and Space*, 19: 351–70.

Healy, M. (1996) *Gay Skins: Class, Masculinity and Queer Appropriation*, London: Cassell.

Heelas, P. (1996) 'Detraditionalisation and its rivals', in Heelas, P., Lash, S. and Morris, D.P. (eds) *Detraditionalisation: Critical Reflections on Authority and Identity*, Oxford: Blackwell.

Hegel, G.W.F. (1821/1967) *Philosophy of Right*, Oxford: Oxford University Press.

Heidegger, M. (1978) *Basic Writings*, London: Routledge and Kegan Paul.

Helmann, C. (1988) 'Dr Frankenstein and the industrial body: reflections on "spare part" surgery', *Anthropology Today*, 4: 14–16.

Hennessy, R. (1995) 'Queer visibility in commodity culture', in Nicholson, L. and Seidman, S. (eds) *Social Postmodernism: Beyond Identity Politics*, Cambridge: Cambridge University Press.

—— (2000) *Profit and Pleasure: Sexual Identities in late Capitalism*, London: Routledge.

Herzfeld, M. (1999) 'Of language and land tenure: the transmission of property and information in autonomous Crete', *Social Anthropology*, 7(3): 223–37.

Hill, J. (1986) *Sex, Class and Realism: British Cinema 1956–1963*, London: British Film Institute.

—— (2000) 'Failure and Utopianism: representations of the working-class in British cinema of the 1990s', in Murphy, R. (ed.) *British Cinema of the 1990s*, London: British Film Institute.

Hirsch, F. (1976) *The Social Limits to Growth*, Cambridge, MA: Harvard University Press.

Hobsbawm, E.J. (1992) *Nations and Nationalism Since 1780: Programme, Myth, Reality*, Cambridge: Cambridge University Press.

Hodgson, G. (1988) *Economics and Institutions*, Cambridge: Polity Press.

Hollander, A. (1988) *Seeing Through Clothes*, London: Penguin.

Hollows, J. (2000) *Feminism, Femininity and Popular Culture*, Manchester: Manchester University Press.

Holmund, C. (1993) 'When is a lesbian not a lesbian? The lesbian continuum and the mainstream femme film', *Camera Obscura*, 25(6): 145–78.

Holquist, M. (1990) *Dialogism, Bahktin and his World*, Austin, Texas: University of Texas Press.

hooks, b. (1990) 'Marginalising a site of resistance', in Ferguson, R., Geves, M., Minh-ha, T.T. and West, C. (eds) *Out There: Marginalisation and Contemporary Culture*, New York: New Museum of Contemporary Art and MIT Press.

Hoschild, A. (1983) *The Managed Heart: Commercialisation of Human Feeling*, Berkeley, CA: University of California Press.

Huff, T.E. (ed.) (1981) *On the Roads to Modernity, Conscience, Science and Civilisations: Selected Writings by Benjamin Nelson*, Totowa, NJ: Rowman and Littlefield.

Hughes, G., McLauglin, E. and Muncie, J. (2001) *Crime Prevention and Community Safety*, London: Sage.

Hunt, L. (1998) *British Low Culture: From Safari Suits to Sexploitation*, London: Routledge.

Hunter, I. (1992) 'Aesthetics and cultural studies', in Grossberg, L., Nelson, C. and Treichler, P. (eds) *Cultural Studies*, London: Routledge.

Hutnyk, J. (1998) 'Clifford's Ethnographica', *Critique of Anthropology*, 18(4): 339–78.

Jackson, P. (1999) 'An explosion of Thai identities: peripheral genders and the limits of queer theory', IAASCS Second International Conference, Manchester Metropolitan University.

Jameson, F. (1981) *Postmodernism, or, The Cultural Logic of Late Capitalism*, London: Verso.

Jancovich, M. (2001) 'Naked ambitions: pornography, taste and the problem of the middlebrow', http://www.nottingham.ac.uk/film/scope.

Jokinen, E. and Veijola, S. (1997) 'The disoriented tourist: the figuration of the tourist in contemporary cultural critique', in Rojek, C. and Urry, J. (eds) *Touring Cultures: Transformations of Travel and Theory*, London: Routledge.

Jones, L. (1994) *Bulletproof Diva: Tales of Race, Sex and Hair*, New York: Doubleday.

Joyce, P. (1994) *Democratic Subjects: The Self and the Social in Nineteenth-Century England*, Cambridge: Cambridge University Press.

Kahn, J.S. (2001) *Modernity and Exclusion*, London: Sage.

Kaplan, C. (1996) *Questions of Travel: Postmodern Discourses of Displacement*, Durham, NC: Duke University Press.

Kapp, Y. (1979) *Eleanor Marx: Family Life 1855–1883*, Vol. 1, London: Virago.

Kay, J.P. (1832) *The Moral and Physical Condition of the Working-Classes Employed in Cotton Manufacture in Manchester*, London: James Ridgway.

Keith, M. and Pile, S. (1993) *Place and the Politics of Identity*, London: Routledge.

Killick, A.P. (1995) 'The penetrating intellect: on being white, straight, and male in Korea', in Kulick, D. and Willson, M. (eds) *Taboo: Sex, Identity and Erotic Subjectivity in Anthropological Fieldwork*, London: Routledge.

Kipnis, L. (1999) *Bound and Gagged: Pornography and the Politics of Fantasy in America*, Durham, NC: Duke University Press.

Kipniss, M. (1993) 'Transparent commodities', *Rethinking Marxism*, 6(3): 1–21.

Kishlansky, M. (1997) *Monarchy Transformed: Britain, 1603–1714*, Harmondsworth: Penguin.

Kopytoff, I. (1986) 'The cultural biography of things: commoditization as process', in Appadurai, A. (ed.) *The Social Life of Things: Commodities in Cultural Perspective*, Cambridge: Cambridge University Press.

Kroker, A. (1985) 'Baudrillard's Marx', *Theory, Culture and Society*, 2(3): 56–70.

Kuhn, A. (1995) *Family Secrets: Acts of Memory and Imagination*, London: Verso.

Kulick, D. (1998) *Travesti: Sex, Gender and Culture among Brazilian Transgendered Prostitutes*, Chicago: University of Chicago Press.

Kulick, D. and Willson, M. (eds) (1995) *Taboo: Sex, Identity and Erotic Subjectivity in Anthropological Fieldwork*, London: Routledge.

Laing, S. (1986) *Representations of Working-Class Life 1957–1964*, London: Macmillan.

Lamont, M. (1991) *Money, Morals and Manners: The Culture of the French and the American Upper Middle Class*, Chicago: Chicago University Press.

—— (1992) *Cultivating Differences: Symbolic Boundaries and the Making of Inequality*, Chicago: University of Chicago Press.

—— (2000) *The Dignity of Working Men: Morality and the Boundaries of Gender, Race and Class*, Cambridge, MA: Harvard University Press.

Lapovsky Kennedy, E. and Davis, M.D. (1993) *Boots of Leather, Slippers of Gold: The History of a Lesbian Community*, New York: Penguin.

Lash, S. (1990) *The Sociology of Postmodernism*, London: Routledge.

—— (1994) 'Reflexivity and its doubles: structure, aesthetics, community', in Beck, U., Giddens, A. and Lash, S. (eds) *Reflexive Modernisation: Politics, Tradition and Aesthetics in the Modern Social Order*, Cambridge: Polity Press.

Lawler, S. (1999) 'Getting out and getting away', *Feminist Review*, 63: 3–24.

—— (2000a) 'Escape and escapism: representing working-class women', in Munt, S. (ed.) *Cultural Studies and the Working-Class: Subject to Change*, London: Cassell.

—— (2000b) *Mothering the Self: Mothers, Daughters, Subjects*, London: Routledge.

Levitas, R. (1998) *The Inclusive Society? Social Exclusion and New Labour*, London: Macmillan.

Lingis, A. (1994) 'The society of dismembered body parts', in Boundas, C. and Olkowski, D. (eds) *Giles Deleuze and the Theater of Philosophy*, London: Routledge.

Linklater, A. (1998) *The Transformation of Citizenship*, Cambridge: Polity Press.

Lipset, S.M. (1959) *Social Mobility in Industrial Society*, Berkeley, CA: University of California Press.

Longhurst, B. and Savage, M. (1996) 'Social class, consumption and the influence of Bourdieu: some critical issues', in Edgell, S., Hetherington, K. and Warde, A. (eds) *Consumption Matters*, Oxford: Blackwell Publishers.

Lovell, T. (2000) 'Thinking feminism with and against Bourdieu', *Feminist Theory*, 1(1): 11–32.

Lucey, H. and Reay, D. (2000) 'Social class and the psyche', *Soundings: Journal of Politics and Culture*, 15: 139–54.

Lury, C. (1993) *Cultural Rights: Technology, Legality and Personality*, London: Routledge.

—— (1997a) *Consumer Culture*, Cambridge: Polity Press.

—— (1997b) 'The objects of travel', in Rojek, C. and Urry, J. (eds) *Touring Cultures*, London: Routledge.

—— (1998) *Prosthetic Culture: Photography, Memory and Identity*, London: Routledge.

—— (2000) 'The united colours of diversity: essential and inessential culture', in Franklin, S., Lury, C. and Stacey, J. (eds) *Global Nature, Global Culture*, London: Sage.

Mac an Ghaill, M. (1994) *The Making of Men: Masculinities, Sexualities and Schooling*, Buckingham: Open University Press.

MacKintosh, M. (1990) 'Abstract markets and real needs', in Bernstein, H., Crow, G., MacKintosh, M. and Martin, C. (eds) *The Food Question: Profits versus People*, London: Earthscan.

Macpherson, C.B. (1962) *The Political Theory of Possessive Individualism*, Oxford: Oxford University Press.

Mahony, P. and Zmroczek, C. (eds) (1997) *Class Matters: 'Working-Class' Women's Perspectives on Social Class*, London: Taylor and Francis.

Marcus, L. (1994) *Auto/Biographical Discourses*, Manchester: Manchester University Press.

Marcuse, H. (1964) *One Dimensional Man: The Ideology of Industrial Society*, London: Sphere Books.

Martin, B. (1996) *Femininity Played Straight: The Significance of Being Lesbian*, New York: Routledge.

Martin, E. (1989) *The Woman in the Body*, London: Routledge.

—— (1994) *Flexible Bodies: Tracking Immunity in America from the Days of Polio to the Age of AIDS*, London: Routledge.

—— (1997) 'The end of the body', in Lancaster, R. and DiLeonardo, M. (eds) *The Gender/Sexuality Reader*, London: Routledge.

Martinsson, L. and Reimers, E. (2002) 'Towards a disharmonious pluralism: discourse analysis of official discourse about social diversity', Knowledge and Discourse Conference, Hong Kong.

Marvin, S. (2002) 'Understanding the city from the centre', *URBIS: Of the City*, Manchester: Manchester Metropolitan University.

Marx, K. (1857/1970) *The German Ideology*, London: Lawrence and Wishart.

—— (1967) *Capital*, Vol. 1, New York: International Publishers.

Massey, D. (1991) 'Flexible sexism', *Environment and Planning D: Society and Space*, 9(1): 270–81.

—— (1994) 'Power-geometry and a progressive sense of place', in Robertson, G., Marsh, M., Tickner, L., Bird, J., Curtis, B. and Putnam, T. (eds) *Travellers' Tales*, London: Routledge.

Mauss, M. (1925/1990) *The Gift: The Form and Reason of Exchange in Archaic Societies*, New York: Norton.

Maynard, M. (1998) 'Feminists' knowledge and the knowledge of feminisms: epistemology, theory, methodology and method', in May, T. and Williams, M. (eds) *Knowing the Social World*, Buckingham: Open University Press.

McCarthy, C. (2000) 'Reading the American popular: suburban resentment and the representation of the inner city in contemporary film and TV', in Fleming, D. (ed.) *Formations: A 21st-Century Media Studies Textbook*, Manchester: Manchester University Press.

McClintock, A. (1995) *Imperial Leather: Race, Gender and Sexuality in the Colonial Context*, London: Routledge.

McKeon, R. (1987) *Rhetoric: Essays in Invention and Discovery*, Woodbridge: Ox Bow Press.

McMylor, P. (2001) 'McIntyre: virtue ethics and beyond', British Sociological Association Annual Conference, Manchester.

McNall, S.G., Levine, R.F. and Fantasia, R. (eds) (1991) *Bringing Class Back In*, Boulder, CO: Westview Press.

McNay, L. (1999) 'Gender, habitus and the field: Pierre Bourdieu and the limits of reflexivity', *Theory, Culture and Society*, 16(1): 95–119.

Medhurst, A. (1999) 'The Royle family', Material Cultures Conference, Coventry.

Mellor, R. (1997) 'Cool times for a changing city', in Jewson, N. and McGregor, S. (eds) *Transforming Cities*, London: Routledge.

Mercer, K. (1987) 'Black hair/style politics', *New Formations*, 3: 33–54.

Mercer, K. and Julien, I. (1988) 'Race, sexual politics and black masculinity: a dossier', in Chapman, R. and Rutherford, J. (eds) *Male Order: Unwrapping Masculinity*, London: Lawrence and Wishart.

Miller, T. (1993) *The Well-Tempered Self: Citizenship, Culture and the Postmodern Self*, Baltimore, MD: Johns Hopkins University Press.

Milner, A. (1999) *Class*, London: Sage.

Moi, T. (1991) 'Appropriating Bourdieu: feminist thought and Pierre Bourdieu's sociology of culture', *New Literary History*, 22: 1,017–49.

Mooney, G. (2000) 'Class and social policy', in Lewis, G., Gewirtz, S. and Clarke, J. (eds) *Rethinking Social Policy*, London: Sage.

Moran, L. (1997) *The Homosexuality of Law*, London: Routledge.

—— (2000) 'Homophobic violence: the hidden injuries of class', in Munt, S. (Ed.) *Cultural Studies and the Working-Class: Subject to Change*, London: Cassell.

Moran, L. and Skeggs, B. (2001a) 'Property and propriety: fear and safety in gay space', *Social and Cultural Geography*, 2(4): 407–20.

—— (2001b) 'The property of safety', *Journal of Social Welfare and Family Law*, 23(4): 1–15.

—— (2003) *Violence and the Politics of Sexuality*, London: Routledge.

Morley, D. (2000) *Home Territories: Media, Mobility and Identity*, London: Routledge.

Morris, L. (1994) *Dangerous Classes: The Underclass and Social Citizenship*, London: Routledge.

Morris, P. (1991) 'Freeing the spirit of enterprise: the genesis and development of enterprise culture', in Keat, R. and Abercrombie, N. (eds) *Enterprise Culture*, London: Routledge.

Munro, R. (1996) 'The consumption view of self: extension, exchange and identity', in Edgell, S., Hetherington, K. and Warde, A. (eds) *Consumption Matters*, Cambridge: Blackwell.

Munt, S. (1995) 'The lesbian *Flaneur*', in Munt, S. (ed.) *Mapping Desire*, London: Routledge.

—— (ed.) (2000) *Cultural Studies and the Working-Class: Subject to Change*, London: Cassell.

Musselwhite, D. (1987) *Partings Welded Together: Politics and Desire in the Nineteenth Century Novel*, London: Methuen.

Narayan, K. (1993) 'How native is the "native" anthropologist', *American Anthropologist*, 95(3): 19–34.

Nast, H. and Pile, S. (eds) (1998) *Places through the Body*, London: Routledge.

Nava, M. (1996) 'Modernity's disavowal: women, the city and the department store' in Nava, M. and O'Shea, A. (eds) *Modern Times*, London: Routledge.

Nayak, A. (1999) '"Pale warriors": skinhead culture and the embodiment of white masculinities', in Mac an Ghaill, M. (ed.) *Thinking Identities: Ethnicity, Racism and Culture*, Basingstoke: Macmillan.

Nead, L. (1988) *Myths of Sexuality: Representations of Women in Victorian Britain*, Oxford: Blackwell.

Nestle, J. (1987) *A Restricted Country*, Ithaca, New York: Firebrand Press.

Newbury, D. (2001) 'Telling stories about photography: the language and imagery of class in the work of Humphrey Spender and Paul Reas', *Visual Culture in Britain*, 2(2): 69–89.

Nietzsche, F. (1969) *Genealogy of Morals*, New York: Vintage.

O'Neill, J. (1999) 'Economy, equality and recognition', in Ray, L. and Sayer, A. (eds) *Culture and Economy after the Cultural Turn*, London: Sage.

Ong, A. (1999) *Flexible Citizenship: The Cultural Logics of Transnationality*, Durham, NC: Duke University Press.

Ortner, S. (1991) 'Reading America: preliminary notes on class and culture', in Fox, G.R. (ed.) *Recapturing Anthropology: Working in the Present*, Santa Fe, NM: School of American Research Press.

Ossowski, S. (1963) *Class Structure in the Social Consciousness*, New York: Free Press.

Oxley, D. (1997) 'Representing convict women', in Duffield, I. and Bradley, J. (eds) *Representing Convicts*, London: Leicester University Press.

Papastergiadis, N. (1999) *The Turbulence of Migration*, London: Routledge.

Partington, A. (1990) *Consumption Practices as the Production and Articulation of Differences: Rethinking Working-Class Femininity in 1950s Britain*, Birmingham: University of Birmingham.

Pateman, C. (1988) *The Sexual Contract*, Cambridge: Polity Press.

—— (1989) *The Disorder of Women: Democracy, Feminism and Political Theory*, Cambridge: Polity Press.

Patrick, A. (2001) 'Defiantly Dusty: a (re)figuring of "feminine excess"', *Feminist Media Studies*, 1(3): 361–79.

Pavletich, J. (1998) 'Emotions, experience, and social control in the twentieth century', *Rethinking Marxism*, 10(2).

Pearson, K. (1904) *National Life from the Standpoint of Science*, 2nd edition, Cambridge: Cambridge University Press.

Perkin, H. (1989) *The Rise of Professional Society: England since 1880*, London: Routledge.

Peterson, R. and Kern, R. (1996) 'Changing highbrow taste; from snob to omnivore', *American Sociological Review*, 61: 900–7.

Peterson, R. and Simkus, A. (1993) 'How musical tastes mark occupational status groups', in Lamont, M. and Fournier, M. (eds) *Cultivating Differences: Symbolic Boundaries and the Making of Inequality*, Chicago: Chicago University Press.

Phillips, L. (1988) 'Hegemony and political discourse: the lasting impact of Thatcherism', *Sociology*, 32: 847–67.

Pitez, W. (1985) 'The problem of the fetish I', *Res*, 9: 5–17.

—— (1987) 'The problem of the fetish II', *Res*, 13: 23–45.

Plummer, K. (1996) 'Intimate citizenship and the culture of sexual storytelling', in Weeks, J. and Holland, J. (eds) *Communities, Values and Intimacy*, London: Macmillan.

Polanyi, K. (2001) *The Great Transformation: The Political and Economic Origins of our Time*, Boston, MA: Beacon Press.

Poovey, M. (1995) *Making a Social Body: British Cultural Formation 1830–1864*, Chicago: Chicago University Press.

—— (1998) *A History of the Modern Fact*, Chicago: University of Chicago Press.

Porter, R. (ed.) (1997) *Rewriting the Self: Histories from the Renaissance to the Present*, London: Routledge.

Postone, M. (1993) *Time, Labour and Social Domination: A Reinterpretation of Marx's Critical Theory*, Cambridge: Cambridge University Press.

Pratt, M.L. (1992) *Imperial Eyes: Travel Writing and Transculturation*, London: Routledge.

Preteceille, E. and Terrail, J.P. (1985) *Capitalism, Consumption and Needs*, Oxford: Basil Blackwell.

Prieur, A. (1998) *Mema's House, Mexico City: Transvestites, Queens and Machos*, Chicago: University of Chicago Press.

Probyn, E. (1993a) *Sexing the Self: Gendered Positions in Cultural Studies*, London: Routledge.

—— (1993b) 'True voices and real people: the "problem" of the autobiographical in cultural studies', in Blundell, V., Shepherd, J. and Taylor, I. (eds) *Relocating Cultural Studies*, London: Routledge.

—— (2000a) *CarnalAppetites: FoodSexIdentities*, London: Routledge.

—— (2000b) 'Shaming theory, thinking disconnections: feminism and reconciliation', in Ahmed, S., Kilby, J., Lury, C., McNeil, M. and Skeggs, B. (eds) *Transformations: Thinking Through Feminism*, London: Routledge.

Putnam, R. (1995) 'Bowling alone: America's declining social capital', *Journal of Democracy* 6(1): 65–78.

Rabinow, P. (1977) *Reflections on Fieldwork in Morocco*, Berkeley, CA: University of California Press.

—— (1986) 'Representations are social facts: modernity and post-modernity in anthropology', in Clifford, J. and Marcus, G.E. (eds) *Writing Culture: The Poetics and Politics of Ethnography*, Berkeley, CA: University of California Press.

Radin, M.J. (1993) *Reinterpreting Property*, Chicago: University of Chicago Press.

Reay, D. (1997) 'Feminist theory, habitus, and social class: disrupting notions of classlessness', *Women's Studies International Forum*, 20(2): 225–33.

—— (1998) *Class Work: Mothers' Involvement in their Children's Primary Schooling*, London: University College Press.

—— (2000a) 'Children's urban landscapes: configurations of class and place', in Munt, S. (ed.) *Cultural Studies and the Working-Class: Subject to Change*, London: Cassell.

—— (2000b) '"I dont really like it here but I don't want to live anywhere else". Life on large estates', *Antipode*, 32(4): 4,410–28.

Reed, E. (1995) 'The cycle of abuse: personal and political, *Rethinking Marxism*, 8(3): remarks section.

Regan, S. (2001) 'Economic analysis: saving grace', *The Guardian*, London.

Ricoeur, P. (1980) 'Narrative time', *Critical Inquiry*, 7(1): 169–90.

—— (1983) *Time and Narrative*, Vol 1, Chicago: University of Chicago Press.

—— (1990) *Soi-même comme un autre*, Paris: Seuil.

Robbins, B. (1986) *The Servant's Hand: English Fiction from Below*, Durham, NC: Duke University Press.

—— (2001) 'The village of the liberal managerial class', in Dharwadker, V. (ed.) *Cosmopolitan Geographies: New Locations in Literature and Culture*, London: Routledge.

Roberts, I. (1999a) 'Bring 'em back alive', in Beynon, H. and Glavanis, P. (eds) *Patterns of Social Inequality*, Harlow: Longman.

—— (1999b) 'A historical construction of the working-class', in Beynon, H. and Glavanis, P. (eds) *Patterns of Social Inequality*, London: Pearson.

Roemer, J. (1982) *A General Theory of Exploitation and Class*, Cambridge, MA: Harvard University Press.

—— (1986) 'Should Marxists be interested in exploitation?', in Roemer, J. (ed.) *Analytical Marxism*, Cambridge: Cambridge University Press.

Rosaldo, R. (1989) 'Death in the ethnographic present', in Hernadi, P. (ed.) *The Rhetoric of Interpretation and the Interpretation of Rhetoric*, Chicago: Duke University Press.

Rose, N. (1989) *Governing the Soul: The Shaping of the Private Self*, London: Routledge.

—— (1992) 'Governing the enterprising self', in Heelas, P. and Morris. P. (eds) *The Values of Enterprise Culture: The Moral Debate*, London: Routledge.

Rose, S.O. (1999) 'Cultural analysis and moral discourses: episodes, continuities and transformations', in Bonnell, V.E. and Hunt, L. (eds) *Beyond the Cultural Turn*, Berkeley CA: University of California Press.

Rotman, B. (1980) *Mathematics: An Essay in Semiotics*, Bristol: Bristol University.

Rouse, R. (1991) 'Mexican migration and the social space of postmodernism', *Diaspora*, 1(1): 13–27.

—— (1995) 'Thinking through transnationalism: notes on the cultural politics of class relations in the contemporary United States', *Public Culture*, 7(2): 353–402.

Rowbotham, S. and Beynon, H. (eds) (2001) *Looking at Class: Film, Television and the Working-Class in Britain*, London: Rivers Oram Press.

Rowe, K. (1995) *The Unruly Woman: Gender and the Genres of Laughter*, Austin: University of Texas Press.

Rowling, N. (1987) *Commodities: How the World was Taken to Market*, London: Free Association Books.

Rubin, L.B. (1972/1992) *Worlds of Pain: Life in the Working-Class Family*, New York: Basic Books.

Rueschemeyer, D. and Mahoney, J. (2000) 'A neo-utilitarian theory of class', *American Journal of Sociology*, 105(6): 1,583–91.

Rybczynski, W. (1986) *Home: A Short History of an Idea*, London: Heinemann.

Said, E. (1978) *Orientalism*, London: Routledge.

Sandlos, K. (2000) 'Unifying forces: rhetorical reflections on a pro-choice image', in Ahmed, S., Kilby, J., Lury, C., McNeil, M. and Skeggs, B. (eds) *Transformations: Thinking Through Feminism*, London: Routledge.

Savage, M. (2000) *Class Analysis and Social Transformation*, Buckingham: Open University Press.

—— (forthcoming) 'Assets, resources and capitals: working with Bourdieu'. Paper presented to Assets group, Department of Sociology, University of Manchester.

Savage, M., Bagnall, G. and Longhurst, B. (1999) 'The ambiguity of class identities in contemporary Britain', British Sociological Association Conference, Edinburgh.

—— (2001) Ordinary, ambivalent and defensive: class identities in the Northwest of England', *Sociology*, 35(4): 875–92.

Savage, M., Barlow, J., Dickens, P. and Fielding, T. (1992) *Property, Bureaucracy and Culture: Middle-Class Formation in Contemporary Britain*, London: Routledge.

Sayer, A. (2000) 'Markets, embeddedness and trust: problems of polysemy and idealism', Research Symposium on Market Relations and Competition, Centre for Innovation and Competition, University of Manchester.

—— (2001) 'What are you worth? recognition, valuation and moral economy', British Sociological Association Annual Conference, Manchester.

Seabrook, J. (2000) *Nobrow: The Culture of Marketing and the Marketing of Culture*, London: Methuen.

Seiter, E. (1990) 'Making distinctions in TV audience research: a case study of a troubling interview', *Cultural Studies*, 4(1): 61–85.

—— (1999) *Television and New Media Audiences*, Oxford: Clarendon Press.

Selbourne, D. (1994) *The Principle of Duty: An Essay on the Foundations of the Civic Order*, London: Sinclair Stevenson.

Silverstone, R. (1999) 'Rhetoric, play, performance: revisiting a study of the making of a BBC documentary', in Gripsrud, J. (ed.) *Television and Common Knowledge*, London: Routledge.

Sinn, G. and Sinn, H.W. (1994) *Jumpstart: The Economic Unification of Germany*, Cambridge, MA: MIT Press.

Skeggs, B. (1994a) 'Situating the production of feminist ethnography', in Maynard, M. and Purvis, J. (eds) *Researching Women's Lives from a Feminist Perspective*, Basingstoke: Taylor and Francis.

—— (1994b) 'Refusing to be civilized: "race", sexuality and power', in Afshar, H. and Maynard, M. (eds) *The Dynamics of Race and Gender*, London: Taylor and Francis.

—— (ed.) (1995) *Feminist Cultural Theory: Process and Production*, Manchester: Manchester University Press.

—— (1997) *Formations of Class and Gender: Becoming Respectable*, London: Sage.

—— (2001) 'The toilet paper: femininity, class and mis-recognition', *Women's Studies International Forum*, 24(3–4): 295–307.

—— (2002) 'Who can tell? Reflexivity in feminist research', in May, T. (ed.) *Issues and Practices in Qualitative Research*, London: Sage.

Sklair, L. (2001) *The Transnational Capitalist Class*, Oxford: Blackwell.

Slater, D. (1997) *Consumer Culture and Modernity*, Cambridge: Polity Press.

Slater, D. and F. Tonkiss (2001) *Market Society*, Cambridge: Polity Press.

Smith, A. (1757) *Theory of the Moral Sentiments*, London: Liberty Press.

—— (1776/1970) *The Wealth of Nations*, Harmondsworth: Penguin.

Smith, A.-M. (1994) *New Right Discourse on Race and Sexuality*, Cambridge: Cambridge University Press.

Smith, D.E. (1988) 'Femininity as discourse', in Roman, L.G., Christian-Smith, L.K. and Elsworth, E. (eds) *Becoming Feminine: The Politics of Popular Culture*, Lewes: Falmer Press.

Smith, M. (1994) *Invisible Leviathan: the Marxist Critique of Market Despotism beyond Postmodernism*, Toronto: Toronto University Press.

Smith, P. (1996) 'Unified capital and the subject of value', in Gordon, A.F. and Newfield, C. (eds) *Mapping Multi-Culturalism*, Minneapolis: University of Minnesota Press.

Smith, S.M. (1999) *American Archives: Gender, Race and Class in Visual Culture*, Princeton: Princeton University Press.

Solomon, R.C. (1999) 'Justice v vengeance: on law and the satisfaction of emotion', in Bandes, S. (ed.) *The Passions of Law*, New York: New York University Press.

Sombart, W. (1902) *Der Moderne Kapitalismus*, Leipzig: Duncker und Humbolt.

Sorenson, A.B. (2000a) 'Employment relations and class structure', in Crompton, R., Devine, F., Savage, M. and Scott, J. (eds) *Renewing Class Analysis*, Oxford: Blackwell.

—— (2000b) 'Symposium on class analysis: towards a sounder basis for class analysis', *American Journal of Sociology*, 45(6): 1,523–58.

Soysal, Y.N. (1993) 'Construction of immigrant identities in Europe', *European Identity and its Intellectual Roots*, Cambridge.

Sparke, P. (1995) *As Long as it's Pink: The Sexual Politics of Taste*, London: Harper Collins.

Spivak, G. C. (1990) *The Post-Colonial Critic: Interviews, Strategies, Dialogues*, London: Routledge.

—— (2000) 'Claiming transformation: travel notes with pictures' in Ahmed, S., Kilby, J., Lury, C., McNeil, M. and Skeggs, B. (eds) *Transformations: Thinking Through Feminism*, London: Routledge.

Stacey, J. (2000) 'The global within: consuming nature, embodying health', in Franklin, S., Lury, C. and Stacey, J. (eds) *Global Nature, Global Culture*, London: Routledge.

Stallybrass, P. (1998) 'Marx's coat', in Spyer, P. (ed.) *Border Fetishisms: Material Objects in Unstable Spaces*, London: Routledge.

Stallybrass, P. and White, A. (1986) *The Politics and Poetics of Transgression*, London: Methuen.

Standing, K. (1999) 'Lone mothers' involvement in their children's schooling: towards a new typology of maternal involvement', *Gender and Education*, 11(1): 57–73.

Stanko, E. (1988) 'Fear of crime and the myth of the safe home: a feminist critique of criminology', in Yllo, K. and Bograd, M. (eds) *Feminist Perspectives on Wife Abuse*, London: Sage.

Stanko, E. and Curry, P. (1997) 'Homophobic violence and the self "at risk": interrogating the boundaries', *Social and Legal Studies*, 6(4): 513–32.

Stanley, L. (2000) 'From "self-made woman" to "women's made selves"? Audit selves, simulation and surveillance in the rise of public woman', in Cosslett, T., Lury, C. and Summerfield, P. (eds) *Feminism and Autobiography*, London: Routledge.

Stansall, C. (1986) *City of Women: Sex and Class in New York, 1789–1860*, New York: Alfred A. Knopf.

Stanworth, M. (1984) 'Women and class analysis: a reply to Goldthorpe', *Sociology*, 18(2): 153–71.

Starr, M. (2002) 'Reading the economist on globalisation: knowledge, identity and power', paper presented at the conference on 'Cultural Returns: Assessing the Place of Culture in Social Thought', St Hugh's College, Oxford, September 2002. Revised February 2003.

Ste. Croix, G., de (1981) *The Class Struggle in the Ancient Greek World*, London: Duckworth.

Stedman Jones, G. (1971) *Outcast London: A Study in the Relationship Between Classes in Victorian Society*, Oxford: Clarendon.

Steedman, C. (1997) 'Writing the self: the end of the scholarship girl', in McGuigan, J. (ed.) *Cultural Methodologies*, London: Sage.

—— (1998) *Enforced Narratives; Notes Towards an Alternative History of the Self, Autobiography and the Social Self*, Lancaster: Lancaster University.

—— (1999) 'State sponsored autobiography', in Conekin, B., Mort, F. and Waters, C. (eds) *Movements of Modernity: Reconstructing Britain 1945–1964*, London: Rivers Oram.

—— (2000) 'Enforced narratives: stories of another self', in Cosslett, T., Lury, C. and Summerfield, P. (eds) *Feminism and Autobiography: Texts, Theories, Methods*, London: Routledge.

Stevenson, N. (2002) 'Cosmopolitanism, multiculturalism and citizenship', *Sociological Research Online*, 7(1): www.socresonline.org.uk.

Stewart, K. (1996) *A Space on the Side of the Road: Cultural Poetics in an 'Other' America*, Princeton: Princeton University Press.

Stocking, G.W.J. (1987) *Victorian Anthropology*, New York: Free Press.

Stolcke, V. (1995) 'Talking culture; new boundaries, new rhetorics of exclusion in Europe', *Current Anthropology*, 36(1): 1–24.

Stoler, A. (1995) *Race and the Education of Desire: Foucault's History of Sexuality and the Colonial Order of Things*, Durham, NC: Duke University Press.

Strathern, M. (1991) *Partial Connections*, Maryland: Rowman and Little.

—— (1992a) *After Nature: English Kinship in the Late Twentieth Century*, Cambridge: Cambridge University Press.

—— (1992b) 'Qualified value: the perspective of gift exchange', in Humphrey, C. and Hugh-Jones, S. (eds) *Barter, Exchange and Value: An Anthropological Approach*, Cambridge: Cambridge University Press.

—— (1999) *Property, Substance and Effect: Anthropological Essays on Persons and Things*, New Brunswick, NJ: Athlone.

Susman, W.I. (1979) '"Personality" and the making of twentieth-century culture', in Higham, J. and Conkin, P.K. (eds) *New Directions in American Intellectual History*, Baltimore, MD: Johns Hopkins University Press.

Sutton, D. (1985) 'Liberalism, state collectivism and the social relationships of citizenship', in Langan, M. and Schwarz, B. (eds) *Crisis in the British State, 1880–1930*, London: Hutchinson.

Svensson, B. (1997) 'Auto/ethnography', in Reed-Danahay, D.E. (ed.) *Auto/Ethnography: Rewriting the Social Self*, Oxford: Berg.

Sweet, M. (2000) 'A case of suffering for no art', *Independent on Sunday*. London.

Taguieff, P.-A. (ed.) (1991) *Face au Racism. Vol One, Les Moyens D'Agir*, Paris: Editions La Decouverte/Essais.

Tasker, Y. (1998) *Working Girls: Gender and Sexuality in Popular Culture*, London: Routledge.

Taylor, C. (1989) *Sources of the Self: The Making of the Modern Identity*, Cambridge: Cambridge University Press.

—— (1994) 'The politics of recognition', in Goldberg, D.T. (ed.) *Multiculturalism: A Critical Reader*, Oxford: Blackwell.

Tedman, G. (1999) 'Ideology, the state, and the aesthetic level of practice', *Rethinking Marxism* 11(4).

Thompson, E.P. (1966) *The Making of the English Working-Class*, Harmondsworth: Penguin.

—— (1978) *The Poverty of Theory*, London: Merlin.

—— (1993a) *Customs in Common*, Harmondsworth: Penguin.

—— (1993b) 'The making of a ruling class', *Dissent*, Summer: 380–95.

Thompson, G. (1999b) 'How far should we be afraid of conventional economics: a response to Ben Fine', *Economy and Society*, 28(3): 426–33.

Thompson, J. (1996) *Models of Value: Eighteenth-Century Political Economy and the Novel*, Durham, NC: Duke University Press.

Thornton, S. (1997) *Club Cultures*, London: Routledge.

Tipton, S. (1982) *Getting Saved from the Sixties*, London: University of California Press.

Tomkins, S. (1995) 'Shame-humiliation and contempt-disgust', in Sedgwick, E.K. and Frank, A. (eds) *Shame and its Sisters: A Silvan Tomkins Reader*, Durham, NC: Duke University Press.

Trautmann, T.R. (1997) *Aryans and British India*, Berkeley, CA: University of California.

Tyler, C.-A. (1991) 'Boys will be girls: the politics of gay drag', in Fuss, D. (ed.) *Inside Out: Lesbian Theories/Gay Theories*, London: Routledge.

Urry, J. (2000) *Societies Beyond the Social: Mobilities for the Twenty-First Century*, London: Routledge.

Valocchi, S. (1999) 'The class-inflected nature of gay identity', *Social Problems*, 46(2): 207–24.

Vicinus, M. (1974) *The Industrial Muse: A Study of Nineteenth-Century British Working-Class Literature*, London: Croom Helm.

Vincent, D. (1981) *Bread, Knowledge and Freedom: A Study of Working-Class Nineteenth-Century Autobiography*, London: Europa Publications.

—— (1991) *Poor Citizens: The State and the Poor in the Twentieth Century*, London: Longman.

Visweswaran, K. (1994) *Fictions of a Feminist Ethnography*, Minneapolis: University of Minnesota Press.

Vitellone, N. (2002) '"I think it more of a white person's sort of awareness": condoms and the making of a white nation in media representations of safer (hetero) sex', *Feminist Media Studies*, 2(1): 19–36.

Wahrman, D. (1995) *Imagining the Middle-Class: The Political Representation of Class in Britain, c. 1780–1840*, Cambridge: Cambridge University Press.

Walkerdine, V. (1988) *The Mastery of Reason: Cognitive Development and the Production of Rationality*, London: Routledge.

—— (1989) 'Femininity as performance', *Oxford Review of Education*, 15(3): 267–79.

—— (1990) *Schoolgirl Fictions*, London: Verso.

Walkerdine, V. and Lucey, H. (1989) *Democracy in the Kitchen: Regulating Mothers and Socialising Daughters*, London: Virago.

Walkowitz, V. (1989) *City of Dreadful Delight: Narratives of Sexual Danger in Later Victorian London*, London: Virago.

Wallace, M. (1993) 'Negative images: towards a black feminist cultural criticism', in During, S. (ed.) *The Cultural Studies Reader*, London: Routledge.

Waquant, L. (1989) 'Towards a reflexive sociology: a workshop with Pierre Bourdieu', *Sociological Theory*, 7: 26–63.

—— (1991) 'Making class: the middle-class(es) in social theory and social structure', in McNall, S.G., Levine, R.F. and Fantasia, R. (eds) *Bringing Class Back in Contemporary Historical Perspectives*, Boulder, CO: Westview Press.

—— (1999) '"Ce vent puniqui vient d'Amérique"', April', *Le Monde Diplomatique*, April(77).

—— (2000) 'Durkheim and Bourdieu: the common plinth and its cracks', in Fowler, B. (ed.) *Reading Bourdieu on Society and Culture*, Oxford: Blackwell.

Warde, A., Tomlinson, M. and McMeekin, A. (2000) 'Expanding tastes? Cultural omnivorousness and social change in the UK', Manchester, CRIC, University of Manchester.

Warren, C.A.B. (1988) *Gender Issues in Field Research*, London: Sage.

Watt, I. (1957) *The Rise of the Novel*, London: Chatto and Windus.

Weeks, J. (1981) *Sex, Politics and Society: The Regulation of Sexuality Since 1800*, London: Longman.

Weiner, A.B. (1992) *Inalienable Possessions: The Paradox of Keeping-while-giving*, Berkeley, CA: University of California Press.

Werbner, P. (1999) 'Global pathways. Working-class cosmopolitans and the creation of transnational ethnic worlds', *Social Anthropology*, 7: 17–35.

Wheen, F. (1999) *Karl Marx*, London: Fourth Estate.

Williams, L. (1997) 'Review Essay', *Journal of Contemporary Ethnography*, 25(4): 516–20.

Williams, P. (1991) *The Alchemy of Race and Rights: Diary of a Law Professor*. Cambridge, MA: Harvard University Press.

Williams, R. (1973) 'Base and superstructure in Marxist cultural theory', *New Left Review*, 82: 3–16.

—— (1988) *Keywords: A Vocabulary of Culture and Society*, London: Fontana.

Willis, P. (1977) *Learning to Labour: How Working-Class Kids Get Working-Class Jobs*, Farnborough: Saxon House.

—— (2002) '"Taking the piss": double consciousness and the sensuous activity of manual labour', Labour Studies Conference, Department of Sociology, University of Manchester.

Willis, P., Jones, S., Cannan, J. and Hurd, G. (1990) *Common Culture*, Milton Keynes: Open University Press.

Wilmer, V. (1989) *Mama Said They're be Days Like This: My Life in the Jazz World*, London: The Women's Press.

Wolpe, A.-M. (1988) *Within School Walls: The Role of Discipline, Sexuality and the Curriculum*, London: Routledge.

Woolgar, S. and Ashmore, M. (1991) 'The next step: an introduction to the reflexive project', in Woolgar, S. (ed.) *Knowledge and Reflexivity: New Frontiers in the Sociology of Knowledge*, London: Sage.

Woolgar, S. and Latour, B. (1979) *Laboratory Life: The Construction of Scientific Facts*, London: Sage.

Wouters, C. (1986) 'Formalization and informalization: changing tension balances in civilizing processes', *Theory Culture and Society*, 3(2): 1–21.

Wray, M. and Newitz, A. (eds) (1997) *White Trash: Race and Class in America*, London: Routledge.

Wright, E.O. (1979) *Class Structure and Income Determination*, London: Academic Press.

—— (1985) *Classes*, London: Verso.

—— (1997) *Class Counts: Comparative Studies in Class Analysis*, Cambridge: Cambridge University Press.

—— (2000) 'Class, exploitation and economic rents: reflections on Sorenson's "Sounder Basis"', *American Journal of Sociology*, 105(6): 1,559–71.

Yeatman, A. (1994) *Postmodern Revisionings of the Political*, London: Routledge.

Yeo, E. (1993) *The Contest of Social Science in Britain: Relations and Representations of Gender and Class*, Lancaster: Lancaster University.

Zelizer, V. (1988) 'Beyond the polemics on the market: establishing a theoretical and empirical agenda', *Sociological Forum*, 3(4): 614–34.

—— (1994) *The Social Meaning of Money*, New York: Basic Books.

—— (1996) 'Payments and social ties', *Sociological Forum*, 11(3): 481–95.

Ziff, B. and Rao, P.V. (1997) *Borrowed Power: Essays on Cultural Appropriation*, New Brunswick, NJ: Rutgers University Press.

Zizek, S. (1994) *The Sublime Object of Ideology*, London: Verso.

—— (1996) '"I hear you with my eyes": or the invisible master', in Salecl, R. and Zizek, S. (eds) *Sic 1: Gaze and Voice as Love Objects*, Durham, NC: Duke University Press.

—— (1997) Multiculturalism, or, the cultural logic of multinational capitalism', *New Left Review*, 225: 28–52.

—— (2002) 'Are we in a war? Do we have an enemy?', *London Review of Books*, 23: 3–6.

Zukin, S. (1987) 'Gentrification: culture and capital in the urban core', *Annual Review of Sociology*, 13: 129–47.

Zweig, M. (2000) *The Working-Class Majority: America's Best Kept Secret*, Ithaca: ILR Press.

Index